ONCE UPON A PRIME TIME

MY JOURNEY ON INDIAN TELEVISION

ANANTH MAHADEVAN

EMBASSY BOOKS
www.embassybooks.in

Once Upon A Prime Time © Ananth Narayan Mahadevan

First Edition 2020

Published in India by:
Embassy Book Distributors
120, Great Western Building,
Maharashtra Chamber of Commerce Lane,
Fort, Mumbai 400 023, India
Tel: (+9122) -30967415, 22819546
Email: info@embassybooks.in
www.embassybooks.in

ISBN: 978-93-88247-72-6

Cover Design by Sonal Churi

Cover Photograph by Ravi Mahadevan (Aspect Ratio)
Location courtesy: Don Bosco School, Matunga

Layout and typesetting by Sonal Churi &
Gangaram Dhuri (Brand Soul Creations)

Printed & Bound in India by Repro India Ltd., Navi Mumbai

❝ Television history is a doctoral topic and this book has so many precious diamonds that we would not have known if they weren't documented. This treat will take readers back and forth into the existence of television. ❞

DR SWAPNA PATKER, *Clinical Psychologist, Author, Corporate Trainer*

❝ Mahadevan has an almost feral intellectual ferocity that ought to intimidate, but comforts just about everyone around him. He transcends effortlessly between print, television, cinema and stage as actor, writer, director. ❞

R K BAJAJ, *Editor, Channel Head, the RKB Show host*

❝ When you write a book on any industry, you either take the outsider's bird's eye view approach or you take an insider's intimate details approach. You don't do both. And you don't do both because you can't do both.

But when you read this book, you realise that if you are Ananth Mahadevan, you can do both. And do it so brilliantly.

Ananth straps you down gently on his roller coaster of the television industry and hurtles you on a back-to-the-future ride like never before.

He stops at every milestone that you remember, and many that you had forgotten, and brings a lump in your throat with nostalgia.

It's not merely a history of television. It's a living picture in three dimension—of the programmes, the people, the ups and downs, the intimate anecdotes involving the giants of the industry, and with Ananth himself a witness—much like the common man of R K Laxman.

If you are averse to unputdownable binge reading, don't touch this book. You have been warned. ❞

BHARAT DABHOLKAR, *Ad Guru, Actor, Director*

66 Amazing memories of the golden age of television, brought back to life by a master raconteur; it's real, witty and shows that we can love a book which is not sensational or gimmicky! Unmissable. Read it again and again and again! 99

VIVECK VASWANI, *Film Producer, Screenwriter, Teacher, Actor*

66 Full of delightful anecdotes and a wonderful history of prime time television. 99

LILLETTE DUBEY, *Actress, Theatre Director*

66 The story of Indian television engagingly told and peppered with personal anecdotes. A definite must read for those who grew up on the halcyon days of Doordarshan and for those who missed the bus to know about the golden era of Indian television. 99

NANDITA OM PURI, *Author, Columnist*

66 A real page turner... great trip down memory lane... 99

BENJAMIN GILANI, *Actor, Professor - FTII, Pune*

66 The book encapsulates the journey of TV in India through an interesting perspective. Mahadevan underlines the important role played by many well-known filmmakers shaping this powerful medium in the last 30 years. What makes this special are some hitherto lesser known facts and behind the scenes reality. Interspersed with interesting anecdotes and keen observations the book is a must read for all associated with media including viewers. 99

AMIT KHANNA, *Filmmaker, Author, Analyst*

This book is dedicated.

"Getting there is half the fun,
Being there *is all of it........"*

CONTENTS

Foreword by Hema Malini xi

Acknowledgements xv

Prologue - And Then There Was Television xix

Episode 1 - The Beginning

The Magic Lantern 2

Viva Mexico! 13

The Comic Buccaneer 23

Changing Lanes 29

Face in the Crowd 41

The Smoke and Light Show 55

Here's Rajni 61

Short Cuts 67

Three's Company 83

Soldier Blue 91

The Good Doctor 97

The Gods Must Be Crazy 107

Derailed 117

Classics Illustrated 125

Elementary, My Dear Watson 139

The Television Inferno 151

Double-Edged Sword..................................... 159

History Repeats.. 173

Star Trek 181

Episode 2 - The Middle

Oh, What a Lovely War! 195

The New Wave... 205

The Last Metro 219

Shaikh, Rattle and Roll.................................. 231

The Invasion of the Serial Snatchers 241

The Business of Entertainment 249

The Twilight Zone.. 255

Bachchan's Billions 263

Episode 3 - Not the End

The TV Supermall 275

The Last Laugh 283

Reality Bites 293

Silence of the Lambs...................................... 305

Epilogue - An Episodic Story.............................. *313*

FOREWORD

It was always fortuitous to be present at the right time and place in life. Looking back at the rewarding decades I enjoyed as an actress and danseuse, several experiences cross my mind. I doubt if I could have had it better in any other era. From dance recitals to cinema to television, I've had the opportunity of running the entire gamut.

That is what draws me to this book, appropriately titled, as it narrates the story of a memorable era. Technology has always played a key role in redefining the media, as I reconciled with changing times.

Of course, the paradigm shift–from the cinema screen to a 20-inch monitor–was difficult for most of the popular film stars of the 1980s to reckon with. They were wary, wanted to test waters before making up their mind. In my case, the migration was a studied and calculated one.

Initially, the idea to make a dance-based drama was conceived as a classic film. But then the material couldn't be confined to a two-hour screen time and so, the clarion call of television was heeded. I decided to take the plunge as a producer-director-actor in my first foray into television, *Noopur*. In the journey of the girl who discovered the world and relationships through her love for dance,

I discovered the medium and its vast scope for storytelling.

That is where *Once Upon A Prime Time* comes in. Incidentally, the author played a pivotal role, that of one who chronicled my life, in *Noopur*. It was also the first time we ever met and worked together. I am glad that Ananth took the initiative to put on record this commercial phase of television that was dominated by stalwarts for nearly two decades. Like film negatives, these memories too need to be restored and archived for posterity, as they tell many an untold tale worth cherishing.

Having run parallel to the television industry ever since the inception of sponsored programmes in 1983, Ananth's innings has been a long and unbroken one.

The book reads like an autobiography, but covers every major player who was responsible for the nostalgia that Indian television now evokes. Even as a lot of new candidates jumped in to get a piece of the pie, the medium attracted prominent film figures. Gulzar, Basu Chatterji, Yash Chopra, Ramanand Sagar, Ramesh Sippy, Sai Paranjpye, Hrishikesh Mukherjee, B R Chopra and Shyam Benegal, to name a few. They all had stories to tell, in a style quite different from their big screen successes.

As I browsed through the book, I let myself be drawn into the years when television permitted filmmakers to break away from the formula and explore every possible genre without the box-office sword hanging on their heads. This led to family dramas [soaps, they were called] like *Hum Log* and *Khandaan*, comedies like *Yeh Jo Hai Zindagi* and *Ghar Jamai*, contemporary satires like *Nukkad*, classics like *Mujrim Haazir, Srikant* and *Mirza Ghalib*, mythologicals in *Ramayana* and *Mahabharata* and chunks of history in *Buniyaad* and *The Sword of Tipu Sultan*.

The book traverses the monopoly of Doordarshan right up to the decade that introduced satellite television flooding our homes with innumerable channels and dividing attention span. The time when my own *Noopur* and *Women of India* which, along with other mega serials, scored unheard of rating points above 50, stands in stark contrast to the decimal points of today's shows.

The story of the arrival of the new millennium, and with it the advent of the daily soaps, is also a revealing feature of the book. It alienated a lot of veterans who, despite being superior storytellers, found the new model of work rather intimidating.

Attitudes, style and audience tastes underwent a sea change. I have been witness to these days when my attempts to revive and retain the values of the early days of television was met with scepticism. Television as a medium was throwing up new role models and challenging both the auteur and the new age software minds.

It is unusual for a practitioner to have run parallel to an industry, but Ananth has virtually achieved that and penned a biography of Indian television over three decades. His interactions with major filmmakers and the recounting of their thoughts and experiences is the real take-away here. The chapters not only look at the "opera of soaps" but also take you behind the scenes and give you a glimpse into the characters that, at times, even overshadowed the actors, who, saddled with such popularity, were faced with an identity crisis in real life. Many facts of trivia woven into the stories, such as Kishore Kumar singing the title song for the television serial

Yeh Jo Hai Zindagi or Shekar Kapur shooting a scene all night to attain perfection, bring so much reality to the narrative that you almost feel like you are a part of the production crew in many of the projects being described. While keeping the glamour in place, Ananth also shows the flip side, that of sweat and toil and a garnishing of good luck that went into many successful television shows. The result is that the reader gets a feeling of getting up close to the journey of television - from a black and white single- channel wonder to streaming videos on our smartphones.

Considering that most of our television serials haven't been immortalised on digital discs, as is prevalent in the West, *Once Upon A Prime Time* assumes greater significance.

I, for one, wholeheartedly welcome this book which could be a reference book, both, for connoisseurs and a new generation that is eager to obtain a bird's eye-view of the history of television and its players in India.

Wishing Ananth, his written work, and the publisher the very best for *Once Upon A Prime Time*.

Hema Malini

Acknowledgements

The graduation from a pencil to a pen, had me fascinated. The fountain-pen habit inculcated in us, as opposed to the ball-point pen, helped improve the handwriting. I chose them, to put pen to paper for the opening pages of this book, instead of the key-board route.

P. G. Wodehouse did rattle me when he wondered if his life was gripping enough for an autobiography. To compound my fears, Pulitzer Prize winner Michael Cunningham observes, "one always has a better book in one's mind, than one can manage on paper." Indeed, this book would have pixelated in my mind, if it wasn't for a firm but friendly nudge from those I can only thank now.

When I first mooted the idea of this book, two friends were instrumental in spurring me on. Mona Shourie, producer and co-founder of Future Studios (Mumbai) was emphatic. "Just write it" she exclaimed. Journalist turned publicist Hilla Sethna's continued insistence was infectious. As the book sees the light of day, it is my misfortune that both have left us. I feel a sense of remorse for not having completed the book earlier.

It is with a sense of immense gratitude to many others, that I round off this exercise. A big 'thank you!' is in order to Nandita. C Puri, for having facilitated the journey of this book from manuscript to print. More so, to Dr. Swapna Patker for her thoughtful introduction to my publisher Sohin Lakhani of Embassy Books, who along with his enterprising editor-in-chief Aruna Joshi, lost no time in accelerating production, besides backing up with invaluable inputs.

To Hema Malini for having graciously acceded to my request to write the Foreword to the book. She has amalgamated her illustrious journey with the context of this book, very admirably.

The artistic conglomerate of Sai Paranjpye, Aziz Mirza, Kundan Shah, Hrishikesh Mukherjee, Basu Chatterji, Gulzar, Govind Nihalani, Ramesh Sippy, Yash Chopra, Ravi Chopra and Amitabh Bachchan who willingly shared their experience, to make this journey an enjoyable one.

Of course, I owe a big one to all my producers and directors who thought it appropriate to employ me as an actor or director during this trek of 38 years. They, along with the television channels, have shaped my career, and in doing so, this book.

To the stalwarts like Amit Khanna, Bharat Dabholkar, Aanand Mahendroo, Pankaj Parashar, Rahul Rawail, R.K. Bajaj, Ashish Vidyarthi, Viveck Vaswani and others for their words of encouragement and inspiration.

To my editors Aruna Joshi and Shahu Buchar for patiently making this book ship-shape for the reader.

And last, but not in the very least, a round of applause to Ravi Mahadevan, a rather under-rated but immensely gifted photographer for the front-cover and flap pictures that he devised and shot.

A book, like a film or a television show, is a collective effort. I hope any omissions in this list will not be held against me.

So, read on......

PROLOGUE

...AND THEN THERE WAS TELEVISION

December 2017. I woke up to find that my television was gone. In its place sat an unfamiliar apparition. Someone had, in the stealth of the wintry night, wrenched the plug and replaced the television I had come to befriend for over three decades, with what they assured me, was the new age tube. Eventually, many a software production group and digital platform claimed responsibility, but no one deemed it necessary to appear apologetic.

Immediate victims of the reductio-ad-absurdum were the founding-fathers of sponsored broadcasting in the country. The flutter of their flustered feathers was barely heard, and far from heeded. Prime time television had donned an obverse mask and assumed a new definition. This was akin to the upgrading of towns, as concrete structures claimed, whilst they displaced the architecture of heritage homes in my green Kerala hamlet, Thrissur.

I was switching channels. In my mind. I harked back to the summer of 1964. As a toddler on vacation at our ancestral home in Kerala, I remembered my maternal uncle lugging up the stairs, a rather complicated looking wood-panelled box sporting a calibrated plastic screen, embellished below with a few knobs. As I eyed the Telerad brand label curiously, he read my thoughts. With that typical Palakkad Tamil-Malayalam twang he explained: "This is called a radio. It plays music and news from radio stations. But you haven't seen anything yet. There is something more amazing coming our way. It has already hit the West. On a box similar to this, you can watch films, just like you do at the cinemas." "Even as they screen it at the Jos theatre [our favourite local haunt in Thrissur] we get to see it on this box?", I enquired, my voice betraying naivety and wonder. A dismissive nod, and he continued to walk up the narrow wooden steps to his room, taking care to avoid grazing the wall on his right. He had conjured a vision I could only marvel at. In one plain remark, he had managed to jog my imagination of a future that awaited us.

History, meanwhile had readied my favourite apparatus for me in 1936, when the British Broadcasting Corporation (BBC) flagged off the first black-and-white, four-hours-a-day television service, followed by the United States in New York on April 30, 1939 with a broadcast of the opening of the World Broadcasting Fair in New York. It took a major part of the 1950s for other countries to begin television broadcasting on a wide scale. 1953 marked the first full-fledged programme in colour, transmitted by CBS in the USA. Commercial broadcasting in the world happened around the same time. Times were changing, and fast. Everybody could now 'see' things unfold in front of them. The Lumiere Brothers' "train moment" had come home.

As seemed to be an Indian norm, television was nearly twenty years late in coming. On a nondescript floor of Akashvani Bhavan in New Delhi, officials, in the absence of air-conditioning machinery, were cooling with ice slabs, a closed-circuit television, that the Philips company from Holland had chosen to abandon after an exhibition had concluded in the city. This was the raw material for India's first television indulgence. Operating with a small transmitter and a make-shift studio, over a radius of 25 kilometres in September 1959, the origins of *Doordarshan* [a literal Hindi language translation of 'tele-vision'], India's first public broadcasting television service, began with two one-hour programmes a week, on guarded topics like community health, citizens' duties and rights, and traffic and civic sense.

The television census recorded an initial figure of around 180 sets in the country. In 1961, the government availed of a grant from the UNESCO to upgrade to a more equipped infrastructure at Akashvani Bhavan. Daily transmission kicked off in New Delhi in 1965, but television was still a part of its parent company, All India Radio [AIR]. Broadcasts were extended to include a school educational project. One of the earliest shows, *Krishi Darshan,* [launched on Republic Day, 1967] toed the central government's policy of catering to farmers and rural development. The service was extended to Bombay and Amritsar in 1972. Finally in 1976, television services were delinked from radio. It took a while though, to bring both radio and television under The Broadcasting Corporation of India [1990, *Prasar Bharti*], wresting it from direct government control.

The first real signs of turbulence began on the 'autonomous' *Doordarshan* in 1977, 18 years after its inception. The station opened with the soulful composition of Ustad Ali Ahmed Husain Khan and Ravi Shanker. The signature tune, though not as memorable as All India Radio's curtain-raiser, gradually played itself back in our mind down the years. But beaming waves without interruption was a tall task in those days. The constant disruptions were backed up with the apologetic *"rukawat ke liye khed hai"* [regret the interruption] sign.

So the arts, in order of appearance as I saw it, were theatre, radio, cinema. And then there was television. I was more intrigued by the nickname it eventually earned. The idiot-box. Initially, I attributed the metaphor to the kind of programmes they produced for the tube. It dawned later that the word unwittingly also reflected viewer addiction. The two of them appeared to complement each other! Still, television hadn't ignited criticism, yet. It was a cause for celebration. A reason to welcome technology of the time into our lives. To raise a toast to the evolution of the term "home-entertainment". It kept you glued to the clock, so as not to miss a show that had been programmed in your mind. Time had assumed a different dimension. Be it the absurdly expensive seconds of advertising or, years later, guest speakers being eased off during a debate on a crisis bothering the nation, because "I am afraid that's all the time we have".

Television came to be equated with time travel even if only in the present. People, images and happenings from across the world converging on to a single monitor evoking varied levels of interest from people from different walks of life. During its start-up days, one experienced the traditional hesitation from the old order to accept a technological intrusion into family domain. But the myopic vision soon gave way. Just like the subsequent reconciliation to computers, mobile phones and virtual reality. From Carnatic and Hindustani music recitals to film song sequences, holy sermons, live cricket matches [no multi-cameras though, only white flannel, no ultra- slow motion replays, stump mikes or third umpire] and news bulletins, the "audio" became "visual". Television was on its way to becoming a way of life, dictating a new schedule in households. Right up till half past ten at night when the lady on screen gleefully called it a day and the station went off air, leaving a blank screen reverberating with static waves. I was to learn much later that about one percent of the static visible on the screen was due to radiation from the Big Bang that created the universe!

Circa 1982: Doordarshan turned a full fledged National broadcaster. The box has since been a constant companion, subsequently an occupational hazard. Whilst our cinema sinfully indulged in what Jean-Luc Godard would have dubbed "the American cultural occupation of India", the tube offered to undo the creative corrosion that had seeped in with distorted "musicals" and the sweeping influence of James Bond. As an opportunity, television was elbowing for space next to theatre. Initially constrained by distribution oligarchy, where one was at the mercy of the government channel's policies, television was a gauntlet that only the valiant picked up as a business and creative option of the future.

For the intrepid and enterprising professional, television posed a mammoth challenge. For unlike cinema and even the theatre, where darkness bonds you and the proceedings, small screen audiences were almost, always 'somewhere else'. The assumption that television was 'free', prompted the housewife to cook her favourite dish even as she strained to pick up the dialogue on the set in the living room. The unexpected guest, the ill-timed phone calls and the wailing kids all contributed their mite in destroying the impact of what artistes had spent months to so thoughtfully create.

Nonetheless, it jump-started an all-new generation of writers, actors and creative heads, who stumbled and stuttered through its nascent days. And yet, an unwritten law of honesty and integrity prevailed, compelling the creative heads to digress from the routine and make it inventive, if not a masterpiece. However, followed a middle-order, which, as many observers would insist, was a complacent sector that fell short of capitalizing on a good start to an innings. Then, a rather sudden and unexplained descent into a vapid state of art, transformed those humble beginnings into mini classics. Surely, one isn't naïve enough to deny that audience tastes have undergone a metamorphosis. These trigger- happy, remote- toting viewers have unintentionally pushed all semblance of creativity under a commercial microscope. But what makes all the difference is, that, while shows were initially designed by film-makers, today they are largely whipped up by executive producers and communication school diploma holders.

Between being a product of a plucky past, and a deer caught in the headlights of a confounding present, I often feel like a fiddler on the roof. Here's looking back at a career not many, including me, would have envisaged. In these thirty-six odd years, very few time capsules have passed wherein I haven't been featured either as an actor or director. A record of sorts, as some observers prefer to see it. I bow, humbled. I am but a survivor.

This book, however, isn't meant to be an anthology of Indian television or a couch potato's handbook. Neither is it confined to a personal reminiscence of being there in the midst of the action. Despite being swayed by Laurence Olivier's confession in his book *On Acting* that "it is always fun to talk about yourself", I have attempted to perceive the scenario from the perspective of those who played important parts. I do not profess to sit on judgement of the works of my seniors or peers, but merely to capture their energies which affected me–pleasantly or otherwise. If I have overlooked the regional Indian channels spawned by the soap-opera syndrome, it's only because the formula merely manifests itself in a different language. The logistics are of pretty similar calibration. News channels, of course, have turned out to be a different kettle of fish altogether. For one, they killed the evening newspaper. Their strategy for news stories could give soap scriptwriters a run for their money. Then, there is this affinity for show-business related snippets to garner eyeballs. And on every other occasion it's an unabashed 'rerun' of *The Truman Show*. India, on the rare occasion, is pushing the envelope in an attempt to emulate a channel like CBS or a news anchor like Walter Cronkite. But that's another story.

The hunt for my lost television still continues. The mind's memory box rummages bucolic nostalgia. As I draw open the curtains of a window to the past, I brace myself to look in the eye, all of them–the teething problems, the frustration-ridden moments, the amusing trends, the cavalier players, the unexpected successes, the unresolved paradoxes and the lesson-in-it-somewhere failures. They all run like subterranean streams seeking sunlight. Thoughts outwit the pen as I rewind the rugged landscape of sponsor-driven broadcasting, cherishing the delights whilst cushioning the chaos.

It may appear presumptuous–attempting to condense 36 years of creative turmoil between the covers of a book, but it's the story of a world that set the ball rolling. A world that appears to be fraught with the dangers of infiltration from technology, thought and time. Once inhabited by a creative species who could be looked upon as aboriginals. 'Television warming'? Here, then unfolds their true story.

Of course like some observers claim, all true stories are untrue!

Television, for its major part may be all about episodes, but the story of Indian television itself seems episodic. It nestles itself into a three-episode saga that assumes the shape of a story about storytelling.

EPISODE

THE BEGINNING

New Delhi was the venue for the 1982 Asian Games. It was seen as an opportunity to usher in colour television broadcast in India. And to capitalize on the investment, came the proposal to go the radio way. Throw the field open to commercial players. But with only one government run channel in operation, the initial moves were crucial. The decision had made the box enter my living room... all that was left for me now, was to step inside it!

THE MAGIC LANTERN

The pigeons at Trafalgar Square may find the comparison odious, but their counterparts at the Dadar *kabootarkhana*, an aviary in central Bombay, of the early 1970s, weren't less inviting. But it was beyond the feathered cacophony that I led my unsuspecting father, into the confines of the Dadar Department Store. For, long before I could read Swedish film master Ingmar Bergman's passionate autobiography *The Magic Lantern,* I had discovered mine in that store. The toy projector burnt a forty-rupee hole in my father's pocket, a princely sum in those days for a modest person who manned the administrative section of an engineering and construction company. The demon seeds of my future, the television, were being surreptitiously sown.

The black contraption resembled a coffee grinder as I vigorously churned its wooden handle to make the film spool run and light up the wall of my tiny darkened room with silent images. Moving images I was fascinated by, images that gradually infiltrated my adventurous mind. I regarded the plastic roll in my hand with great care, my very own piece of 35mm film. Instantly, the narrow strips of

16mm films in the projector room of my school auditorium, where we had our initial exposition to cinema, appeared diminutive. As the characters of the film *Gumnaam* [Hindi's cinema's take on Agatha Christie's novel *And Then There Were None*] ran towards an aircraft noiselessly taking off, I was being subconsciously converted to the religion of cinema. Of course I remained oblivious to the fact that good South Indian *Tamizh Brahmana* [it shrunk down to *"Tam Brahm"* eventually] boys do not indulge in such detours from their culture. The only family history of artistic pursuit was my mother's fascination for the veena, an Indian plucked string musical instrument. She had tutored herself in playing one of the most eloquent instruments and then given it all up after marriage, when she migrated during the early 1960s from Thrissur [the town credited as the cultural capital of Kerala] to then, Bombay.

I must have missed the appalled look on my father's face as I interrupted his conversation with an acquaintance of his, a Tamil theatre actor. The rich aroma of filter coffee brew wafted into the Matunga bylane from the traditional Sharda Bhavan café across the street, as I, all of eight, craned my neck towards the tall actor and posed the objectionable question, "do you think you have a role for me in your play?" My father spared him the embarrassment of answering. I found myself being whisked away from my dreams as he began to reiterate the importance of education. Subsequently, for several years, Mahadevan Senior made sure that radio and television remained a conjugated version of a line from a commercial for a popular television brand. 'Neighbour's pride, my envy'. Cricket scores were updated by pressing one's ear to the wall to pick up the faint roar of the live commentary on the radio in the adjoining apartment. The sonorous voice of Ameen Sayani presenting the hit parade on *Binaca Geetmala* was however interrupted by weak signals on Radio Ceylon. My young neighbour and best buddy, Jaideep Mukundan, obliged by stealthily turning up the volume.

Art found an outlet in the books I borrowed from my school library at Don Bosco's. Back home, I was left to devour serialized stories by Dr Lakshmi in *Kalki* or other authors in *Ananda Viketan,* [both very popular Tamil weeklies] as my mother read them out loud. I was upset with myself for not having learnt to read and write in Tamil and Malayalam, a process I had begun in Kerala before school beckoned in Bombay. However, the narrations were enough to ferment in me a growing desire to tell tales. In the format of episodes.

Thrice I came close to witnessing a film shoot. Once [I was in fourth grade] on the way to school, I noticed a man driving a car with the door open and leaning out awkwardly. I wondered aloud what the man was up to. My mother who was accompanying me remarked that it was probably a stunt for a film being shot. I looked around for a hidden camera but there wasn't any. The next time I spotted it loud and clear. It was right under our nose, below our apartment in Wadala. The actors, the paraphernalia, the works. I leaned out of the second-floor balcony, foolishly hoping the camera would pick me up in the distance. I even made efforts to find out what the name of the film was, so I could catch myself in it on release. Of course that was as far as I got. Then after many seasons, across the railway tracks, in the distance I noticed [what I would learn years later] huge 'solar' lights. Unmistakably, a film shoot in progress on a building under construction. The two specks I strained to see, were, I was told, popular Hindi film actors Vinod Khanna and Shashi Kapoor enacting an action scene for a film called *Chor Siphaee*. Excited, I borrowed my friend's powerful binoculars and tried to get as close as possible. That night I dreamt of performing in front of the camera. It was a raw, passionate dream of desire bleached out only by the rays of the rising sun.

Dreams and desires, like water, have a knack of finding their own level. So today, instead of authoring a paper on the cyber knife robotic radiology that can blast away a tumour, or having a hand in tenecteplase, the life saving clot buster that could abort a heart attack, [as you can see, the zeal to keep abreast of developments in a career that was not to be, is still alive] I am reduced to penning a book on cathode ray tube 'emissions' and celluloid cravings that I was denied in my growing years. If I had access to Bob Hope those days, I would have sought refuge in his cryptic comment to dissuade my father from making me a doctor. "Think of the hundreds of lives that would be saved!"

But my father stood vindicated. Education held me in good stead. Whilst I pursued the sciences, I tutored myself in the arts. University debates and dramatics vied for attention with the hapless frog and earthworm on the dissection table. The Don Bosco institution in the green canopy of Matunga was among the earliest to adopt the Cambridge syllabus and examination system in India. So Shakespeare, Physics, Chemistry, Biology and Advanced Mathematics became part of the curriculum from the sixth grade itself. The class was brimming with ambitious candidates who raised the bar with healthy competition. It was like playing the best bowlers in the world. My biology teacher C. Rai still vouches that few could dissect the mud ridden earthworm cleaner than me. That was a citation I yearned to achieve in the performing arts too, each time I dissected a role. It's another matter that dissections are being phased out and teaching methods with computer simulated models being adopted. Much like actors' faces being scanned and superimposed on body doubles. Today, my biology teacher wonders if I could introduce his nephew, a budding songwriter to composers who could foster a career for him in the world of music. Is that how the cookie crumbles?

I think there still exists a subconscious guilt complex in me. Of not putting to good use the education we were so studiously subject to. That could be one reason I opted for a medical representative's job after my graduation. It sucked me into the medical profession, of course stopping a long way from being a doctor. I was once posted in what the pharmaceutical company executives felt was "an area of great potential" for the sales of antibiotics. The red light area at Kamathipura with the seedy Alexandra cinema, the titles of Hollywood potboilers translated into cheesy Hindi, the overflowing drains with their stench, the faces of women caged in the windows above and the forlorn look on their faces finally got to me. I felt horribly sick, my mind replaying the putrid atmosphere and even destroying my appetite. This job had to go. It was six months later that my degree in Chemistry met my pet hobby, journalism, at the offices of *The Chemical Age of India,* a technical journal where I could still cling on to the knowledge I had earned whilst getting a window for writing. It was as though the Universe had stage-managed my career at this point. For, below the offices of the journal at the Eucharistic Congress building in Colaba, was the tunnel to my wonderland.

The Blaze minuet screened previews of films for the print media before their theatrical exhibition. I befriended Commissariat, the manager, and sneaked into the shows, little aware that one day I would be managing these events. In 1980, V P Sathe, the director of Bombay Publicity, the agency that handled film producers and distributors' accounts noticed me, the odd-man-out at his screenings. He was a veteran in the field besides helming scripts for renowned filmmaker Raj Kapoor in the company of K A Abbas. He checked out my writing abilities with sample advertisements and must have been suitably impressed, for soon after, he recruited me as a copywriter. Even at a starting salary of a not-too-flattering seven hundred rupees a month, I was enjoying the process. Every element of the jigsaw suddenly fell into place. Advertising, journalism, theatre, television and films all converged into a common melting pot at the agency, Bombay Publicity. The 1980s were to become a defining decade of my career. The punishing posting at Kamathipura was a blessing in disguise. Or else, who knows, I would have graduated to becoming a senior sales executive in some pharmaceutical firm. Incidentally, Kamathipura too has changed. The women are migrating to distant suburbs as the lease on their cages has become unaffordable. Alexandra too ceases to exist as a cinema. It is now a dargah, a place of prayer. All sins have been atoned for.

I had read somewhere that the world is inhabited essentially by two erudite entities: the scientist, and the artiste. But somewhere down the line, there is a vital difference. For, while the scientist is constrained to deduce a formula in a one-dimensional mathematical calculation, the artiste has to go beyond the deductive derivation. Instead, their vision demands a three-hundred-sixty degree spectrum. There are no set rules and the formula could be turned on its head. Come to think of it, the artiste's job was tougher! I was needlessly undermining myself. It was a noble profession after all! And so the deed was done. My hobby morphed into a career. In hindsight, the sophomoric move wasn't too bad a deal. Even as my mother expressed displeasure at every opportunity, I conveniently construed this rewarding amalgam, as "the application of a scientific approach to the arts".

Beginnings are like opening nights. They are first impressions that spread like wildfire. They could either open up a generous window of opportunity or dent your confidence. For me, it had to be the theatre and the Bard of literature, Shakespeare. It would eventually pave the way for television and cinema. I couldn't have asked for a more auspicious baptism. My debut on stage in 1977 at the Tejpal auditorium [at the historic Gowalia Tank], almost on the heels of my graduation exam, was under the watchful eyes of the redoubtable thespian Yusuf Khan [Dilip Kumar], who was the guest of honour for the evening. With him in the audience my enthusiasm was buoyed. The garrulous Polonius in Hamlet must have rented a puny corner in his memory. As I rattled away,

"The actors are here my Lord,
the best actors in the world,
either for tragedy, comedy, history,
pastoral, pastoral comical, historical pastoral,
tragical comical, tragical comical historical pastoral,
scene undivided or poem unlimited,
Seneca cannot be too heavy nor Platus too light,
for the law of writ and liberty,
these are the only men!"

The audience cheerfully put their hands together. My first ever applause on a professional platform! A few years down the line, during the late 1980s, in the thick of my television stint, when I rubbed shoulders with Yusuf *saab* again at a press meet, he left me with the line "I like the way you conduct yourself". Those words served as an elixir, that nothing need be achieved at the cost of dignity.

Inspite of *Becket*, [an adaptation of Jean Anouilh's play, *The Honour Of God*] a film that I am still in awe of, I hadn't dared to entertain the British star Peter O' Toole in my dreams. So I had to pinch myself to believe that it was actually happening to me in my first film. It was the first quarter of 1983, just as television was being readied to invade us. A British crew was in India to film Rudyard Kipling's classic, *Kim*. The flight from Bombay to Jodhpur will remain etched in my memory. It was the first flight of fancy coming true. On location, as I walked across O'Toole's tent, I stopped with child-like anticipation. An aide signalled me to step out of range. "Peter's in there," he warned, sounding like an apostle to St Peter himself! As the Lama in the film, O'Toole regarded me, playing his assistant, and whispered "you are speaking too fast". My film baptism had begun in right earnest. I was contracted for a day with the thespian. But it ballooned into a week, as O'Toole, with contact lenses to hide his blue eyes, lounged in front of a storm fan to cool off in the sweltering Jodhpur summer. The lenses dried up in his eyes resulting in a long drawn ophthalmology. The entire unit, that also featured the late veteran actress Nadira, had to stay put till he recovered in his plush suite at the Umaid Bhavan palace. "Have we had our picture taken?" His phonetic voice enquired, ever so thoughtfully, after my portions had wrapped. It was a recurring request I had made, ever since I set foot on location. He had his personal assistant click a picture and instructed her to mail it to me. The postman never arrived. I still gaze at Sir O'Toole in a polaroid snap, which I managed to swipe off the continuity girl's file. The only evidence of my screen space with the towering thespian.

It was a slow but sure first step into theatre and films. Come 1984, with television looming large in the wings. I just had to hang in there. Only, my father wasn't around to witness it. It had been nearly eight years since his sudden demise after a bout of brain tumour. In later years, he had shed his didactic stand and even provided me with fodder for my first ever inter-school elocution contest. I was to speak on Gandhi, for three minutes. Even as I exceeded the time limit, the judges went for their bells like a fire station springing to life. I calmly stated "I'm sorry but it isn't easy to encompass Gandhiji's exploits in three minutes. So I beg you to give me a minute more." The audience clapped, as the judges smiled and relented. It was my father who had forewarned and armed me with those words. He wasn't so generous though, whenever I sought his help for essay writing in school. "Write it yourself or you will never learn". Though the extra time robbed me of the top spot in the competition, my second place was more popular with my teachers and friends who were mighty entertained by that bit of improvisation. A few years later, my father all of forty two, went "back to school" with me. A public speaking course over six weekends, where we enrolled together. The bus journeys from Wadala to the heritage area of Byculla in South Bombay, where the classes were held was akin to my school bus trips. Having your father in the same class as you isn't a commonplace occurrence.

These days I often wonder how he would have reacted to my rebellious adventure if he were around. Looking at your father in a photograph isn't as simple as it sounds. Him, younger than you and the thought that you have outlived his age, is a bizarre feeling. Even today, the conundrum engages my restless mind. Was he better off, not seeing his son smother his dreams of being a doctor, chemical engineer or research scientist? Or would he still have had a pat on the back for me, like the time when I had triumphantly brought home an inter-collegiate debate trophy? Then again I am paranoid about him turning away from the television set in sheer protest. Maybe, maybe not? It's an answer I'll never get, but will always yearn to know. My mother has reconciled in silent defiance. In the years ahead she was to bemoan my demeanour... "your eyes have lost their innocence". It set me thinking. In all the wild rush to improve performance levels, were we subconsciously replacing the element of innocence with calculable benefits? Is that what draws me to animals and birds....their quality of innocence that we as humans have lost? Today I want to gift her a *veena* and ask her to play all over again. But she laughs away the very thought. I realise that fires can't be rekindled in hearths that have turned cold.

Ironically, these days, my works on television and cinema, occupy the grooves of a technologically powered magic lantern, that does not demand to be hand-churned like a coffee grinder. My brother Ravi, a photographer by profession and techno-savvy by choice, in his enthusiasm, has had one of my rooms converted into a home theatre where a digital projector and a Blu-Ray player do the rest. Those obsessive images are back, this time on a bigger screen. Life seems to have come full cycle. I casually check into the departmental store at Dadar. They initially wonder what I am talking about. It is a new generation that is shuffling impatiently at the smartphone and video-gaming counters. One of them tells me that my magic lantern, has been off the shelf for years. They do not make them anymore.

Just like my father's dreams.

VIVA
MEXICO!

Circa 1983. Mexico threw up other palatable attractions besides its tacos, nachos and *enchiladas*. The discovery was effected by the visiting secretary for Information and Broadcasting, S S Gill. In fact he shoplifted an entire idea. The soap opera. Gill was aware that the government in India sought refuge in 'non-performance' as a safe and ideal way out. It sounded a subtle warning to the time-servers not to attempt anything off the beaten track. Fortunately, the Secretary was made of sterner stuff. He did not tow the regressive policy line. On his return from Mexico, Gill recounted the strange phenomenon he had witnessed with the excitement of an Archimedes. The serials were influencing Mexican society, even changing it. Gill extolled the concept of television shows on the Indian airwaves. It was a medium waiting to be reinvented and adapted for a wider section of society. Rounding up like-minded, middle-of-the-road filmmakers like Basu Chatterjee, Gulzar, Sai Paranjpye, Kundan Shah and others, he elaborated on how the format could be implemented to advantage here. But the Mexican soap references sounded alien to most of them. "We couldn't figure what the hell he was talking about, and anyway whoever wanted to get into television?" was Kundan Shah's initial reaction.

Gill's approach now assumed near-mercenary proportions. When Kundan Shah landed in Delhi in June 1984 to receive the national film award for his cult farce *Jaane Bhi Do Yaaron*, he found himself being tailed. It was Gill the stalker. "We must do something for television. So when are you coming to see me?" Shah who preferred to be far from the madding crowd of television, hadn't bargained for Gill and his persistence. "Imagine, they were chasing us those days," reminisced Shah in an apparent reference to the striking contrast today.

The government bus, ferrying the national award winners to Janpath, moved at the pace of files in a bureaucratic office. Shah suddenly felt a hand grabbing the scruff of his neck. Surprised, he looked up to see Gill breathing down his back, speaking in monosyllables. "Tomorrow, 9.30, you, me, my office". From the look on his face Shah realised that the Secretary, I&B, wasn't playing dumb charades.

It was the June of 1984. Just five months prior to the assassination of Indira Gandhi. The Golden Temple issue and the Khalistan turmoil of the Punjab had reached a dead end. When Shah walked into Gill's office at the appointed hour, agitated voices reverberated from the adjoining conference room. It was packed with Sikh representatives. Shah wouldn't have won a prize to guess the room temperature. But before he could utter "*balle balle*" his jaws dropped as he spotted Gill leaving *that* conference and heading towards him. It spoke volumes for his seriousness. The point was well taken. Before he could even broach the topic again, Shah found himself assuring the minister that he would come back to him with a television project. Gill exuded a vision and initiative and was all set to give Indian television a change of scene.

Long before Gill's impending revolution, television in India was content with its partisan beginnings, with a mere seven city telecast. Four hours of prescribed programming on stark black and white television sets. Except when an English cricket team came visiting. In the latter half of the 1970s and early 80s, the two government controlled channels, [one central and the other state], swung alarmingly close to what one had heard about television glasnost ["a tortoise crawling towards freedom of speech"] in the Soviet Union. It was said that the main channel there catered to government propaganda, and if you switched on the secondary channel, you had a KGB agent popping up and directing you to watch the first. The policies in India were in similar territory. They were hard-pressed to adhere to governmental diktats of projecting an archetypal middle-class ethos with a family that rallies around social demands.

The television set was now screaming to be part of the household. I had, had enough of invading the privacy of friends and neighbours, picking programmes of my choice and dropping in as an uninvited guest. So on a bright Sunday morning in 1979, it was shopping time, yet again at Dadar. The Zarapkar department store was a block away from where I had once picked up my projector almost eight years ago. A *Crown* brand tag said 'Rs 3000'. I had saved up for that from my *Chemical Age of India* days. I carted it home and carefully housed it in a wooden cabinet with sliding doors. And promptly wrote to my uncle that his picture box had finally arrived.

Living in Bombay, one got an eclectic mix of programmes, truly cosmopolitan in nature. The local Bombay Doordarshan had began to beam shows in 1972 and even its Marathi programmes appealed to a wide cross-section of viewers. Writer C V Joshi's popular series *Chimanrao Gundyabhau* was among the first comedy adaptations in any language. Dilip Prabhavalkar as Chimanrao and Bal Karve as Gundyabhau set an early benchmark for the genre. My "second-language" education stood me in good stead as I relished the early smiles on Indian television. The other Marathi infotainment targeted farmers with *Aamchi Maati Aamchi Manse* [Our land, our people], children [*Kilbil*], and students [*Dainandeen Vigyan, Gyandeep*]. Despite their minimalistic format, I found myself watching, more out of fascination for the medium than the content itself. The regional film on Saturday evenings and the Hindi film on Sundays, were, not surprisingly, rated the most popular. Bombay Doordarshan had two other standard fares. The guide to upcoming shows of the week [*Saptahiki*] and even one on missing persons *Aapan yaana pahilat ka* [*Gumshuda* on the Hindi network]. Gujarati theatre exponent Adi Marzban and the wizened pair of Baban Prabhu and Yakub Syed gave viewers their first taste of stand-up comedy. In *Haas Parihaas,* they reeled in the laughs, blissfully unaware that this format, twenty odd years later would emanate from garish sets, stand up comics and a bench of judges deciding who'd have the last laugh.

Biwi Natiyon Wali, [early 1980s], the soap about a woman who was always at hand to help others was the first Hindi series to attract a faithful viewership. With K P Saxena, the satirist, penning its scripts, this Lucknow Doordarshan production gained popularity on the national charts, and despite no barometer of television rating points during the time, frequent household discussions reflected its reach. Playing in tandem alongside it was Paintal, the Pune Film and Television Institute graduate who played Laddoo Singh Taxiwala in a series of the same name and another to woo the senior citizens called *Dadi Maa Jagi*. Film-based shows, in those days too, wooed more eyeballs. Tabassum, a child actress turned anchor, was television's first celebrity host. Despite lack of colour or an ostentatious set, she roped in stars for *Phool Khile Hain Gulshan Gulshan,* a chat show that star-struck fans eagerly tuned in to on Friday nights. Her proximity to the stars ensured that the biggest names turned up for an often irreverent tête-à-tête, steering clear of gossip and controversies, instead of indulging in homilies and nostalgic moments. Little wonder then, that it still holds the record as Indian television's longest running chat show.

Long before video cassettes and players took over our lives, the Hindi feature film slot on Sunday evenings was the only other outlet besides cinemas, for the movies. It was a window to watch those films from the black and white times that wouldn't play at cinemas again. It vied with the song medley show *Chhaya Geet* for top ratings, proving a cliché, that there is nothing better than star power and glamour to draw audiences. Of course the discerning viewer opted for shows sourced from the USA, Germany and the UK. *Fireball XL5, Here's Lucy,* Charlie Chaplin's shorts, *D'fferent Strokes, Star Trek, Old Fox [Der Alte]* and *Didi's Comedy Show* all gave us a sampling of programming in overseas. Their modest country cousins were a children's show *Magic Lamp*, a quiz contest "*What's the Good Word*", anchored by theatre actress Sabira Merchant, and a weekly Sports-Round-Up by Fredeun Devitre. *Chhaya Geet*, was the first to turn commercial but rather tentatively. I recollect how my friends chuckled loudly when the very first, rather familiar commercial of a popular dental paste [actor Benjamin Gilani modeling for Forhans] a regular curtain-raiser on cinema screens, came on rather apologetically in black and white on the small screen. There was no mistaking the "so-television-has-fallen-prey-too" snigger, by the regular viewers congregating in a neighbour's apartment.

Nothing was really trending until *Hum Log* came along, on 7 July 1984. Even as the humble sets, the languid shooting style and old fashioned filming format came under the hammer from higher creative echelons, audiences overlooked the warts and sought identification with the late Manohar Shyam Joshi's edifice of the reach-out-and-touch characters. My morning train journeys from Wadala to Chhatrapati Shivaji Terminus (then, Victoria Terminus) and from Grant Road to Bombay Publicity, were filled with animated conversations of the previous night's episode. Eavesdropping on these groups was a revealing exercise. The characters in *Hum Log* had, as if, merged with the families of the office-goers debating the decisions taken in the previous night's episode.

That people who create history do not know it, holds good and true for *Hum Log*. Twenty-five years after its telecast, the media paid tribute to the likes of Basesar Ram, Dadi, Nanhe, Badki, Chutki, and Lalloo. The character had gained precedence over the actor. The Doordarshan co-production with emerging software producer Shobha Doctor boasted of no familiar faces or ornate staircase dominated sets. What keeps it alive in memory is that *Hum Log*'s sentiments were echoed by the millions who followed their fortunes, trials and tribulations of the North Indian family. The affable grandfather, the alcoholic son, the rather crude grandmother and all the children with their idiosyncrasies were an addiction on Tuesday and Saturday nights, rounded off by veteran actor Ashok Kumar who brought his own brand of dignity to the summation. It was indeed the icing on the cake. His "*Chhanna Pakaiyya Channa Pakaiyya Chhanna ke upar joga, Badki-Majhli ka jhagda bhai dekhenge hum logaa.*" was an amusing sign-off. The Brechtian technique of weaning people away from the story raised the level of social significance. So popular was this episode summary, that South Indian audiences brought in a regional flavor with veteran Tamil actor Shivaji Ganesan stepping in for Ashok Kumar.

It's the post script however, that dished out the statutory warning. It didn't take long for the *Hum Log* actors to discover that television could throw up stereotypes too. If one wasn't on the lookout, it could trap you in your own image. So, Rajesh Puri remained the prototype Lalloo in practically all his films. Much later, film actors Arun Govil and Deepika Chiklia were to discover to their chagrin, that they have been immortalized as Ram and Sita after the outlandish devotion they sparked off with the viewers of Ramanand Sagar's mythological, *Ramayan* [1986]. Almost six years later I was to witness a rather unflattering incident. It happened on location near a *dargah* on the outskirts of Jaipur while shooting for

Sanjay Khan's historical, *The Sword of Tipu Sultan*. Deepika in all her regalia as Hyder Ali's wife had come to "pray for an offspring" at the holy shrine. In our make–up tents, we were distracted by a commotion outside. I didn't know where they had descended from, but what greeted us was the sight of villagers falling at Deepika's feet and paying obeisance to Sita. The actor's dilemma was palpable. Whether to pride herself on being recognized even behind a traditional Muslim garb or regret the permanent halo around her head. In India, you don't deny the masses their dose of faith. You stand smiling smugly and bless them.

Riding the crest of *Hum Log*, Gill's Mexican syndrome eventually manifested itself as 'prime-time' television. It took all the right cues from Mexico's 1970 commercial soap-opera formulator Miguel Sabido who merged culture and entertainment with great success. Besides being a moral and role-model guide, it satiated one's need to know what was happening in other peoples' lives. Miguel also mooted the theory of soap operas being human communication theories that could boost social infrastructure, something he found lacking in a developing country like India when he had an audience with Prime Minister Indira Gandhi in 1982.

After *Hum Log*, *Yeh Jo Hai Zindagi* by Kundan Shah wrested the prime time slot. And then it didn't rain, it poured. The first few weeks [1984] threw up a royal clutter. I cosied up to Parikshit Sahni's lawyer in *Barrister Vinod* [Mondays], *Hum Log* [Tuesdays and Saturdays], Sridhar Kshirsagar's ode to *Dallas and Dynasty* in *Khandaan* [Wednesdays], Sai Paranjpye's quintessential neighbourhood *Ados Pados* [Thursdays], the delightful *Yeh Jo Hai*

Zindagi [Fridays], Aanand Mahendroo's version of *Three's Company* in *Idhar Udhar*, Basu Chatterjee's crusading *Rajni* and *Darpan* [short stories], Yash Chopra's *Khazana*, and Rajshri's *Paying Guest* and *Wah Janab* amongst others, completing our Sunday mornings. All of them feature in this episodic journey in subsequent chapters. Because they were all part of that unforgettable "opening week night".

*Jump cut to: Circa 2010. This was life after **Hum Log**. But the nostalgia persisted and with it, an urge to revive the series. Doordarshan, in an effort to regain some of its lost viewership, decided to give it a new avatar. For some reason they dropped the "log". The series was simply called **Hum**. No one from the cast of the 1980s original was approached. Quite a few of them openly expressed surprise and disappointment. Yet the attempt was to recreate the original. Shobha Doctor, now played 'mentor'and claimed that it was only a take-off on **Hum Log**. The joint family was replaced by a larger subset.. the inhabitants of a village. And Ashok Kumar by dadi Sushma Seth, to round off each episode. These days they call it Season 2. It took Doordarshan twenty five years to wake up to this seasonal flavour. But then, everything has changed. The joint family is on the way out. There are as many divorces as marriages. Even the neighbours aren't the same. And even if they are, we won't be rushing to their homes to watch **Hum [log]**. History in this case, sadly, doesn't repeat itself.*

THE COMIC
BUCCANEER

It was what the movie moghuls would have called a "blockbuster opening week". Though only 28 percent of Indian audiences had access to television in 1984, the introductory evening shows became the topic of society discussion. Barring *Hum Log*, which had already created a religious viewer bank over the months, the others had their task cut out for them. Popular names from cinema propelled the initial draw. Amol Palekar, Rameshwari [*Ados Pados*], Girish Karnad, Shriram Lagoo [*Khandaan*], Parikshit Sahni [*Barrister Vinod*] amongst others. But this was also the week of the new breed, the television actor. Names from the theatre and occasionally cinema, like Neena Gupta, Mohan Bhandari, Shekhar Suman, Supriya Pathak, Ratna Pathak and Priya Tendulkar would soon give movie stars a run for their popularity. But it was the foursome of Shafi Inamdar [the late actor and a stage regular], Satish Shah, Rakesh Bedi [both Pune Film and Television Institute graduates] and Swaroop Sampat [fresh from a few feature films] in *Yeh Jo Hai Zindagi* who scored brownie points. This despite the fact that the story of their coming together was not the cakewalk that Kundan Shah would have expected, armed even as he was with ministerial approval.

The top guns at Ogilvy & Mather, the agency that offered to pick up the sponsorship tab for the series, began by shooting down Shah's concept. They had taken a fancy for an American soap that had become popular for spoofing social norms and suggested that Shah write an Indian version. After all, the Yankees could do no wrong. Shunted to a corner, Shah found shelter in a 'Mad-magazine-come-alive' concept and conjured a take on the Hindi film industry, which was to, a couple of years later, emerge in the garb of a series titled *Manoranjan*.

The operation at hand needed more 'doctors' and Shah found a cerebral ally in an enterprising new writer and director Manjul Sinha. Together they conjured up a classic American style sitcom with Indian sensibilities, and scheduled a script reading session with the managing director of O&M and businessman S S Oberoi, who had made a marketing success of a herbal dental paste [*Vicco*]. Oberoi, as it turned out, was a buccaneer. Shah was asked to submit a budget. The figures he came up with make for an interesting case study in contrast to what television would splurge in the new millennium. Rs 120,000 for an episode that set aside Rs 8000 as the director's fees and Rs 6000 for the writer. What Shah wasn't aware of was that this created a furore among other producers who thought Oberoi was out of his mind. Eager to grab a piece of the pie, they projected a figure of a mere Rs 30000 for an episode. "But Oberoi had faith in us, and the rest was history", observed Shah.

All this was afoot during an age when Doordarshan was still looking West to strike a balance. The imported software comprised of sitcoms like *Here's Lucy*, and *D'fferent Strokes*, and space shuttles like *Star Trek* and its ilk. The "What you talking about Mr D?" by the diminutive pouting figure of the late Gary Coleman in *D'fferent Strokes* was the most mimicked line after the Indian film *Sholay's 'kitne aadmi the'*. It left Shah wondering as to how the man in the hinterland of Sangli, a remote village in Maharashtra, would reconcile with this "cultural anarchy". These were American soaps in an unfamiliar milieu. *Yeh Jo Hai Zindagi's* primary target was to purge the alien influence and culture.

"June we met, September we were on air", is how Shah trumpeted the route map of *Yeh Jo Hai Zindagi*. The principal characters Ranjeet [Inamdar] and Renu [Sampat], were both offshoots of friends in real life theatre person Ranjit Kapoor and the late Renu Saluja, who had made her mark as a film editor. Kapoor's henpecked, multi-tasking husband whose discipline was suspect, pitted against a domineering wife in the Delhi stage production of *Ek Ghoda Teen Sawar*, were the springboards for the couple in Shah's script. But the wife living in reflected glory [her brother was a police officer] did not appeal to scriptwriter and humourist Sharad Joshi who recommended swapping the cop for a nincompoop. This eventually balanced Ranjit and Renu's characters with the brother-in-law [Rakesh Bedi] playing a parasite.

Kundan Shah initially had in mind Satish Shah who had played "dead" with aplomb in *Jaane Bhi Do Yaaron* [admittedly inspired by the Cuban film *Death of a Bureaucrat*]. "Only the dead body," Shah clarified, "it wasn't in the first draft, but then I incorporated it." Satish Shah actually failed the look-tests for the husband or the brother-in-law. The director knew Satish was imperative but had no inkling how to incorporate him. On the other hand, Shafi was a theatre major but a serial appeared to limit his scope. So a comic spirit that bound the characters and their situations had to be Satish's calling card. It was then that Manjul Sinha, who scripted most of the episodes, had a brainwave of making the rotund actor essay an important cameo in each episode. At first Shah didn't buy the idea but Sinha's convincing powers saw the actor, in chameleon fashion, don different garbs every week.

It was another day at work. The decrepit facades of the foundries along the industrial belt of Sewri accentuated the romance of train travel in rather strung-out fashion. It was like walking into the pages of the Charles Dickens' classic *Hard Times*. But the mood in the carriage was upbeat. As I balanced myself on the footboard watching the locomotive lazily trade tracks, I was all ears to a critical analysis of a show that had become a perfect antidote for the blues. The guessing game afoot was "what would Shah's *avatar* be in tonight's episode of *Yeh Jo Hai Zindagi*?". The same actor playing different roles in the same show was a new gimmick. There was an occasional disapproval that he appeared more of a caricature, than a character, but it didn't really matter to the majority. The commuters were thoroughly entertained. His "*thutty* [30] years of experience", a line performed with much relish, had stuck. Shah, eventually turned out to be what Oberoi called "the pillar of the show". Pleased with his popularity, Oberoi in an aside told him that he deserved a raise and was planning to give him one. Shah humbly turned it down saying it would dampen the spirits of the rest of the team. Oberoi understood and divided the bonus money with the other actors.

The title refrain of *Yeh Jo Hai Zindagi* is still high on the television memory charts. When pop star Ajit Singh composed it, S S Oberoi blew a bugle, "let's get Kishore Kumar to sing it!" Kumar, the maverick actor-singer-composer, had not stepped out of the movie circuit before. In his legendary style, without batting an eyelid, he rattled off a figure of 18,000 rupees, the fees he charged for a film song. Oberoi didn't blink either. He could see the song playing on television every week. Over 52 episodes it would amortize to less than 400 rupees a week. And so Kishore Kumar sang for television. But then *Yeh Jo Hai Zindagi* was one show which had its say, any which way. They dictated to the ministry what slot they wanted, they pencilled in the day and time, and decided what the plots would be. Notwithstanding the fact, that the lack of competition was a major contributing factor to the popularity of such shows. But that they hit the laugh buttons far better than their successors, puts their story in another perspective.

Kundan Shah wished they had the last laugh too, but that was watered down a bit for some time. Shafi Inamdar felt the first signs of television recoil when audiences called out to *"Ranjeet"* during one of his stage performances of *Chung Ching*, the Hindi adaptation of *Move Over Mrs Markham*! It was a spoiler that annoyed him to no end and he wanted out of the series. He was eased out after 24 weeks. Veteran actress Farida Jalal tried to fill in the vacuum as Ranjeet's aunt, but despite her ebullience, the viewers weren't ready for a change in plot and character. So Inamdar resurfaced in episode 44. The show dragged its feet till it hit 72, by then even

Kundan Shah had quit.

Yeh Jo Hai Zindagi could well have conjured the smile emoticon. That I had lived during those times was no small mercy. Besides, it had achieved something else that no one had possibly anticipated. Kundan Shah overheard Rakesh Bedi and Swaroop Sampat saying that during the shoot they had to turn up the windows of their cars to dissuade people from mobbing them. He dismissed it as a manifestation of their newfound exposure, until he decided to check for himself. It was indeed happening. The day of the television star had dawned. Satish Shah milked his cameos in a spate of commercials. Some of them had three Shahs in different garbs running riot. Even Eddie Murphy's *Nutty Professor* would have been amused. But Shah wasn't. To date he objects being bracketed as a comedian.

CHANGING
LANES

In 1983, as Indian television was waiting to forge a footprint, I was in the thick of theatre. Shakespeare, Gogol, Arthur Miller, Richard Nash, Moliere, Ray Cooney, Badal Sircar, Mohan Rakesh and Vijay Tendulkar were some of the playwrights put to the sword by our unbridled enthusiasm. Television which dangled *Hum Log* in our living rooms, appeared to be teasing and taunting our ambitions every night. But entertaining thoughts of graduating to the small screen was met with much circumspection by the *Ank* theatre group director, Dinesh Thakur, who had made a successful screen debut with *Rajnigandha*, director Basu Chatterjee's charming new age look at relationships. Thakur appeared to equate film ambitions to army desertion. The unthinkable act of exploiting theatre as a stepping stone to the movies. Whilst I appreciated his dedication to the stage, his stand left me at a dead-end. Packed performances at Shashi and Jennifer Kapoor's artistically crafted Prithvi theatre in Juhu made for memorable moments but didn't double up as a source of revenue to pay my bills. There had to be an alternate medium, without writing off the incomparable joy of intimate theatre. But something told me I needed to bide my time. Audacity wasn't exactly one of my virtues.

In these circumstances, the run into Sai Paranjpye was fortuitous. Not surprisingly it was "*the theatre*!" as Neil Simon proclaimed in his adaptation of Chekov's short story "*The Sneeze*". I had just performed multiple roles in Simon's exhilarating play *The Good Doctor*. In the company of actor Salim Ghouse who directed the play, I auditioned for, what I was told was, a television play, praying fervently that a twerp like me would pass muster with the director of acclaimed films like *Chasme Baddoor*, *Sparsh* and *Katha*. It was during this audition that I learnt about the big wave that was about to hit television. Paranjpye animatedly explained how Doordarshan was commissioning sponsor-backed fiction shows to be telecast on prime time [9 PM] everyday. They had shortlisted one director for each day of the week and approved a basket of concepts ranging from mystery [*Barrister Vinod*], soap [*Khandaan*], family [*Ados Pados*] to comedy [*Yeh Jo Hai Zindagi, Idhar Udhar*] and short stories [*Darpan, Khazana*]. I listened, excited. This was just what the doctor ordered!

Not surprisingly I found my energies propelled into making things happen. The act of a sexton driven to dire straits by a maniacal dentist, caught Paranjpye's attention for the feather-brained character *Chintamani* in the series she was planning, *Ados Pados*. It was another twist of fate, that Ghouse, the man responsible for my meeting Paranjpye, fell out of favour with her. Playing a theatre director, Ghouse had somewhere let his real-life approach spill over to the sets. A predictable "difference of opinion" with Paranjpye saw him being 'packed off to Canada' after the four initial episodes.

That was probably the earliest exit a character made, a precedent that many soaps followed with the unconvincing but functional "this character will now be played by..." tagline. In years to come, an innovative insurance policy against renegade actors followed. Invariably, the first day of shoot included a 'photo-session' where pictures were clicked. The actors got the hint. If they weren't on their best behaviour they would turn into garlanded portraits on the wall, killed in an unfortunate accident or by the ever-obliging blood cancer. Not to mention the concept of plastic surgery that seems to have found more patronage in television scripts, than on the cosmetic surgeon's table.

For Paranjpye who began her career as a producer with Delhi Doordarshan, television was no stranger. But despite the exalted company of veteran theatre persons and writers like Shama Zaidi, A Prasad, P Kumar Vasudev, Habib Tanvir, Swadesh Kumar and others, only dull education shows ruled. Short of producing hard-core news programmes, she tried her hand at everything. For one who tags herself as "a first-rate writer and a second-rate director", she found television an ideal grooming ground. Her first television film *The Little Tea Shop* (1972), won the Asian Broadcasting Union Award at Teheran. Later that year, she was selected to produce the inaugural programme of Bombay Doordarshan. One of her television plays *Raina Beeti Jaye* with Kulbushan Kharbanda and Sushma Seth later metamorphosed into the National award-winning movie *Sparsh*, with Naseeruddin Shah and Shabana Azmi reprising the roles. And the sleeper hit comedy *Chashme Baddoor*, which established her credentials as the country's first eminent woman director, had its origins in yet another play *Dhuan Dhuan*.

Sakke Shejari, her Marathi theatre production, which was the springboard for *Ados Pados*, was a concept she was deeply fascinated by. "Being a middle-class loner, I was prone to hankering for company. I had turned envious of friends who had relatives and visitors galore in their houses. So the vicarious me took over. I made a mental note of the numerous relationships and interactions of neighbours. In the eventual series, quite a bit came from my play chugging along with a train of new thoughts and observations". Her estranged husband Arun Joglekar, theatre actors Chandu Parkhi and Usha Nadkarni with a whole bunch of kids added to the slice-of-life fun that Paranjpye gleefully helped herself to.

The query, "I hope you have free dates to allot to film our series" tickles me even in hindsight. It was the first time someone had vaguely accorded me 'star' status and respected my time, which I was only too willing to devote. She then proceeded to give me a narration of the episode. I listened in. The smile in her voice as she 'enjoyed' the reading still lingers. She had designed the production in a budget of less than three lakh rupees for each episode. With such a huge cast and a set that was rebuilt for each schedule, this was a lesson in meticulous planning of finances without aesthetics being compromised.

Paranjpye, like her senior contemporary filmmakers Hrishikesh Mukherjee and Basu Chatterjee, resized the middle-class. For her, life virtually began and terminated there. The animated title sequence in *Ados Pados* where every character appeared like a cuckoo in a clock, opening up windows, within hand-shaking distance of each other symbolized their match-box existence in the city. And the "open house" attitude of the neighbours resulted in amusing interplay as characters flitted in and out turning a mundane existence into the peep-hole vision of the director.

As I entered the portals of the famed Natraj Studios in Andheri, I reflected on how I had always wanted to be a fly on those hallowed walls one day. The compound housed some of the biggest names in big screen entertainment. Shakti Samanta, Atma Ram [brother of the much celebrated Guru Dutt] and Pramod Chakravorthy were among the filmmakers who had their offices at Natraj. I had met each one of them with V P Sathe, to discuss publicity campaigns for their films. Bombay Publicity catered to virtually every filmmaker's advertising programmes and was probably the only agency that could boast of releases that occupied a full page in Times of India each day of the year! And there I was in those make-up rooms, readying myself for my first big step.

Toeing the technique of television, Sai brought into play a multi camera set up for the first time on the commercial arena and even preferred to do a major portion of the edit on-line as she whispered to the person on the console "camera 2.. camera 1...camera 3". The three cameras on the set ensured that the scene was covered from all angles eliminating the need for counter shots. It also facilitated attractive match-cuts at the edit table, so that one action flowed seamlessly into another cut. Virtually all American and European shows availed of this technique, cutting short filming and edit hours in the process. Fortunately, Paranjpye opted for theatre style workshops and execution as we grappled with our characters. For a beginner like me, this instilled oodles of confidence. It also took me closer to the unforgiving ways of the camera. My first lesson was eye-control. In one scene expressing surprise and shock, my eyes widened more than they should have. I cringed. I learned to warm up to the economic demands of the camera. It was just the beginning of a long-standing affair with the lenses!

Playing hooky from the job at the agency, predictably left a few senior colleagues' tongues wagging. They didn't take very well to Sathe *saab* granting me licence to accommodate another career. But Sathe was graceful - "Finish your work and go if you have to". Which I did. After all, not everyone got to debut with a Sai Paranjpye show. Neena Kulkarni was exactly how Paranjpye had described her. "You are going to have a very beautiful wife". We projected the ideal foil to each other. Me, Chintamani, sweet, adorable and a twit as Paranjype had perceived him, and she Champakali, the domineering wife who was at her wits' end when her husband brought home an overgrown pumpkin in lieu of his monthly pay or decided to buy the entire stock of spinach in the market because it was going at a throwaway price. *Ados Pados* had a whole bunch of neighbours running riot. Veteran actor and poet Harindranath Chattopadhyay as the classic loner uncle, Arun Joglekar with his pack of kids, and Chandu Parkhi, a thief who callously flitted in and out, were among the characters who raised a chuckle with their idiosyncrasies. Though film stars didn't exactly relate with television in the eighties, the aura of being the director of critically acclaimed films, was good enough in drawing Amol Palekar and Rameshwari towards *Ados Pados*. Movie actors had lesser hang-ups those days and, in fact, were happy to be part of a series. It was in concurrence with the American way of thinking, where several big names performed in theatre and television without any qualms.

The grand-daddy of the cast, Harindranath Chattopadhayay dropped in on the sets one day. I introduced myself and then casually, Neena Kulkarni as "my wife". A few weeks later when her husband Dilip Kulkarni, himself a stage actor, visited the sets, Neena introduced him to Chattopadhyay as "my husband". The foxed look on the veteran's face was a moment frozen in time. It took some explaining to make him realise that I was the screen husband, and Dilip the real one. Years later, and much to her chagrin, I still jocularly refer to her as "my first wife" and wait for the listener's almost never failing words of sympathy, "oh I am sorry" before resolving the mix-up in a gush of laughter.

Chattopadhayay was a personality to experience. And learn from. He had a way with limericks. One of his favourites that he loved to recite was "*I am not afraid of a tiger/I am 60 years of age/I am not afraid of a tiger/Provided it is in a cage*". It was difficult not to be inspired. I used the opportunity to peddle some of my own lines, though I knew that I didn't hold a candle to his work. But he surprised me by saying, "you must write more often. Don't stop here".

The contract that Doordarshan drew up those days was for an initial 13 episodes renewable to 26 or 52. Thirteen episodes done, the channel issued a termination letter. "The series is not given an extension", the letter simply said. The officials probably felt that the comic elements in the show were understated. A loud farce would have worked better for them. *Ados Pados* was probably expected to, as Alec Guinness had put it, "fantasticate the mechanics". Why can't real people be funny? Paranjpye, of course, did not let the diktat influence her sensibilities. She opted to wrap up the show. The days of television rating points weren't in vogue then. Rather, the number of commercials booked was the yardstick. The absence of competitive channels was a determining factor too. A good series caught the imagination of the masses and they sat back to enjoy it. That was it.

On the last day of the shoot, a solemn air prevailed. It seemed like the cessation of a mini lifetime. I offered to refund all my remuneration if she could get them to extend the series by another thirteen instalments. Paranjpye could only react with a "how sweet of you" smile. It was the first of many deaths I was to live. Last days, I was to later realise, were inevitable. But Paranjpye dispelled the gloom with a, "What fun we had. It was terrific."

Trying to put the termination out of my mind, I dwelled on the positives. I was part of the opening of commercial telecast in the country. It would eventually be part of the record books. My only grouse was the quality of telecast. The lush greens of my spinach were washed out on Doordarshan. The channel wallowed in that time warp for years, despite grandiose plans to upgrade its technical finesse. It was, however, a teething lesson for me. Much later in the day, calculated colour correction on my film prints became mandatory. I wouldn't want cinema audiences to grimace like I did when I watched *Ados Pados*.

Time, as is its wont, flew. Two decades later. The spring of 2004. Chintamani stubbornly refuted the adage that public memory is short. When a passerby stopped in his tracks to tell me how he still remembered the 'power-cut' episode, where I am caught complaining to the power company, despite the lights having come back on, it reminded me how characterisation makes a difference. Paranjpye seconds it. "Like I said, I am a good writer and wrote all these lovely characters in. The uncle's band of kids [*mama ka paltan*] all wearing similar dresses cut from the same cloth, the neighbourhood thief who seeks shelter in one of the homes, and a whole lot of quirky people peeping into each other's abodes. "But Chintamani, the fool with a heart of gold, was one of my all time favourites. Only a Chintamani would pick up a sackful of spinach just because the vendor was giving him a discount. And then end up selling it to the neighbours to get rid of it. I have known so many Chintamanis. They never die."

Paranjpye's favourite real-life episode on the sets concerned one Sharad, a teacher in Pune and a dear friend of hers. Life had given him a raw deal. He was plain awestruck that his friend was a film and television director. So he worshipped Paranjpye, massaged her ego and the kickback was a scene he bagged in *Ados Pados*, the role of a baker who had a mundane line to utter. Sharad ended up making a royal mess of it. Fifteen takes later, when he still failed to get it right, Amol Palekar started getting uptight. "Who the hell is this," he muttered under his breath. Arun Joglekar issued a subtle warning, "if you wish to continue on the show, do not utter a word against him. He is a very special friend of the director and has come all the way from Pune." Palekar obediently backed off. After the episode was telecast, Sharad's students made a remark, that was nothing short of inflammatory: "What a shame sir! You call her your friend and all she gives you is an inconsequential part to play". Sharad cut off ties with Paranjpye after that. "After all the trouble I took, this is what I get", she says laughing it off. She followed up with two more serials *Chhote Bade* and *Hum Panchi Ek Chawl Ke*. She was honest enough to admit that both had characters which were spin-offs from *Ados Pados*.

When I ran into Paranjpye years later, I tried to explore the chances of a re-run of *Ados Pados*. "But where are those tapes lying?', there was no mistaking the despair in her voice.... "With Doordarshan? You got to be joking! One of my best documentaries during my Doordarshan stint was on the legendary singer Pankaj Mullick after he had won the Dadasaheb Phalke award. I got him to sing the unforgettable "*aayee bahar*" on the terrace of his house even as his wife was occupied with sorting the rice for dinner. I persuaded P C Boral and even Hemant Kumar [who wasn't on talking terms with Pankaj Mullick] to speak about him. If Doordarshan could misplace this rare recording, *Ados Pados* hardly stood a chance. But I am to blame too. I wasn't thoughtful enough to make a copy either of that or *Ados Pados*".

I hark back again to that all-pervading first week. The summer of 1984, when I converted to my new religion: television viewing. The blurred images have more clarity than those which succeeded them three decades later. Parikshit Sahni got to shed his brother-father image and play a no-nonsense lawyer in *Barrister Vinod*. The ritual of *Hum Log* on Tuesday done with, we switched to *Khandaan* on Wednesday. It brought sheen and opulence, besides a bright new director, Sridhar Kshirsagar on the scene. The presence of stalwarts like Girish Karnad, Shekhar Kapur and Tanuja enhanced its appeal. But when it came to Thursday, the opening night of the telecast of *Ados Pados*, by a strange quirk of fate, I was performing *Kachchua Khargosh*, the Hindi version of the original Marathi play [*Sasa ani Kasav*] on which Paranjpye's film *Katha* was based. As the clock struck nine, I decided to utilize the time of my short exit from a scene. I sneaked out backstage, through the stage door and out behind the Tejpal theatre. I could faintly hear my voice emanate from half a dozen television sets in the neighbourhood. I was on air finally! It was a great elixir. And a funny sense of déjà vu. From cricket commentaries to my debut on the small screen, I still had to have an 'ear to the wall' to savour the moment! There was more surrealism to follow. In the summer of 2003, I ended up moving into the apartment next to Sai Paranjpye's at the Ambar Apartments in Juhu. Paranjpye was now a next-door neighbour! I stepped into her living room to playback my first audition there. It was *Ados Pados* all over again. That bench in the premises below, where we shot the spinach sequence was still there–like a testimony from a time machine.

They say elephants come back to their place of birth to die. I had come back to live!

FACE IN THE CROWD

Entertainment during my school years was restricted to playtime and reading. Owning a television was a status symbol. Unknowingly, I had stumbled on to the concept of an on-going series many years before our television embraced it. Those Tamil language publications that found their way home with weekly precision along with *Ambilimama* [the South Indian version of the popular illustrated folklore magazine *Chandamama*], *Ananda Viketan* and *Kalki*, had serialised stories, initiating me into soaps and mythologicals. The stories had their instalments marked with numbers, and ended on a high note each time, just like episodes on television. In fact, *Vikram-Vetaal* [the Ramanand Sagar project on Doordarshan], was first graphically serialised in *Ambilimama*. Little did I realise those days that I was 'reading' the future of television.

December 1984: The television debut hadn't affected my routine. It was still the morning 8.15 packed-to-the-brim Harbour line suburban train that would take me from Wadala to the Victoria Terminus station from where I would head for the film previews at the Eros cinema minuet in Churchgate. I had donned an additional mantle. That of a film critic. I gathered it was the best way for a self-taught film appreciation course. I started off being published in film weeklies like *Cine Advance* [printed from Calcutta] and *Variety India* [a start-up by M S M Desai, a journalist who had quit the premier film weekly *Screen*], before being noticed by R K Karanjia's first Bombay news tabloid *The Daily*. Rajiv Kunwar Bajaj, an enterprising and dynamic news person was the editor and we hit it off from day one. He became the guiding light that stitched together my formative years as a critic. Bajaj, who led a chequered career in the print media, eventually graduated to becoming a national figure on television with his *The RKB Show*. As both, a news editor and celeb host, Bajaj became an influential force and continues to highlight and debate significant issues that plague Mumbai.

Back to the train journeys, I could sense an air of transformation. The initial stares of co-passengers and their stifled giggles spoke a new kind of "hello". Deciphering those subterranean thoughts was the new pastime. Later, perfect strangers did not shy away from opening conversation, quite often to figure out whether they had guessed my face right. The look on their faces was a probing "what is he doing here on a train?" But that wasn't going to burn a hole in my ego, not for a long time. A vehicle was clearly unaffordable those days. Today, after all these years, I still do not hesitate to hail a three wheeler autorikshaw if the need arises. All you have to do is answer a few simple questions that bother the driver while he glances at you in the rear view mirror. And with unfailing regularity, it's him, the quizmaster who wins this contest, informed as he is, about your work. This was one aspect I admired about the versatile actor Farouque Shaikh. He actually enjoyed 'auto' rides because the parking problem resolves itself and you don't have a driver breathing down your conscience!

If fate had willed otherwise, I would never have been on that train nor would have had a supplement to a modest income. So when Sai Paranjpye told me that my fee would be three thousand rupees for each episode of *Ados Pados*, I considered the offer more than generous. For a reason. When I had completed the last of my graduation exams, a well-meaning friend had advised me to not wait for the results and grab any job, "because they were not easy to come by". So, I stepped into the neighbouring South Indian Welfare School in Wadala where I lived, and applied for a teacher's post. The principal wondered why I wanted a job that paid only three hundred rupees! "Oh, three hundred is good enough!" I beamed. "You really value money, don't you," he said with a wry smile. He did not give me the job. As I looked at Sai Paranjpye's first cheque, I did not know whether I was supposed to be grateful to that school principal. I still accept modest sums with a lot of gratification. It may have bracketed me in the lowest paid actor-director category. It could be a weakness that my producers have turned into their advantage. Each time I am asked "how much", I fear the greed of the greens may deny me the job. Someday, maybe, I will muster courage to attach a monetary value to my work.

January 1985. It was a lazy afternoon at the Bombay Publicity Service. The release orders for the next day had been dispatched. This sugar bowl of advertising, [as the *Times of India* film critic

Abad Karanjia nicknamed it], was also an improvised "coffee shop" for film folk where news percolated all day long. A snippet on the front page of *Mid-Day*, a popular eveninger drew my attention. The report said that Sridhar Kshirsagar, the maker of the aspirational *Khandaan* (the star-studded Indian take on high society American shows *Dynasty* and *Dallas*), was on the lookout for a lead face for a new comedy series he was planning. It was titled *Ghar Jamai* [a husband who stays put at his in-laws' place]. A few telephone calls later I had Kshirsagar's Worli office details. Armed with an appointment, I slipped away from the office at Lamington Road in a taxi, praying that I wasn't the hundredth candidate for the job. I remember that taxi ride like it happened yesterday. My pulse races every time I rewind to it. As I cursed the traffic signals and bumper to bumper traffic, I could well have been in an ambulance fighting to reach a life saving clinic. I prayed hard. As hard as an ambitious twenty-five-year-old could.

Astra Telecast's tastefully done up interiors mirrored the mind-set of its director. I waited at the reception that appeared to suffocate between the front door, an accounts office and an editing suite. I tried to take my mind off its nervous ticking by playing a guessing game of whether Astra stood for 'astral' or '*astra*', as in 'weapon'. A staircase wound its way up to a mezzanine floor dressed in ethnic style, including straw mats neatly laid out. It was an endearing hark back to my Kerala beginnings. But this was no time to revel in nostalgia. I was here to shake the hand of the enigmatic, bearded Kshirsagar, who peppered his English with a Bangalore accent. Kshirsagar was among the earliest to recognize the potential of the small screen and though he hadn't cut his teeth as a filmmaker yet, a discussion with him reflected his command over content and the medium. *Ados Pados* spared me the laboured ritual of an introduction. At least it wasn't "*Ananth who?*". But then, Kshirsagar wasn't peddling false hopes either. After a brief narration of the concept, he diluted my excitement with "we are also considering Pratap Pothen, so you can keep those fingers crossed." Pothen was a popular star in Tamil movies. The thought plagued my mind as I took a taxi back to the office.

Suspense is an element best enjoyed on screen. In real life it can get to you, as I experienced waiting for what could well have been Godot, for all I knew. It took a week for the Graham bell invention to ring in the new. It happened while I was penning one of those corny "*All prints engaged in 2nd week!*" captions for a film advertisement. It was the moment every aspiring actor yearned for. Sridhar's assistant Mohena Singh's voice. "You are on", she said nonchalantly and asked me to come over to meet Sridhar. Momentary blackout, then my mind flashed to Pratap Pothen. What could have transpired? I didn't want to know!

52 episodes of *Khandaan*, the soap with many senior faces, seemed to have made Sridhar feel confident about his associate Mohena Singh's ability. "He set me up with my first directorial venture - *Ghar Jamai* - at the right royal age of 22 or was it 23?! He was one heck of a teacher. He taught me the importance of editing, certainly the most vital part of any audio-visual product. When I later went on to man *Jugalbandi*–an espionage series and other products–from his stable, Kshirsagar admitted graciously 'the scholar ran before the master'".

Satish Shah and Farida Jalal, fresh from their *Yeh Jo Hai Zindagi* popularity, were the best co-stars a newcomer like me could have been pitted against. I had first watched the ebullient Jalal in a film called *Paras* [though *Taqdeer* and *Aradhana* were her early films], and admired her spontaneity. And here I was sharing screen space with her! Kshirsagar sure did things in style. The Windsor Manor Hotel in Bangalore flaunted a banner welcoming the unit of *Ghar Jamai*. I doubt if any other television producer in those days had displayed such a gesture. The month-long schedule to film 13 episodes kept me away from my theatre performances and job. Those were the days when channels didn't await television rating points [TRPs] to decide how the next episode would be written. They followed the American pattern of filming an entire season of 26 episodes before telecast. Of course in the decades that followed Indian television chose to live by the day... and on many an occasion, die by night.

It was the longest period I had stayed away from the city. It initiated me into a career that would demand prolonged absences. A young Rajit Kapur, playing my brother-in-law, shared the room with me. I could sense his irritation as I buried myself into my scripts in preparation for each day's scenes. He was more prone to fun and preferred to frequent the disco to turning a script-worm. No soothsayer in that room could have predicted that he would one day become a regular face in the films of the auteur Shyam Benegal and even bag honours at the National level for his portrayal of the young Gandhi in the veteran's *The Making of the Mahatma*.

Two factors got me locking horns with my character and the script each day. First, I didn't want Kshirsagar and his director Mohena to feel that I was second best to Pratap Pothen, their original choice. Secondly, Sai Paranjpye's off-the-cuff comment. When I broke the news of having bagged the title role in *Ghar Jamai* and described the character to her, Paranjpye felt that the multi-faceted Malayalam actor Nedumudi Venu would have been best suited to play the part. I hadn't seen that coming. Maybe it was the director in her speaking, but it threw a gauntlet at me. But I picked it up. This sitcom of a South Indian [Kannadiga, not *"Madrasi"* as people generalize it] son-in-law in a North Indian household was like a cat among the pigeons. Only, this time the father-in-law was the cat and the son-in-law, the pigeon. I made a concerted effort to steer clear from the caricatured South Indian and play Subbu with just the right accent. It must have worked. A delighted Doordarshan chief Harish Khanna, after watching a preview of the pilot episode, called Kshirsagar and remarked *"kahan se pakad ke laya yeh Subbu"* [where in blazes did you hatch this Subbu?] The name Subbu stuck ever since. In fact Rajit Kapur still addresses me by that name. And onlookers wonder why I answer to his calls of "Subbu".

Bangalore, true to its reputation, had a moderate temperature even in the summer. In the neighbourhood building, a juice-blender whirred as its blades cut through some hapless fruit, reminding me that life followed its unchanged routine oblivious to the scripted excitement and ambitions in my hotel room. As opposed to the domestic blender, my room coffee percolator hissed like a dragon on its last throes of life as it spat out the final bit of foam into the cup. It was my elixir before reporting on location every morning.

I was initially comfortable living in the reflected glory of Shah and Jalal, fully aware that titular opportunities don't happen every day. Besides, it was a learning process. About acting and cameras too! The part required me to be bespectacled. During one particular shot, a strange thing happened. The flare from a light refracted from my glasses and embedded itself in the lens of the camera. We all gathered to look at this rare eclipse on a lens. It seemed like a cataract on the retina of the camera. The attendants wrapped the equipment in a cold cloth and placed it gently in a corner like a sick baby. We had no option but to wait until the image of the flare gradually died down. On another occasion, right in the middle of a long heated scene between me and the wife, Kamia Malhotra, the telephone of the house which we had leased, rang. From the corner of my eye I caught the look of alarm on Kshirsagar's face, but before he could utter "cut", I reached for the phone and answered it, telling the caller that he had the wrong number. The person on the other side couldn't decipher my behaviour and disconnected while I banged the receiver down to resume my dialogue with Kamia. When Kshirsagar exclaimed "cut", the unit was in splits. The response to the interrupting call was in sync with the cranky mood of the scene. I quietly thanked my theatre roots for the presence of mind. The telephone rang again. As the owner answered it, I escaped to the next room to avoid his suspicious gaze.

Kshirsagar was pleased as punch with the results. "It's a hit" he declared with amusing pomposity after watching the initial edits. A week before the telecast [*Ghar Jamai* was replacing his own long-running *Khandaan* on the Wednesday night slot], the buzz had started amongst the early morning crowd. The 8 AM locals were buzzing with, "they are coming up with a comedy called *Ghar Jamai*". I was curious to know how the 'face in that crowd' would fare. It would only be a week before the jury was out.

I guess it took a while for *Ghar Jamai* to sink in as a comedy of manners. For those fed on the staple sitcom diet, this clash of North and South rituals could well have been a "culture shock". But gradually Mr Mehra and Subbu came to 'stay'. Mohena admitted that as a genre, comedy was certainly a tougher option. "It doesn't come easily to me. It obviously didn't come easily to Sridhar too, as he himself confessed. Probably that's why he had me direct *Ghar Jamai*. But then again, it wasn't a comedy like "*Yeh Jo Hai Zindagi*" which was stomach-clutching funny. This, on the other hand, was about relationships, adjustments, habits and the cultural diversity of opposites under the same roof. It was a more poignantly humourous serial. That's why I think I enjoyed directing it."

On the eve of the premiere telecast, an upbeat Kshirsagar, confident of *Ghar Jamai's* success, was briefing us on how to handle the media and be politically correct. He may as well have lectured us on how to deal with unemployment. For, Doordarshan officials, fuelled by stray feedback that the series ridiculed communities, played safe with the mandatory thirteen episodes and did not keep their word of the promised extension. It was my first tryst with the fickle ways of bureaucracy. And this was only the tip of the iceberg. I was to discover that we were a nation of 'oh-so-easily-hurt people'.

It was also my first brush with the gossip columnists. Harmless in comparison to today's paparazzi, but gossip all the same. The *Illustrated Weekly* [now defunct], a magazine of repute from *The*

Times of India group, on their film and television page reported that an affair was brewing between me and Kamia Malhotra, who played my wife in the series. Though harmless, it did put me in a spot of bother. Then *Stardust* ["the magazine that turns stars to dust" as actor Shatrughan Sinha wrote in jest], followed it up with more yellow linen. It was like an "initiation" into the world of show business. The anointment made veteran film critic Iqbal Masud remark with his typical guffaw "Congratulations! You have made it to *Stardust*! You are now wholly and absolutely corrupted." The grapevine wasn't as effected or influential as the Instagram age. *Ghar Jamai* went off air but stayed alive in memory as a unique culture conflict.

Stree was a hugely creative idea that Kshirsagar nurtured, a series that was truly inspirational. The docu-drama for national television spoke about women who'd taken on professions which had hitherto been the domain of men. It was revolutionary for the early days of television and was, by far, Kshirsagar's finest concept. I had to be satisfied playing a part in just one episode, thanks to the episodic format. But several actors of substance like Ratna Pathak Shah, Rohini Hattangady, Kiron Kher, Farida Jalal and others enacted real-life characters so early on in their careers. It was the first series on women empowerment, a theme that the pro–millennium shows sought refuge in, quite often to camouflage their stereotyped characters and arguably regressive plots.

Amidst all this, Kshirsagar had planned a small screen magnum opus based on the Navy. He drilled in the fact that I wouldn't be landing title roles all the time. I had to be part of an ensemble too.

I understood. It was an obvious truth. But naval red-tape, script scrutinies and possibly unfeasible budgets stalled his ambitions. I could sense his dismay when in the late 1990s, DD Metro, the satellite arm of Doordarshan commissioned a series on the life and times of Indian Coast guard officers titled *Sea Hawks* toplined by Om Puri, Niki Aneja and Anup Soni among other popular television names. Kshirsagar's dream had achieved fruition elsewhere. *Sea Hawks*, a UTV production saw directors Anubhav Sinha and Shivam Nair successfully cut their professional teeth before taking on the big screen challenge.

Kshirsagar, of course, wouldn't be caught sitting back and relaxing. In an attempt to be prolific, he plunged headlong into one series after another. The detective series *Jugalbandi* and family soap operas *Manzil, Gulmohar Lane* and *Anand*, all of them with his regular actors, Girish Karnad, Benjamin Gilani, Tinnu Anand, amongst others. These, however, lived in the shadow of *Khaandaan*. And when the results weren't as exciting, the pressure began to tell. No one really knew when he had reached for the bottle for succour. During a shoot of *Manzil* in Bangalore, I thought I was seeing things. The morning shift had barely begun. I watched him step into his car and open the glove compartment. I turned away trying hard to ignore what I saw. I couldn't bring myself to see one of my favourite directors use a crutch to prop himself up. Expectedly, the shows lost their sheen and were downscaled on the viewer charts. Kshirsagar was grappling with the whys and hows of the turnaround. For him, it was a twisted John Huston situation. "I don't try to guess what a million people will like. It's hard enough to know what I like." But I guess Huston must have said that in better times.

The nineties were in their final throes. The new millennium was knocking on our doors. Astra Telecast had but become a pleasant memory. Mohena moved to Bangalore where she turned an independent producer. Kshirsagar was confined to his South Bombay apartment, harbouring plans of a comeback. Around the time, I was directing my first major series *Chamatkar* on the Sony Television channel with actor Farouque Shaikh playing the man who could hear things and read your mind. The success of the series brought me in contact with producer Dinesh Bansal who had just made an impressive debut with *Kurukshetra* [on the Zee network] helmed by the veteran filmmaker Lekh Tandon. I had a brainwave. I suggested to him that we revive *Ghar Jamai*. I was all for second seasons, long before Indian television and digital platforms made a bee-line for it. The thought struck the right chord with Bansal who was willing to purchase the rights from its original creator.

Reconnections can be demanding. From a time when I had rushed to grab the main part in his series, to the day I was going to approach him to buy the rights of that very product, was a far cry. Kshirsagar agreed to meet me. As I rang the bell of his Nepean Sea Road apartment I switched back to the evening I had pressed the button outside the door of Astra Telecast. That was more than ten years back. There was a mirror on that door, where wannabes like me would settle their distraught hair to look their best before they entered. It didn't take me long to discover that this was a two-way mirror. Inside the assistants would have a hearty laugh at the aspirants giving their hair a quick finishing touch. The mirror on this day, was Kshirsagar's face. I could see myriad reflections as he sat me down in his enclosed balcony. The house exhibited a huge collection of books, statuettes and some original Tanjore paintings of Hindu Gods. The style certainly hadn't diminished, though the energies seemed to have ebbed. Sridhar indulged in philosophy, "I was foretold by the forces that someone would come into my life and revive my career". The irony was too blatant for me to take. He was in need. He agreed to sell the rights of *Ghar Jamai* for a mere twenty thousand rupees. His other scripts too were there for the taking, he said. I heard him out patiently, only too happy to be of some comfort to the man who was instrumental in shaping my career. *Ghar Jamai's* second season duly acknowledged his creation in the opening credits– *"Based on characters created by Sridhar Kshirsagar"*. I wish I could have been a bigger help. But his other scripts did not find favour with the new breed of channel creatives. Today, I occasionally leaf through them. He had painstakingly etched those character sketches and stories. I replace them in the rack. Mementos of a director whose career curiously turned dormant.

The millennium was well into its fifth year. One afternoon, I solemnly leafed through a report in the *Mid-Day*. It said television producer and director Sridhar Kshirsagar had breathed his last. The very newspaper that led me to him, completed the obsequies.

Life had come full cycle, in its royal theatre of the absurd.

THE LIGHT
AND SMOKE
SHOW

Ghar Jamai's sudden demise after its first season had saddened me. It was a role and show that I had pinned a lot of hopes on. This was the second time, after *Ados Pados*, that a show was being discontinued because someone up there in New Delhi's Mandi House seemed to lack a sense of humour. Quite naturally, it weaned me away from Wednesday's prime time, a slot that I had looked forward to, for three months. But the curiosity to witness the show that had been allotted that window, got the better of me. Both the genre and the story turned out to be vastly different. This was a grim, dark world that was being attempted on Indian television.

Bharat Rungachary was one of those enterprising young men who started his career as an assistant to filmmaker Hrishikesh Mukherjee. In fact, Hrishi *da* once admitted that Rungachary was the best assistant he had. He had independently shot an interesting documentary on a day in the life of the star, Amitabh Bachchan, that was screened on Doordarshan one evening long before the channel's sponsor-driven era. Rungachary's sights were always set on the big screen and he did, in fact, complete some stylish big-ticket entertainers like *Waqt Hamara Hai, Khatarnaak* and *Baat Ban Jaaye*. Television, however, offered scope to reinvent and he was probably the first director to hit on the drug addiction that was threatening to engulf the college going youth of the time. *Subah* [The Dawn] was the title that sought to create the possibility of respite for youngsters who had thrust themselves into a world of artificial utopia.

Rungachary's Tamilian roots made him familiar with *Avan,* the novel penned by writer and social activist Sivasankari. The story was a trendsetter mapping youngsters from different economic strata and upbringing falling prey to the menace of the dreaded powder. It also facilitated a spotlight on youth, a genre that was missing so far from the channel's commissioned programmes. The novel gave the director enough scope to explore the mindset of youngsters who could be easily swayed into dark alleys. The roles threw up fresh faces like Kumar Bhatia, Ragesh Asthana and Anil Bajaj. My friend, and theatre director, Salim Ghouse made an impactful comeback to the small screen playing a junkie Bharat, who tempts the trio into intoxication. *Subah*'s theme and scenes whipped up the expected "unsuitable for family audiences" whispers in the corridors of Mandi House, but the series lasted the prescribed 13 weeks.

Subah had a striking initiation to its episodes. Rungachary had succeeded in getting the expertise of popular music director

R D Burman for the moody title number. The composer's signature rendition of *"eh zamane tere, saamne aa gaye"* was the extra edge a series of this kind could do with.

Rungachary was always brimming with ideas. My interaction with him lasted for several years, but work was limited to a brand ambassador commercial of a South Indian finance company. He went much before his time. Much before he could see the fructification of his dream concepts. I suspect a dual reason. The stress of box-office performance coupled with family pressures.

Matching the restlessness of Rungachary was a South Bombay boy who made his debut in Kshirsagar's ensemble of *Khandaan*. Viveck Vaswani's enthusiasm for theatre, films and show business in general, was unbridled. After *Khandaan* had completed its run, his prying eyes fell on a script written by Ravindra Wagh, a teacher from his alma mater, The Cathedral John and Connon school. Vaswani turned Wagh's story on its head to explore the influence of drugs among the elite South Bombay crowd. The series was titled *Nai Dishayaen*. Vaswani chose to play the affected boy in a show that was funded with an initial one lakh rupees by Ravi Gupta from Trikaya Advertising. What he had devised as a college production assumed enviable proportions as he succeeded in enticing his *Khandaan* co-stars, Girish Karnad and Jayant Kriplani, to topline the project. Being a fanboy of Navin Nischol the star, made Vaswani reach out to him to play his father. Nischol's reaction was cryptic. "This clearly indicates that my days as a hero are over"! Parikshit Sahni and Anju Mahendru completed the ensemble cast for the pilot episode shot by debuting camera person Kiran Deohans. He was, in the years to come, to carve a niche for himself as a celebrated cinematographer in Hindi cinema. Vaswani had this eye for talent. That he introduced Shah Rukh Khan to the film business, hence came as no surprise.

The pilot episode of *Nai Dishayen,* shot with frugal facilities at Vaswani's own apartment and the terrace of a Nariman Point building that offered a 360 degree view of the bay city, found its way to Mandi House for approval. That was when things ground to a halt. Vaswani waited for the postman forever and even wrote reminder letters, but the reply was nowhere in sight. Tired of the wait, he decided to travel to Delhi and camped at a cousin's place while seeking appointments with the officials at Mandi House. Finally, a lady named Pramila Kalhan heard him out. Vaswani was quite curt in his approach. "I am not saying approve my work. But at least take a decision instead of wasting the precious time of a young filmmaker". Kalhan turned out to be an influential political journalist. Before he knew it, Vaswani found himself in an article written by her for the *Hindustan Times* that proclaimed the "angst of a young filmmaker who had dared to take on the mandarins of Mandi House".

Even as he was being subject to admonitions by his friends for committing hara-kiri, the article attracted the attention of an influential politician who suggested that he meet then Prime Minister Rajiv Gandhi. The PMO's office, as expected, took time in fixing a meeting and Vaswani found himself spending his days with a kindly lady at a furniture store in Khan market who had virtually "adopted him". When the Prime Minister finally gave him an audience, Vaswani requested closure to the long-standing episode. "Approve it or trash it, but please finish it once for all". Gandhi found the request absolutely fair and personally instructed the department heads at Mandi House to watch the episode and come back with an answer.

The following day when Vaswani walked into the Doordarshan office, he was witness to heads rolling. Bhaskar Ghosh, the head of All India Radio, who had just assumed office as Acting DG, gave him a long stare that seemed to enquire of his deeds at the PMO. He had recruited his entire team of 21 staffers from All India Radio to watch *Nai Dishayaen*. He heartily approved of the product, as did the others. Abhinav Chaturvedi, Delhi actor, joined the cast as the show was granted a Saturday night slot for 13 weeks. Vaswani's grit had won the day.

I was to experience it again years later when he signed me on for my first feature *Dil Vil Pyar Vyar*, a brainchild of his. It was India's first retro-musical that used the published music of R D Burman and went on to become a cult film. Despite the shortfall of funds, Vaswani was resourceful enough to have the film completed and released.

For me, he will always remain the boy who took on a Prime Minister for a television show.

HERE'S RAJNI

At times my clock plays a trick. For that split second the needle seems to step backwards and then it ventures on its course as though cocking a snook at me. For that moment I feel as if time has retraced its step. The Information and Broadcasting Secretary S S Gill was attempting a feat close to that and more. He sought to recapture all those past times, when he thought of the *Mahabharat* as venerable fodder for a mega-series during the inaugural days of the Doordarshan national network. This was much before the popular filmmaker B R Chopra had toyed with the idea. Gill had even broached the concept with new age director Basu Chatterjee. Chatterjee was aware that the auteur, Satyajit Ray too was keen on filming the epic for national television, and how the prohibitive economics did him in. Basu*da*, as he is fondly known, had formed an informal triumvirate with his peers Hrishikesh Mukherjee and Gulzar in the seventies and eighties. In those decades of multi-star cast, formula-driven films, they defied the trend with a homely 'middle-of-the-road' approach. After probing marital disillusionment in his sensitive debut film *Sara Akash* [Clear Skies], he took a charming detour with *Rajnigandha* and *Chhoti Si Baat* and a few years later turned so prolific that it prompted Hrishikesh Mukherjee to ask him to "take it easy" in an article he penned for, the now defunct film monthly, *Star & Style*.

Perhaps Basu*da* never read that article. He was, however, honest enough to admit that it was the lure of money that made him jump on the television bandwagon. His caricaturing ability [he was a cartoonist in the weekly tabloid *Blitz*] stood him in good stead. And that's what made him doodle the character of *Rajni*. Rajni, interestingly, was initially designed on the lines of the popular American series *Here's Lucy*! a housewife who stumbled her way through problems, largely of her own making. Gill, delayed temporarily on the *Mahabharat* track, bought the idea and even assured sponsorship from Mudra, the advertising agency. In 1984, the pilot episode was filmed with movie star Padmini Kolhapure playing Rajni. But when she was faced with the "horror of an episode a week", she quit because it meant "too much time and work"!

Basu*da* had run into celebrated playwright Vijay Tendulkar's daughter, Priya, at a party. But Priya's rather strong demeanour did not blend with the image of the vivacious Lucy. Cinema's other leading ladies, the winsome Moushumi Chatterjee or the spunky Amrita Singh looked better suited to play her. So Basu did a volte-face. Political and social awareness lead to the birth of a character that was the by-product of consumerism. He then effected a 'sex change'. The common man became the common woman, who picked up cudgels against a dysfunctional system. The irreverent Lucy was transformed into a social activist.

Initially, Priya was finicky about draping herself with those modest cotton sarees, but her father who knew Basu*da* well, egged her on to follow his dictum. "I had never set out to make *Rajni* the iconic crusader she eventually grew into. What started off as a caricaturish Lucy, had mushroomed into a spokesperson for harrowed housewives". No public utility was spared. The postman, the gas cylinder agency with its delivery boys, the electrician, the telephone wireman all came in for severe castigation. The stricture on budgets made sets inaccessible. So Basu*da* quietly set up base in his screenwriter Ranjan Bose's apartment, which gave the series its middle-class, lived-in texture. With rebellion hand-delivered at your door-step. The *Indian Express* published a full page 'Letters to the Editor' column, hailing the new social non-conformist and reformer. Television was being taken to heart. For Sunday morning viewers, Rajni was real. Came a time when Priya didn't know what to make of her own popularity.

But others lapped up the idea. Theatre director Dinesh Thakur prudently bought the rights of Vijay Tendulkar's play *Anji*, the tragicomedy of a lady's journey and promptly cast Priya in it. The writing lent itself to an arresting choreography on stage and I found myself playing a philandering Prabhudayal, who leched after Anji. My docile Chintamani of *Ados Pados* and Priya's fiery Rajni were the two images that we were fighting to erase. But it also contributed to the play's immense success. Much as we disliked the misplaced attention, audiences thronged to watch the star rather than the character. All the same, it was like a payback to theatre, a fact that would have suited Thakur. Another profitable fall out for Priya was the increasing number of commercials she was approached for.

Basu*da* himself helmed two of those. "I shot for two or three days for each advertisement, when the trend was to be at it for nearly ten days to make it look like a lot of work. The agencies felt I wasn't doing justice to their films. They stopped giving me jobs after that!"

Circa 1986. A hark back. Bombay Publicity was seeing another of those hectic days. The landline rang. The senior executive Walawalkar, with his spectacles perilously balanced on the bridge of his nose, had this hawk-eye look as he handed over the receiver to me. The man on the line introduced himself as Basu Chatterjee. This was curiously interesting. "Would you like to feature in an episode of *Darpan*? I can pay five hundred rupees". I had never been subject to a more precise and matter-of-fact style of an acting offer. The humble amount was the last thing I wanted to come between me and one of our finest directors. So within the space of a heartbeat I surprised him by blurting, "of course sir, thank you!" As I disconnected the phone with a smile on my face, I could feel Walavalkar's glare. He knew that I would be playing hookey from work. Again.

Darpan [The Mirror] was the first series of short stories that aired on the prime Sunday morning slot. In fact, it was telecast back-to-back with *Rajni* for a full year. It also brought me up close with renowned theatre personality Rohini Hattangady, fresh from her triumph as Kasturba in Richard Attenborough's epic *Gandhi*. On the sets depicting a lower income household, I would prod her on and then be all ears as she spoke about how Attenborough went through the meticulous process of casting her, her scenes with Ben Kingsley and finally how it all climaxed with a limousine driven hospitality at the Oscars. And I had thought that this was the stuff fairy tales were made of!

Basu*da* considers the *Darpan* series his most satisfying work, though I K Behl, the producer, initially felt that the stories were best read and did not lend themselves to visuals. His remark challenged the filmmaker in Chatterjee. "How could anything not be expressed in visuals? At the end of the day I am glad I did *Darpan*". Basu*da* indulged in maniacal schedules those days. He was filming a feature *Zevar* simultaneously and pulling off a balancing act between the big and small screens.

Many years and three shows [*Kakaji Kahein*, a popular political satire with Om Puri, *Byomkesh Bakshi* with Rajit Kapur playing the quintessential Bengali detective and *Humaari Shaadi*, a television feature] later, Basu*da* revisited the short story culture. E*k Prem Katha,* based on love stories from literature, however found no sponsors on Doordarshan's slots. Basu*da* discovered to his chagrin that the sombre days of *Darpan* were over. Dazzled by a new trend of glitz and pace, the channel heads dubbed it "slow" and relegated it to a non prime-time slot. The director had to fight for better sense to prevail and bring the show back on the main network. Chatterjee realised that it would take more than a Rajni tirade to set such anomalies right.

SHORT
CUTS

2002. It is quite possible that I may have missed out on a vital de-link. When did the 'short story' make a quiet exit from the radar of television? The genre which found ready acceptance during the Doordarshan domination and later, even on satellite networks till the turn of the millennium, appeared to have lost its advocates. Any proposal to revive it was met with a cold stare from channel executives as though I was propagating a social taboo. Like programmed robots, they utter, "sorry, we do not have a slot for it", depriving the best works of literature a television exposure.

It would have been a bitter pill for producer Manju Singh to swallow. The actor-turned-television-software-lady [who featured in Hrishikesh Mukherjee's mischievous spoof on double roles, *Gol Maal*] had pioneered the genre in 1984 with her series *Ek Kahani*. It was among the earliest shows on television. In fact it was the celebrated author Amrita Pritam, who mooted the idea of this format for the small screen. For *Ek Kahani*, Singh had a bouquet of stories sourced from various regions of the country. The series premiered with Pritam's own *Junglee Booti* directed by Usha Dixit.

Dixit was closely associated with Singh in dual roles as writer and director. What set apart the 12 episodes from others was their filming in the very regions the stories originated from. Dehra Dun and Gharwal were among the locations that threw up such tales. Local actors who had never faced a video camera enacted several pivotal parts. Like an episode, based on a Tulu story, was shot with actors who were part of a Tulu theatre group. The series was thus truly rooted in Indian soil. Assam's acclaimed director Jahnu Barua featured in the roster of names that helmed the episodes. Quite a few actors who debuted with the series went on to carve a niche for themselves in the future. The names that became familiar were Pallavi Joshi, Ashvini Bhave, Kruttika Desai and theatre personality Meenakshi Thakur, who played the authoress Amrita Pritam.

In 2006, Singh attempted a revival with *Phir Ek Kahani* but the encore wasn't what she would have hoped for. Dixit attributed it to the daily soap syndrome that had flooded the channels. "The channel executives opined that short stories being complete in themselves did not have the ingredients of a daily show to ensure that audiences returned the next day to find out what happens next. Also, it wouldn't make a difference to a viewer if he missed a short story episode, unlike soaps that had daily recall value with strategic hook points".

Back in the mid-eighties, Yash Chopra, the filmmaker who had moved away from elder brother B R Chopra to make popular hits *Daag, Deewar, Trishul, Kala Pathhar, Kabhie Kabhie* and *Silsila*, couldn't resist the bandwagon either. He signalled his television entry with a show titled *Khazana* around the same time as Basu*da*'s

Darpan [1985]. It was, as the title suggested, 'a treasure chest of tales'. I had essayed a guest appearance in his multistarrer *Vijay* and featured in the box-office hit *Chandni* too. Besides working on the advertisement copy of his films at the agency. So the call from his office for a part in *Khazana* didn't come as a surprise. On that morning, Chopra seated me down in his Juhu bungalow and addressed me with an air of apprehension. He was fighting shy of revealing that my character in the episode did not speak a single word and had to rely on reactions alone. He needn't have had any hiccups. It was a dimension that excited the actor in me. It was also a reaction that Chopra was pleasantly surprised by, considering that most actors rely hugely on the spoken word. The episode paired me with actress Zarina Wahab, who had, along with Jaya Bhaduri, Rameshwari and Deepti Naval, been labelled as the girl-next-door favourite with films like *Chitchor* and *Gharaonda*. I was to, years later, direct Wahab in only my second feature film *Dil Maange More*, an irreverent romantic comedy, where she played mother to the ebullient Shahid Kapoor.

I was a young father in the *Khazana* story, who loses his newborn son. There was this climactic scene where he digs a grave to bury the infant. I preferred to play it with solemn grief. Tears swelled up in my eyes, but I didn't weep. It was all pent up within me. The director Deepak Sarin, whose first film *Nakhuda* was for the Yash Raj banner, however, had different ideas. Tears being rationed wasn't his idea of emotion. "*Phoot phoot ke rona*" [cry out hysterically], he insisted. I had no option but to adhere to his instructions. He proceeded to convince me that it was the only language the audience comprehended. Almost two decades later

I still find myself trying to come to grips with the subtlety meter. Few wish to relate to reality and its legumes. And the *Khazana* incident wasn't the last I heard of either. Another mouthful was awaiting me later in my tryst with short stories.

Filmmaker Joginder Shelly's decision to bring the works of famed writer Mohan Rakesh to television was a laudable effort to give literature a wider reach. The series *Mitti Ke Rang* [Colours of the Soil], came on without any pre-launch hype, as Doordarshan arbitrarily slotted it on a Tuesday at 9 PM. Shelly received a call on a hot Saturday afternoon from officials who told him that *Mitti Ke Rang* was on in two days time. That left him with no scope for any promotions. Despite no fanfare, it registered high on the viewership charts from its very first episode settling down to an average rating of 52% eventually, proving that pristine stories sifted, condensed and decanted meaningfully fetch their own viewership.

The short story, *Mr Bhatia*, about a compulsive racecourse gambler featured the late Mohan Gokhale and me. We shot all over South Bombay, at the Racecourse, in public transport and on the streets. Filming in the city was relatively hassle free then, as weighed against the compounded tax caps of latter years. After watching a preview of *Mr Bhatia,* a friend remarked to Shelly, "What's wrong with Ananth Mahadevan? Where's the performance?". I was disheartened, until Shelly conjugated it as a compliment. "The effort should never show, that's what acting is all about". I was glad I had not repeated the *Khazana* experiment, despite acting still being defined by theatrical parameters. Gokhale, later, went on to star as *Mr Yogi* in Ketan Mehta's thirteen episode Saturday prime time series about an eligible bachelor who couldn't decide which of the thirteen girls was right for him. Based on *Kimbal Ravenswood*, by Gujerati novelist Madhu Rye, the subject was ideally suited for the small screen. Could its episodic format be the reason why *Lagaan* maker Ashutosh Gowariker's 2009 film of the novel *What's your Rashee*? failed to draw eyeballs like Mehta's series did? *Mr Bhatia* was the only time I shared space with the talented Gokhale. He was poised to achieve a lot more, if he hadn't passed on way before time.

Long before the stars had resolved the dilemma of "to be or not to be" on the small screen, Vinay Dhumale who was predominantly into Marathi television programming, convinced names like Nana Patekar, a firebrand stage performer, and director Shekhar Kapur to perform for television. The series of short stories was called *Mahanagar*, the title probably a back handed tribute to Satyajit Ray's film, a classic mirror of city life. I remember meeting Dhumale at the heritage Bharatmata theatre in Lalbaug, the belly of Bombay that once housed all its mills. The area since then has undergone a sea change. The mills traded their existence with shopping complexes and corporate houses and the Bharatmata cinema itself has been the target of demolition, on many an occasion. It has, however, hung in there by the skin of its teeth as the sole bastion of the regional Marathi cinema, graduating from its archaic carbon arc projectors to digital image projection. I don't remember any filming to have happened there, before *Mahanagar*. So for Vinay Dhumale it was a first. He was canning a portion of the first instalment. I was cast as an executive who sells out to a big corporate chief played by Shekhar Kapur. Whistle blowers are not as recent a corporate phenomenon as we think. Being in the thick of the mega-series *The Sword Of Tipu Sultan* those days, I sported a bald pate to play Pandit Purnaiya. It did not suit Vinay Dhumale's picture of the character in *Mahanagar* and he had second thoughts about casting me. Not to be undone, I assured him he would get what he wanted. I scurried to my wig maker in the over-crowded Shivaji Mandir theatre area in Dadar and implored him to make one for me overnight. The man was considerate enough to cast aside his other commitments and do the job. Of course, I had to foot the bill. Armed with the headgear I took the taxi to Pune where Dhumale was at work. Pune then, in the late 1980s, was still a quaint little city, unaware of the concrete facelift awaiting it in the new millennium.

Dhumale took one look at my wig and I knew he had aspersions. All right, it was a hurried job. It didn't look natural enough on my head. My worst fears came true. Dhumale riddled me, rather politely, whether I would like to play another minor character, that of a journalist, and be done with it. That was when the survivor instinct in me reared its defiant head. I actually began to convince the man that it wasn't the wig. It was just that he was so used to me with my natural hair that anything else would take time to reconcile with. I must have put up a pretty good act, because he didn't take long to let me keep the part. That evening on the sets of *Mahanagar*, I decided that I wasn't ever going to give up without a fight. A reversal of fortunes was always a possibility, provided one didn't throw in the towel.

Benjamin Gilani, the Forhans toothpaste model, was a co-actor in *Mahanagar*. He had an impressive roster of films and television work and was a fighter in his own way. So it seemed the most natural thing to get down to discussing the vagaries of the performing arts. We were into the third year of the 1990s. Nearly a decade had flowed under the bridge since I had made my debut with *Ados Pados*. Of course, Gilani had many more years of experience. We looked back at those years and delved into an audit of those who had survived and those runners who had stumbled along the way. Strangely, of all the actors who had made a mark in 1984, not more than a dozen were 'alive' and kicking. "It's not how much you do, but how long you last", remarked Gilani with a sense of calm assurance. Words that still ring in my ears. Words I have clung on to, for the sheer strength of the truth in them. Fellow actors Rakesh Bedi, Rajesh Puri, Virendra Saxena, Pawan Malhotra and Satish Shah are among those who haven't wilted with the passage of time. They continue to perform not *because* of a myriad of channels, but *despite* the system's befuddled approach. They have clearly lasted the distance.

The beard gave an intellectual appeal to Shekhar Kapur's face. The seed of breaking into international frontiers - the genesis of *The Bandit Queen*–must have been germinating in his hyperactive mind. As I lunched with him in his hotel room on one of those off-days from the *Mahanagar* sets, Shekhar Kapur did a neat job of not letting the cat entirely out of the bag. He was, however, dropping a hint. He confessed to badly wanting to opt out of Boney Kapoor's forthcoming project titled *Prem*, but was wondering how to break it to Kapoor. He thought aloud, even castled me, looking for an answer. I felt he should go right ahead and speak his mind. Which is what I assume he did, because the next time I heard about *Prem*, it mentioned Kapur's then assistant, and actor, Satish Kaushik in the credits as director.

I guess the lava to break away from the routine and step on to a bigger stage, was getting molten in that Pune hotel room. It manifested itself in a miniscule way, when we shot for a scene that night. Dhumale insisted we shoot a four-page exchange of dialogue in one shot! Shekhar and I walked down the West End theatre road in the middle of the night as the camera did a parallel track. The rigorous rehearsals assured that the shot was canned in a single take. Dhumale, clearly satisfied with the performance, was about to scream a "wrap", when Shekhar felt that we could better the take. Dhumale let him have a go at it. Each time Shekhar felt it could go one shade better. Each time Dhumale let him have his way. Till the clock struck three. The tinkle of the milkman's cycle warned us of the breaking of dawn. We were into the twentieth odd re-take. I was wondering how long he would keep at this. To everyone's relief, Shekhar finally gave a nod of satisfaction and cried a halt. I watched the telecast a few weeks later. Dhumale had retained the first take.

Shekhar Kapur had moved on to bigger pastures. He was ready to film *The Bandit Queen* based on Mala Sen's scorching biography of the controversial dacoit. The film, when exhibited in 1996, was hugely acclaimed. Every time I met Kapur after that I would reiterate my interest to work with him. He played the artful dodger and would get away with a, "what kind of a role do you want?" The last we met was at the Marriott in Juhu in 2008, on a Friday when my film *Victoria No 203*, a remake of the 1980s hit caper by Brij

Sadanah, opened. "So, are you here to get drunk?" he asked me, shook my hand and left. I smiled. Kapur had clearly drifted a long way from home.

A couple of years later, Dhumale moved on to *Avshesh*, a series that attempted to excavate forgotten Indian tradition through the eyes of students of arts and culture. Apart from Tom Alter, Dr Shriram Lagoo and me, it had some first timers. It featured tabla player Nayan Ghosh, classical danseuse Nandita Puri, singer Peenaaz Masani and painter Milon Mukherjee in the cast. Quite often the sets saw an animated discussion on the arts, telescoping with the elements in the script. We shot for the initial bunch of four episodes in rain-lashed Pune. When the clouds descended onto the *Singhgad* fortress, the area resembled a page out of Grimm's Fairy Tales. We kept ourselves warm with the generously sweetened tea and hot fried *bhajiyas* [fritters] from a vendor dispensing from an improvised wooden stall. On one such day, in the midst of the shoot, I realised that Alter was missing. I scoured the area and after a while spotted him below the hillock, gathering plastic packets and bottles that had been inconsiderately littered by tourists. A man with American antecedents doing this on his adopted Indian soil was a regurgitation for the senses. But then, Alter was more Indian than most of us and that's what made him go far beyond the image of the "*gora*" Britisher that Indian cinema routinely saddled him with. Environment, sports and the arts were engrained in his system. His sudden demise in 2017, after he had essayed a part in my film, a biopic on India's first practicing lady doctor, *Doctor Rakhmabai*, left a deep void in several lives.

Avshesh was shaping up like a textbook of infotainment. And then one day, just like that, we heard no more of it. Dhumale's funds had drained out. An ambitious series was left incomplete for want of buyers. And Dhumale like *Avshesh*, faded into virtual oblivion.

Kirdar [The Character] called for a director of Gulzar's stature. It was a series tailor made for the man who ventured into memorable cinematic alleys like *Mere Apne, Parichay, Koshish, Aandhi, Khushboo, Kinara, Kitab, Ijaazat* and *Namkeen*. One of the stories in the 1993 made-for-Doordarshan series was, interestingly, inspired by Billy Wilder's 1950 American film *Sunset Boulevard*. The film has remained a personal favourite and along with *Fedora*, is my reference point on the fickle world of film business. The veteran actress Nadira reprised Gloria Swanson's superstar who was fading into obscurity, Om Puri her butler cum husband, while I played the journalist eager to reveal her story.

The location at the Hermes Villa bungalow on Versova beach was reeking with nostalgia, smattered as it was with black and white photographs from Nadira's early films. It was my first time as an actor with Gulzar and I eagerly imbibed the tips of sensitivity and subtlety. But the filming was more memorable for the companionship I struck up with Nadira. My earlier tryst with her had been at Jodhpur where she was part of the cast of the British production of Rudyard Kipling's *Kim*. The sweltering desert heat drove the ladies in the unit to some childish mischief. They had no qualms slipping ice-cubes down everyone's back. Whilst others protested, Nadira squealed in delight at the tingling sensation. It was like airconditioning for her.

Her pictures, put up on the wall of the Villa as props, made her go down down memory lane and replay episodes that recreated a bygone era. I took a fancy to one of her photographs from *Aah* where she had romanced Raj Kapoor. She graciously autographed it for me while adding almost subconsciously, "I am very lonely, come and see me some time". Though I never got down to visiting her at her Peddar Road residence, we spoke on regular occasions. Then a decade later, another familiar headline broke. "Yesteryear star dies lonely and uncared for". Like another poignant Billy Wilder film. The autographed frame stares at me from the mantelpiece in my theatre room. Signed as Furhet, her real name. She was a steadfast being. I could almost hear the recluse do a Gloria Swanson with a flourish, "Mr De'Mille, I am ready for my close-up"!

Kirdar was telecast on Doordarshan and received critical acclaim, consolidating Gulzar as a master story-teller. 1986 marked another medley of short stories. Prem Kishen, the veteran actor Prem Nath's son who debuted as a leading man in the Rajshri film *Dulhan Wahi Jo Piya Man Bhaye*, teamed up with producer and businessman Sunil Mehta to form a software company, Cinevista. They took the story-telling syndrome forward. *Kathasagar* [an Ocean Of Tales] was a series I regret missing out as an actor. *Kathasagar's* biggest accomplishment was getting celebrated director Shyam Benegal [*Ankur, Manthan, Bhumika, Mandi, Trikaal*] on board. Benegal's keen eye for human behaviour accorded the tales a must-watch rating. Works by masters like Guy De Maupassant, Leo Tolstoy, O. Henry, Anton Chekov and others were adapted into an Indian context while retaining the essence of the original. "*The Necklace*" by Guy De Maupassant, "*A Cup of Tea*" by Katherine

Mansfield, and Tolstoy's "*God Sees The Truth, But Waits*" were episodes of varying charm. Benegal admitted that his foray into episodic story telling was both fascinating and challenging. He equated them to mini features. Other episodic directors included Kundan Shah, Anil Ganguly and Kishen Sethi. Each of the stories featured a star from cinema and that contributed hugely to its appeal and ratings. Ashok Kumar, Sharmila Tagore, Shammi Kapoor, Om Puri, Saeed Jaffrey, Utpal Dutt, Vijayendra Ghatge, Urmila Matondkar, Neena Gupta, Supriya Pathak and Waheeda Rehman top lined different stories, essaying the protagonists. The first season comprised of 44 episodes, its success ensuring that *Kathasagar* was resurrected later as *Kathasagar* 2, this time with writer-director Ved Rahi helming the show.

Cinema's much loved funny man Asrani, a gold medallist from the Pune Film and Television Institute, had experimented with production and film making. But *Chala Murari Hero Banane*, his first film as director did not emulate his idol Mehmood's success story. Mehmood, a successful comic actor had chosen to capitalize on his popularity and made quite a few films like *Mastana, Garam Masala* and *Kunwara Baap*, a rip-off of Charlie Chaplin's *The Kid*. But the film making experience did pave way for a software company that Asrani floated with his actress wife, Manju Bansal, helming a series of short stories titled *Kashmakash* [The Dilemma]. Its opening episode reunited me with *Ados Pados* co-actor Rameshwari where I played her husband who is given to a lot of self-importance. Although Asrani had promised to feature me in a few more episodes of the 13 part series, Doordarshan policies dictated that different faces be cast. *Kashmakash* was among the last of the popular short story series on Doordarshan.

Just as it seemed that the genre would fade out with the advent of multiple channels, in 1999, Zee TV, one of the very first satellite networks, staged a revival in a specially programmed forty- five minutes slot. Titled *Rishte* [relationships], it comprised 166 stories of relationships that pushed the envelope, executed by different producers and directors. These were names that were on the threshold of gravitating towards their first feature films. It was the *Rishte* series that made producer- directors of names like Anurag Basu, Imtiaz Ali, Sridhar Rangayan, Jayant Gilatar and Renuka Shahane. Hansal Mehta who reinvented himself with films like *Shahid* and *Aligarh* in the new millennium, was a discovery of *Rishte*. He was just a bright lad, engaged in filming a cookery show [*Khana Khazana*], when an episode of *Rishte* was allotted to him. He recruited the writing talent of a "poor ambitious boy from Meerut who had come looking for work" by the name of Vishal Bharadwaj. His short story did the trick for Mehta. The episode *Highway* featured Ashish Vidyarthi and Shefali Shah. It garnered rave remarks from filmmakers like Subhash Ghai and Shekhar Kapur and pushed Mehta into the category of a film director. Bharadwaj too has, in the years to follow, left Meerut far behind, re-discovering Shakespeare's works for the Hindi screen.

Sujit Sen, an erudite Bengali scholar who had scripted films like *Saaransh, Arth, Hum Hai Rahi Pyar Ke, Angaar* and others primarily for the *enfant terrible* of contemporary cinema Mahesh Bhatt, had this compelling story of a policeman [Vikram Gokhale] on the verge of retiring, being sent to apprehend a murderer. As he is transporting the prisoner [Suneel Sinha] back by rail, he learns of an inconvenient truth. The man had executed an act, that the cop may have shied away from, the uniform preventing him from taking the law in his hands. In a moment of decision, he lets the prisoner escape sullying his blemishless career. But of course, there comes a twist in the tale. The killer gives himself up to the law to save the cop from such ignominy. I perceived a short movie in the script and, disregarding the rules of television, shot it in a widescreen format. My producer, Dinesh Bansal, who had this impression that comedy was my comfort zone, [I was making the second season of *Ghar Jamai* for him around the same period] wasn't too certain whether I would capture the essence of Sujit Sen's script. He returned after his annual American sojourn and sat down to watch the episode, titled *Mujrim* [The Criminal], with much trepidation. He confessed, that what he saw, pleasantly surprised him. I had always wanted to experiment with different genres. I had made a determined effort not to be typecast as an actor, and I wasn't going to let myself be tied down to any one genre as director. Bansal's heartwarming response was a moment that quietly whispered into my senses that, maybe, at long last, I was getting into filmmaker mode.

Rishte attracted an impressive number of eyeballs each week. One-offs don't demand a story recap and can be watched anytime. Its success prompted me to attempt another one on the occasion of Teacher's Day, titled *Sir*, penned again by Sen. It was a poignant story of a teacher-pupil relationship, where the teacher in turn ends up learning some truths of life from his own student. Bengali and Hindi stage actor Joy Sengupta played the young tutor, while

I smuggled myself in as the kid's father. Farouque Shaikh had warned me not to let that actor in me languish for long. Zee followed up *Rishte* with another short story concept called *Guldastaa* [Bouquet], which had its share of engaging anecdotes too. Both *Rishte* and *Guldastaa* provided the perfect cocoons for a whole tribe of film hopefuls, from actors to producers and directors to carve a future for bigger things.

Playing multiple characters never ceased to fascinate. I continued angling for a part whenever I smelt that a short story series was afoot. Once, I spotted Basu Chatterjee filming with Priya Tendulkar a story set in a Mumbai public transport bus. Here was my chance to do an encore with Basu*da* I thought and jumped into the moving bus. Basu*da* looked at me and said nonchalantly "Why do you want another part? You are engaged with so much work already!" That was indeed a pointed one. As short as the initial telephone call he made. But hardly sweet.

As though on cue, story-telling resurfaced in theatre. Writer, performer and director Mahmood Farooqui and his partner Danish Husain, exponents of the art of *Dastaangoi*, the 16th century Urdu vocal art of story-telling, began demonstrating their skills to discerning audiences. They were joined many-a-year later by stage veteran Naseeruddin Shah. The performance of the trio, with their impeccable Urdu, was music to the ears. In 2010, when theatre actor and director Nadira Zaheer Babbar dramatized a tribute to *dastangoi* in her play *Hum Kahen Aap Sunen*, it provided me with an opportunity to shake off the dust that I was gathering as an actor. The play performed all over the country and revived the art of story-telling. In the company of the veteran actress who had founded her group, *Ekjute*, thirty years ago, I finally rediscovered the platform that pushed my limits as an actor. I had found my way from theatre to television and back.

THREE'S COMPANY

The long and winding road ahead could not have been the Beatles classic. Rather, it resembled the world's longest and most congested automobile rally.

I craned my neck to figure out why we weren't moving. It was nearly an hour since the bus loaded with Aziz Mirza and Kundan Shah's team of actors and technicians had left their Bandra office, but hadn't progressed beyond the suburb of Sion, just about 7 km away. The temperature in the bus was hitting a level of discomfort. The bumper to bumper traffic was not helping either. Not to mention the 16-hour ride ahead to reach the location in interior Maharashtra. I almost rued embarking on this one. But then Mirza and Shah had a *Yeh Jo Hai Zindagi* and *Nukkad* going for them. Also the *Circus* was hitherto unexplored territory on television. Besides there was a certain Shah Rukh Khan, an actor who had made his mark with a series called *Fauji*. He was playing the son of the Apollo Circus owner and was being talked about as an exciting new prospect on the scene. So I braved the all-night journey to Ratnagiri where the 'Big Top' as the circus was called had pitched its tents. Mirza and Shah were made to look like Mary's little lamb… every town the circus went, the duo was forced to go, of course, to record their episodes.

Shah and Mirza had the latter's acclaimed filmmaker brother Saeed Mirza for company. The three were nicknamed the *Brahma-Vishnu-Mahesh* of television, a godly triumvirate that systematically created, destroyed and recreated. It was soon after Saeed's socially edgy film *Mohan Joshi Haazir Ho* [based on the late actor and activist Balraj Sahni's brother Bhisham Sahni's book] that the camaraderie began. Shah had completed *Jaane Bhi Do Yaaron* and Aziz was ticking with a nervous energy that conformed to television demands. They took turns at playing Captain.

As the shadows lengthened on D'Mello Road, Aziz Mirza spent his evenings observing the truckers congregate at this old Bombay area overlooking the docks. It was an exercise he often indulged in. Observing the uncharacteristic character. Amongst them was Pedro the alcoholic who had life and death all tied up. The nearby shrine had assured him his daily binge of country liquor as long as he lived and a coat and canvas shoes when he died. Pheku was another one, who had announced in a crowded bus that this was his last bus journey because he had just inherited shares worth crores. In reality all he had was a broken-down bicycle. Mirza ran a hot knife through these traits, scooped up a slice of life and retold them in the street-corner comedy *Nukkad*. "More Frank Capra, than Maxim Gorky's *Lower Depths*", he muses.

Nukkad was inhabited by the ragamuffins of every walk of life. There was the local toughie, [Dilip Dhawan], the vacuous cop on his beat, [Ajay Wadavkar] the idealistic lady teacher, [Rama Vij] owner of the dingy restaurant by the corner, [Avatar Gil] the resident beggar, [Suresh Bhagwat] the cycle mechanic, [Pawan Malhotra] the domestic maid, [Sangeeta Naik] and of course the chronic drunk, Khopdi [Sameer Kakkad]. Quite often I was witness to the hectic activity behind the scenes at Natraj Studio where the street had been erected. It was like a theatre workshop out there. Though I never became part of the cast, ["why can't we find a role for you?" Mirza wondered loudly sprawled on the sofa] merely mingling with them was education. At one point the writers had hit a road-block. Admits Aziz, "The improvisations were like walking a tightrope. Observers were appalled by my tweaking the script at the slightest hint of betterment."

The serious undertones in a comedy like *Nukkad* made all the difference. One of Mirza's favourite episodes was the *Hidden Camera* story, where the *Nukkad* members learn that a spy cam was picking up their movements. It prompts them to put their best foot forward for the world to see. But by doing a make-over on themselves, they begin to lose their real identity. Shah however roots for the '*Mindi*' [Cipher] episode. Ganshu the beggar decides to turn his beggar trade into a small enterprise [Aatma Service Centre] so he could qualify for a bank loan. He applies for five thousand rupees but does not know how many 'zeroes' follow the figure 5. It ends up with an extra zero making it fifty thousand. The bank officer is only too glad to comply as he has to meet his loan disbursal target.

Nukkad didn't succumb to the clichéd portrayal of a corrupt cop.

In fact Ganpat *havaldar* was a misfit, because he was honest. I remember watching the 20-odd minute episodes taking up the best of three days to film. Both Shah and Mirza could not reconcile to the never-ending format of a series in the subsequent decades. "Those days every episode was shot after a lot of thought. It was like making a short film every week". Until Prime Minister Rajiv Gandhi cried a halt to the series, on grounds of it being subversive. Mirza and Shah couldn't figure out the reasons. The series was withdrawn, but questions were raised in Parliament. "I'd like to know how many people have actually entered the 21st century, argues Mirza '*Nukkad* in fact posed the question.. *who is going into the next century*? Even today farmers continue to commit suicide. So only the rich enter the 21st century and get richer!"

Aziz Mirza's words were mirrored in the dusty streets of Ratnagiri, a district in Maharashtra with a nominal population in those days. *Circus* had followed *Nukkad* and raised curiosity levels. The Circus with its animal and dung odours overpowering our senses, provided the only escapism besides cinema and the community television sets. Mirza had gathered quite a handful of talent including Renuka Shahane and the would-be-director Ashutosh Gowariker. I played a doctor tending to a child who was bedridden and wants to visit the circus. My prescription takes them by surprise. I convince the circus authorities to "bring the circus home". A friendly elephant is transported from the circus and entertains the child in his backyard. If wishes were elephants, children surely would ride them. The circus also had a dapper Shah Rukh Khan playing the owner's son who has returned from foreign shores with business ideas that did not accommodate this model of show business.

The Big Top is threatened with closure. Until the characters rally around to dissuade him.

The fire in Khan's belly was smouldering even during his *Circus* days. Prowling around the location like a restless leopard, he confessed how films were the final frontier, his voice loaded with the anticipation of success in no small measure. Of course I had no inkling that I would one day be cast as his father in *Baazigar* [director team Abbas-Mustan's take on Ira Levin's bestseller *A Kiss before Dying*], a hugely popular film, in which he avenges my death in a blood spilled climax. Khan's mother had first kindled this fire. She was an ardent admirer of Dilip Kumar, the thespian who had the audacity to turn down David Lean's *Lawrence of Arabia*. But in one of those cruel ironies of life, she did not live to see the day. Her son however continued to play Mirza's favourite. *Umeed*, [Hope] a series on nationalized banks was Mirza challenging you to" try making a show on such a dry terrain"! It was to be Khan's swan song in television fiction.

The initial sparks were lit at actress Hema Malini's house. I was playing a prominent part in her first, dance-based television series *Noopur*, [The anklets] She sprung a question on me, "What do you think of this boy Shah Rukh from *Fauji*?" "The energy!" I noted. "Esha and Aahana are very fond of him". Her daughters were moppets who must have been his earliest fans. The phone rang at television actor Viveck Vaswani's Cuffe Parade apartment where Khan had sought asylum. Vaswani, not to let the opportunity slip by, dragged him out of bed and drove him down all the way from Cuffe Parade to Malini's bungalow in the star-spangled, Gulmohar lined bylanes of Juhu. Vivek revealed that all throughout the one-hour drive, Khan insisted that he was in two minds and would meet the lady out of sheer courtesy. Once they reached her bungalow, though, he was eating out of her hands and wasted no time in agreeing to play the lead in her first directorial feature *Dil Aashna Hai* [The Heart Knows The Truth]. Though Mirza's *Raju Ban Gaya Gentleman* co-produced by Viveck Vaswani [with G P Sippy] was his first film that opened in cinemas, Hema Malini's film was the one he had taken on before any other.

Khan had successfully evaded the television image death trap. In sharp contrast to many candidates who still harbor the question "if he can do it why not us?" But none have lasted to tell the tale. Sameer Kakkar after *Nukkad* wasn't fortunate either. He turned into an epitome of Khopdi, the drunkard. Although Mirza decries the trend, there was very little he could have done to help. "It is a perennial sore point with an illiterate industry. After all he is an actor playing a character called Khopdi. When they want a beggar they call for 'Ghanshu'. They are not even aware of his name. Sad but true". A film called *Shahenshah* with Amitabh Bachchan walking tall playing a vigilante, recruited almost the entire *Nukkad* gang to play themselves. Mirza could only play mute spectator.

Years later in 2009, I thought I saw Kakkar again. Yes, it was him. An almost unrecognizable Khopdi. Kakkar had returned after a long hiatus in America and was attempting a change of image on a satellite channel show. He was evidently missing the infectious energy and creativity of *Nukkad* and its gang.

Today Mirza is rather wary of doing television. "From street corners in *Nukkad* to film studios and stars in *Manoranjan*, [Show-Biz] an over-the-top ode to the workers of the film industry, from police station to railway stations, *Intezaar*, *[The Long Wait]*, shot almost entirely on a railway platform and the romance-inducing surroundings I had it all covered". Another season of *Nukkad* didn't look feasible. The street corners weren't the same anymore, infested as they were with cyber cafes and communication centres. They lacked "character". Moreover Mirza has never been prone to indulge in e-mail or the social network. Instead he prefers to take off on a long road trip to Jaisalmer in Rajasthan or a hill resort like Nainital. "The destination isn't important, the journey is" he proclaims. Driving through thirty kilometers of marble vendors, experiencing a bustling township of not more than a kilometer, or savouring the earthy pickle in a *dhabha* [an open Indian wayside inn] looking at faces he would never see again, is his favoured pastime. And of course playing bridge with his friends, has bridged many a gap in his life. One keen, concerned look at him, though revealed that the darkness that fell after Nirmala, his wife left him, probably still enveloped his life. So instead of turning left towards home in Bandra from the Film City road, he instinctively hits the right towards the Ahmedabad expressway. For this high plains drifter, the world has become one huge Big Top, a free-wheeling home.

SOLDIER
BLUE

"I have nothing to offer but blood, toil, tears and sweat." Winston Churchill's words seem to have multiple connotations. As though specially coined for my work culture. The other side of the picture was, of course, the military context in which Churchill spoke. The armed forces called for diligence, discipline and dexterity. Even as we doffed our caps in respect to the men on the border, the actor in me was yearning to don their colours. *Prehari* [The Sentinels] based on India's Border Security Force [BSF], provided just the departure I was waiting for. The traits played on my mind as the wheels of the vehicle dug into the dirt tracks lined with sand dunes before we hit the road to Barmer in Rajasthan, where the series was being filmed. The afternoon sun had a metallic sheen that converted the rugged desert landscape into a surreal canvas, giving you the feel of being on some other lonely planet. The drive that the role demanded had begun.

Uniforms have never ceased to fascinate me. Being in one automatically triggered a transformation of persona. *Prehari* had anecdotes of the BSF and their encounters with infiltrators from across the Line of Control. The setting was real. Barmer was a stone's throw from the Pakistan border. And with Benjamin Gilani, again, for company, the battles began in right earnest. The BSF were a neglected tribe in cinema. Heroism was restricted to the army men. It felt so good to put a foot forward on their behalf.

Earlier, such forays into allied territory on television had carved a niche for themselves amidst the deluge of soaps. In 1991, Kavita Chowdhary's *Udaan*, based on the true story of her elder sister Kanchan Choudhary Bhattacharya who after several hardships went to become the first female Director General of Police, provided major source material. It was a childhood conflict that provoked Kanchan's decision to be an IPS officer. The sight of her father being beaten up over a property dispute and the humiliating inaction of the police despite her pleadings, led to her bearding the lion in its own den. Kavita herself played the protagonist Kalyani in *Udaan*, who feels neglected when all attention is showered on a boy born in their family. Her father, played by veteran theatre and film actor Vikram Gokhale rids her of her insecurities and she makes it her mission to battle gender discrimination. Shekhar Kapur played a cameo, the man in Kalyani's life. After Kshirsagar's *Stree*, this was the first major television show on women empowerment. I watched *Udaan* with a lot of interest for its marked departure from the prevalent staid themes. It was in the scheme of things then to accord it a sequel, albeit years later. Strangely it was the only series Kavita did. These days 'Kalyani' lives in my neighbourhood in North Mumbai. Her sister passed away at 72 after fighting an ailment. The conversation with Choudhary invariably swerves towards her return to television with another *Udaan*. But just like it is with other veterans, I see a pall of disillusionment on her face. It is a veiled, not-oft encountered virtue of someone from television's original brigade wanting to make a valid point and be done with it.

It took a true blue soldier to make a series [*Fauji*-1989] on one of his own. It also called for a fan like worship of Errol Flynn's *Robin Hood* to Dilip Kumar's hinterland characters in *Ganga Jamuna*. Colonel Raj Kapoor was one star-struck army man who was wooed into show business by the sight of singer Mohammed Rafi drawing more crowds than the country's first Prime Minister Jawaharlal Nehru in Lucknow. When he first ran into Dilip Kumar he hugged him so hard that the latter's shirt sleeve came off! Years later when the Colonel was his neighbour at Sunset Heights in Mumbai's Pali Hill, Dilip Kumar reminded him "you owe me a shirt". From the borders of the country to its heartbeat of a city, was like switching from one army to the other. Retiring from the forces in 1977, after serving in the 1971 war against Pakistan, Kapoor felt he was earmarked for cinema, though, earlier on, he was brainwashed into thinking that films were mere *nautanki* and suited only those not destined to do anything else. "Only, in film making there is but one General, all the others are jawans" was his declaration.

The semi-autobiographical *Fauji* was initially meant to be a film. Convincing army personnel and the Defence Minister was another task. The Colonel was asked by the ministry "not to do it... these Indian films on the forces are never authentic". He first ran into the 23-year-old lad named Shah Rukh Khan at Gulmohar Park in New Delhi. Kapoor's brother-in-law auditioned him along with a bunch of others and let them loose on the training ground. The colonel put them through a grind unfamiliar to them. Not surprisingly three of them dropped out with a curt, "we haven't come here to join the army". Only Khan kept up with Kapoor. It ended in a sparring match with both donning boxing gloves. "I goaded him to hit me and he finally did. I could sense his aggressive nature. It was a presence that the camera loved. "My Abhimanyu Rai was born, though honestly I hadn't pencilled him in for the part. He was a bit of a bum though, turning up late for shoots. Once, I ran behind him with a stone and that put an end to his punctuality ills. The other 'bums' weren't a piece of cake either. The Colonel had recruited a barber on the set to clip their Samson locks. Yet the cadets continued to sport long hair. "I later discovered that they were bribing the barber". Corruption had seeped into the 'army', courtesy the civilians.

The (then) General of the Indian army stamped his mark of approval on the first episode of *Fauji*. The series came on, on Wednesday nights, and a star was born. Shah Rukh Khan lived up to his mother's *duas* [blessings], "*Mera ladka bahot upar jayega*" [my son will scale the peak of success]. "*Fauji* made him, he made *Fauji*." admits Kapoor. Years later, on an episode of *Jeena Isi Ka Naam Hai* [This Is Life], an Indian version of the popular British show, *It's My Life*, Khan acknowledged him. "He was grateful to me, I am grateful to him. We're quits!" As I could gather, they don't have provision for needless sentiments in the army.

Perhaps it was gratitude that made Khan recall Colonel Kapoor in 2009. *Fauji* 2 was on the anvil. For the latter, television was like the spider's web–he was stuck with it. Moreover, here was an opportunity to throw up another potential star. The auditions happened at a feverish pace. He was hoping that Shah Rukh would make an appearance as the father of junior Abhimanyu. The filming began at the Indian Military Academy in picturesque Dehra Dun. But, then out of the blue, they cried halt. Something wasn't working. A difference of opinion with the commissioning channel only complicated matters. The Colonel's dream was aborted. His worst fear about television's changing work-ethics had manifested itself. There were those days when he had roughed up a Doordarshan official for demanding a bribe. Now here he was, hard-pressed to beat a system to put his point of view across. It would take a while for another Shah Rukh to materialize. "I say chaps!" as Abhimanyu once trumpeted!

Probably the brightest of the Anand brothers–Dev, Vijay and Chetan was the eldest Chetan. His *Neecha Nagar* [Lowly City, 1946] was the first Indian film to win the Golden Palm at Cannes. But he appeared to have a way with executing war movies like *Haqeeqat* [The Reality], a black-and-white feature on the 1962 Chinese invasion of India and later *Hindustan Ki Kasam* [1973]. The wars that India fought post-independence told several tales of valour that could be condensed into a television series. Anand shortlisted the recipients of India's highest gallantry award, the Param Veer Chakra, and paid tribute to them in a series of the same name. Farouque Shaikh played Major Somnath Sharma of the Kumaon regiment in the curtain-raiser in 1988. The 17 episodes featured prominent actors like Naseeruddin Shah, Pankaj Dheer, Kanwaljit Singh, Puneet Issar, Annu Kapoor and Sunil Lahiri. Anand had cast carefully, matching the original heroes' faces as far as possible. The series continued to underline his knack of recreating the war fields and garnered critical acclaim. Not surprisingly, *Param Veer Chakra* still remains the most accomplished combat series on Indian television.

The desert sands were scorching in the blazing afternoon sun. Benjamin Gilani and I pretended not to be affected as we crouched in them, returning the fire of the 'infiltrators'. The BSF personnel's participation ensured that the ammunition was all real. It was an experience handling all those AK 47s and carbines. The thrill of firing a real carbine made *Prehari* worth the while. For one combat sequence, we were aware that a bomb was to go off after a few seconds behind us. We braced for the moment. Boom, it went up raising a cloud of sand. We performed our act of grimacing and dispersed for lunch. One BSF officer across the lunch table munched on a salad and confided in hushed tones, "that explosive wasn't a dummy. It wasn't supposed to be placed there, so dangerously close to you guys. But don't let this reach the authorities". We first absorbed the fact as we dug into our meal, but it set me thinking that death played on our minds only if we let it. Sometimes being blissfully unaware helps. My 'death' in the series, though, deeply saddened my aunt, who was like a mother to me. She chided me for "doing such scenes" and couldn't bear the thought of me tethered to a bier and cremated. She wouldn't understand if I quoted Kurt Vonnegut, "If you die horribly on television, you will not have died in vain, you will have entertained us".

I had to reconcile to the fact that television was being taken more seriously than life itself!

THE GOOD DOCTOR

The late 1980s. The ubiquitous cell phone hadn't reared its head yet. So it was left to my modest landline to play communicator. I wasn't prepared for the call that day. It was eleven and an uneventful morning routine was staring me in the face. Until the bell rang. It was director Hrishikesh Mukherjee's unmistakable Bengali twang. "What are you doing", he enquired. I confessed I was up to nothing remarkable. He urged me to get out of the house pronto and show up at the location where he was filming a series called *Rishta*. Before one could ask, "Where's the fire?", he hung up. I accomplished a shave and bath session in record time. Then put paid to my driver's siesta preparations. We drove out to the Juhu bungalow where the shoot was happening. The unit hands had a frowning gaze as they saw me enter hurriedly. It was obvious that they were kept waiting. I went up to *dada* [big brother] as we addressed Mukherjee and apologized for being late. "No you are not", he growled and hurried me into a make-up routine. "A basic foundation will do", he told the make-up artiste. All pleas to at least let me in on the character I was to play fell on deaf ears. I had to make do with reading the scene and assuming that my pitching of a husband's part would be correct. I was aware that Hrishi*da* worked real fast but there was something not normal here.

As the camera rolled and I spoke my lines, what caught my eye was a figure that crossed my line of vision and shuffled his way towards the video monitor where Hrishi*da* was stationed. He ignored the new entrant and focused on the monitor. *Dada's* "cut" and "okay" had a dramatic tenor about them. The shot was canned in a single take. The figure turned out to be an actor half bent, in an apologetic posture. An animated conversation followed. Finally, *Dada* dismissed him saying he had "already cast someone else" and announced that he was moving on with the next shot. The actor looked around, guilt written all over his face. Somewhere his eye caught mine. I later learnt that the actor, a Marathi stage and film regular, had not turned up on time for an early morning call sheet. So, I was summoned and asked to step in, before the actor knew what hit him. That was Hrishikesh Mukherjee for you. Quick on the draw!

It was my good fortune, that the connection with Hrishi*da* wasn't confined to absorbing his delightful cinema. *Satyakam, Anari, Guddi, Anand, Namak Haram, Arjun Pandit, Gol Maal, Chupke Chupke and Aalap* were some of the films that had me before showtime at the cinemas, on their opening days. I first met the filmmaker in 1980 at the Blaze mini theatre in Colaba, where the agency had arranged a press preview of one of his later films, *Khubsoorat*. With the film's media booklet [a modest four-page catalogue] in hand, I tiptoed towards him and requested him to autograph it. "Why my autograph?" he humbly questioned. The answer would have taken all evening, so I substituted it with a smile. The next time I heard that voice was in the summer of 1986, when he took his first bow on television. The film producers, Vimal and Vinay Bhatia, with whom I had earlier done a series called *Khari Khari*, a sitcom on house-helps who gather to gossip about their masters, put me on to him. As he came online, I gathered that dreams do come true after all, depends how carnal your craving is. His bungalow '*Anupama*' [named after the film he made with Dharmendra and Sharmila Tagore], at Carter Road on the seafront in Bandra, had a tree growing right in the centre of the living room. *Dada* had refrained from cutting it and built the house around it. On seeing me walk in, he came straight to the point. The new show and my character. That was a trait in the man. He neither wasted time nor film stock. Both life and film were edited beforehand.

Hum Hindustani was the first series he designed. It was produced by Rajendra Bhatia along with his sons Vimal and Vinay. They had made the popular romcoms *Aaj Ki Tazaa Khabar* and *Jungle Mein Mangal* for the big screen. They could claim credit to have wooed an auteur like Hrishi*da* to television. *Hum Hindustani* had its origins in the Manhattan black-out of the early 1980s. Exactly a year later, the city reported a baby boom. The series, a satire on the diverse cultures in India, had an entire colony of men from different communities landing up at a maternity home with their pregnant wives. As the wives deliver the newborns, a fire engulfs the hospital. Veteran actor Ashok Kumar playing the chief doctor manages to rescue the babies but cannot identify the parents. So the babies are distributed amongst the couples and the doctor sits back to watch the parents eyeing everyone else's baby. They even end up identifying their habits in a neighbour's offspring and loving it more than their own, suspecting it to be theirs. The doctor finally lets them into his secret. The babies were never exchanged. Each couple had indeed been given their own. But if one could still love the other's child as one's own, then it would take national integration the extra mile.

After *Ghar Jamai*, predictably, I played the South Indian in *Hum Hindustani*. The show also brought me face to face with the granddaddy of Indian actors, "*dadamuni*". He commanded a respect seldom bestowed on others. When it came to billing, even if he had a cameo in a film, Ashok Kumar would be the first name in the credits above that of the star who played the leading man. The actor's energy seldom betrayed his age. He had digressed into healing through homeopathy and had a cure for almost every ill. Like Hrishi*da*, he was the quintessential good doctor spreading cheer. During breaks on the set, we would rewind to the days of his beginnings in Himanshu Rai's ambitious Calcutta studio Bombay Talkies, Devika Rani's time and Hindi cinema's glorious pre-independence era when actors used to sing in their own voice on screen. Once, at the Subodh Mukherjee owned Filmalaya studios in Andheri, we sat across sipping a cup of tea and turning pages of his history book, when I suddenly felt a sharp thud on my left shoulder as though someone had hit me hard. I looked back to catch the offender but could see no one. Instead, I saw a huge "solar" light that had broken loose from its clamp and fallen from the wooden scaffold above. As the light hands rushed towards the scene, Ashok Kumar announced that I had had a close shave. Apparently, the studio floor was jinxed. Lights have fallen before too, he revealed and even killed a man. He was witness to it during his hey days. The light's edge slicing my shoulder is a feeling that yet hasn't subsided. With the "haunted stage" theory adding fuel to the fire.

I couldn't resist the invitation to visit him at his home and landed up one sweltering afternoon at his Chembur bungalow, where he had lived all his life. No one answered the bell at the gate, so I tentatively dragged it open only to be greeted by a three-dimensional spectre of a huge hound doing an eye-level leap on me. Before I could gather my wits, I heard the thespian's frantic shout and the dog's feet found the ground just short of me. Profusely apologizing and cooking up the frightening consequences if he hadn't stepped out on time, *dadamoni*, made extra efforts to soothe my nerves. That was one long afternoon for the memory books. He spoke of his illustrious innings and even his late wife whom he missed so much. Evenings were lonely, he observed. He spoke of his famous singer-actor brother Kishore Kumar's antics and how his whimsical ways punctured the egos of his producers. I couldn't resist telling him about my favourite scene in the jaunty jalopy comedy, *Chalti Ka Naam Gadi* where he suddenly gestures to Madhubala to remain seated, even as he is lecturing her. Spontaneity that was rarely matched. He came across as an incurable romantic. They don't make leading men like Ashok Kumar anymore.

Hum Hindustani had its run of 26 episodes but spelt a new chapter of bonding for me. Hrishi*da* had this diary where he had his actors' birthdays noted. Unfailingly on the 27th of October each year, a seven o'clock call would typically sound like *"beta, aaj tumhara janamdin hai na*! May God bless you with a long life and success". It invariably brought a lump to my throat. I could do with the man's blessings! Along with his impeccable humour. One such incident relates to *Anand*. "I made a film called *Anand*", he would begin in sheer humility, in his Bengali accent. When he was filming the story of the cancer struck patient [Rajesh Khanna], who laughs off the remainder of his life, his distributors expressed a desire to know something about the story before striking a deal. The conversation, in *dada's* own words, went like this:

Distributor: *Anand ki kahani kya hai?* [What's *Anand* all about?]

Dada: *Ek aadmi ki kahani hai jisko cancer ho gaya hai* [It's about a man afflicted with cancer]

Distributor: *phir kya hota hai?* [what happens next?]

Dada: *phir woh mar jata hai* [Then he dies!]

Apparently the distributors thought he was crazy and abandoned all thoughts of buying the film. That *Anand* went on to be one of his most memorable hits and Rajesh Khanna's best essayed part, doesn't exactly reflect a complimentary image of those distribution heads. Khanna who had virtually bulldozed his way into the project, was wary about a newcomer [Amitabh Bachchan] being cast in the pivotal character of the doctor. "This character's crucial. Maybe you should lookout some more before deciding" suggested Khanna. "You better look out for this young man," replied *dada*, "or he'll overshadow you before you know it". More portentous words had never been spoken. Bachchan went on to do a flamboyant Peter O. Toole to Khanna's subdued Richard Burton in *Namak Haram*, *dada*'s ode to *Beckett*. Subsequently, Khanna, despite negotiating the more demanding character, waged quite a battle to extricate himself from the sledgehammer effect of Bachchan's performance.

In his last feature, *Jhoot Bole Kauwa Kate* [1998], Hrishi*da* came up against conflicting disciplines. The *new-age*, semi-professional ways of functioning caught him unawares. Disillusioned, he asked me to meet him. When I called on him, he was bed-ridden and even lacked the spirit to leave the room. But the passion smouldered. He spoke in metaphors. "Ananth I have made ninety-nine films. Why should I make a hundredth film? No point in just 'another film.'" He was hung up on a short story, *The Dressing Table*, written by the late composer Salil Chowdhary. A poignant story of a newly-wed couple whose life changes when they get a dressing table bought in a flea market after a communal riot. He asked me whether I would assist him. "I know you are a full-fledged director now, and it would not be right to ask you to assist me, but I need like-minded people in my days of failing health. I could give you co-director billing". I was too overwhelmed to react. I heard myself saying "*Dada*, it would please me to be your unit hand if you say, but will not lose out on the opportunity of working on this film".

I would have found my calling much earlier if *The Dressing Table* had been made. *Dada* had found a producer, a certain P D Gupta, whose initial enthusiasm set the film rolling. I brought in writer Sujit Sen to script the film. Sen had penned two of my *Rishte* episodes for television and, later, my first feature *Dil Vil Pyar Vyar* [2002]. Besides, his filmography included such acclaimed screenplays as *Saaransh* and *Arth*. Our enthusiasm must have been infectious. *Dada* slowly found his footing and shook himself out of his stupor. Sen, always looking for a real-life snippet, felt there was a story in this too. The story of a man who migrated from the bedroom to the living room. Sen and I worked on the initial drafts of *dada's* interpretation of Salil Chowdhary's story. But the joy was short lived. One day *dada* called us and we sensed the distress in his voice. He seated Sen and me in the living room. "There's bad news, Ananth, we are not doing this film". Gupta, as most producers did, saw no 'business sense' in the project. *Dada's* resolve not to compromise did him in. I was heartbroken. What Gupta had failed to see was the stature he would have gained after backing such an important film. Hrishikesh Mukherjee's swan song! He wriggled out, *dada* retraced his steps to the bedroom and never stepped out again. Sen, too, quietly passed away after a few years. It was like characters fading out in the journey of my life. I haven't heard of Gupta since. He is probably still looking for that all-evasive business potential.

Dada barely recovered from the setback. His gout problems had aggravated. He spoke to me from his bed often. In the fag end of the last millennium, when I had made *Ghunghat Ke Pat Khol*, my first feature for television, he watched the film during both its weekend telecasts and commended me on the effort. At the foot of his bed, we discussed life and cinema. One of his statements will continue to sound a warning bell for me. "Ananth, in India to be outstanding, all you have to do is be mediocre". I must confess that I picked up the finer points of editing watching him cut away to the right reactions. The exercise on the cutting machine of *Hum Hindustani* and his subsequent shows, *Dhoop Chhaon* and *Talash*

[1992], were lessons no institute could have imparted.

His pet mongrels were his companions on bed. "I have four dogs, these three and myself". And then one day Tupur, his grand-daughter called to inform me that he was in the intensive care ward of the Leelavati hospital. As I stepped into the dimly lit room, my mind was grazing across *Anand* all over again. I wanted to make him smile, but felt odd trying. Self-consciously, I gazed at him but couldn't bring myself to speak. There are these awkward and difficult moments when you feel so helpless wanting to say something, knowing the person cannot talk back. Every thought would appear artificial. Every word would be false cheer. I guess he sensed my agony. People often say my face is a dead give-away of my thoughts. He gestured for a piece of paper to write something. The movement of his hands suggested that he did not want to be seen like this and told me not to come visiting. It was tough holding back the tears. I had this uncanny feeling that this was probably the last time I would see him. The life-giving good doctor of *Anand* deserved better. I remember his words when my aunt had passed away. "Do not grieve so. Death should be faced with as much dignity as life".

The phone doesn't ring on the 27th of October anymore. I have never really celebrated birthdays, but his voice infused a lot of cheer into the day. "Death should be faced with dignity" was a line that stayed with me for long. I used it in my new feature "*Life is Good*!" and dedicated the film [coincidentally based on a Sujit Sen script] to him.

My birthdays, are not the same anymore. Ever since *Anand* left Ananth.

THE GODS MUST BE CRAZY

S S Gill was merely an accomplice, revealed Ravi Chopra, scion of B R Films, one of the most prolific film production companies since the 1960s. It was then Prime Minister Rajiv Gandhi who prescribed three commandments for national television in 1985. Former Prime Minister Jawaharlal Nehru's insightful travelogue *Discovery of India* and two major Sanskrit epics of India—*Ramayan* and *Mahabharat*. Television doctors sprung up like rabbits to dispense the 'mytho' pill. After all, if there was one element man couldn't go wrong with, it was God. Filmmaker Ramanand Sagar who had initially peddled the popular fable *Vikram our Vetaal* for a telecast slot, opened the innings with *Ramayan* [January 1987]. But the war over the rights of *Mahabharat* was fought in court. Though Doordarshan had assigned the rights to B R Films, an aggrieved party, who had applied for it earlier, knocked at the doors of justice. Doordarshan's contention that they could assign a show to whoever they thought fit, won the day. So the Chopra camp set about to film *Mahabharat*. Only, they hadn't bargained for the popularity of the genre.

The telecast of *Ramayan* on Sunday mornings at 9, set up some bewildering benchmarks for television viewership. Deserted streets, garlanded television sets accorded the status of domestic temples, and kitchens shutting shop were stories that homespun fables were made of. But they all did happen. On the sets of another series I was performing in, I was fed with news of how Ramanand Sagar would 'break down' as he filmed the scene of Ram's banishment into the jungle, at the Umargaon studios, about hundred and fifty kilometers from Bombay. No one's sensibilities were affected by the adrenaline rush in the performances or even the modest computer-graphic effects like arrows finding each other in mid-air and neutralising themselves. What was important was that the Gods had kept their date with mankind. Sunday mornings assumed the mantle of a pilgrimage.

All of which brought the *Mahabharat* to a grinding halt. The first four episodes were canned in 1986, but were denied a slot thanks to *Ramayan* showing no signs of vacating. As appeasement, the Chopras were offered a series on the last Moghul emperor *Bahadur Shah Zafar*, whilst *Ramayan* made merry for another two years. It hardly bothered its pious followers that the purists dismissed the show as a bow-and-arrow tele-twaddle. The actors playing Ram [Arun Govil], Seeta [Deepika Chiklia] and Laxman [Sunil Lahiri] were anointed with godly status and found themselves almost banished from roles that portrayed mortals. In an attempt to milk the holy cow fully, the series transgressed to

Uttara Ramayan in 1988, when the roadblocks to *Mahabharat* were eventually lifted. B R Chopra however still did not deem it fit to lock horns with the unprecedented viewership of *Ramayan*. It took a lot of convincing by his team before he relented.

For most observers, the choice of the author was a point of intrigue. But, the Chopras maintained that the celebrated Urdu poet and writer Dr Rahi Masoom Reza was best suited to pen the *Mahabharat*. The officials at Doordarshan had a rider. "How could a Muslim write a Hindu epic?" Chopra contested that with "there was nothing called a 'Hindu epic'". The *Mahabharat* happened in a pre-Muslim era where all Indians were of the same fabric. It all finally boiled down to the channel demanding a narration of the scripts. The Chopras grudgingly gave in, mentally prepared to quit the show if the scripts weren't approved. Ravi Chopra recounts the scene of the narration. "As Rahi *sahab* read out the first four episodes, S S Gill's eyes virtually popped out. The writing took them by surprise. The green light was unanimous."

It didn't, however, end there. When the show was slotted on air, the Vishwa Hindu Parishad put their aggrieved pen to paper with a "how could you guys do this?" notice. The Chopras offered them a taste of the pudding and served the first episode hot. The Sangh wrote back. This time, a letter of apology.

My tryst with writer Dr Rahi Masoom Reza was unexpected. In the early 1990s, I was commissioned by filmmaker B Subhash [who had made the money spinners *Disco Dancer* and *Tarzan*] to direct a television film. Since Dr Rahi Masoom Reza had scripted most of his features, he was brought on to write the film. That was a stroke of good luck. To have the man in vogue himself for a debut project! While I dropped in at his Pali Hill residence on successive afternoons to work on the script of *Sambandh*, a film on the prevalent terrorism in Punjab, I capitalized on the opportunity to satiate my hunger for some answers. How comfortable was he navigating the philosophy of another religion? He attributed it, to what he deemed, 'the hand of God'. "I don't know what comes over me. I go home, have lunch and sleep. Then, I feel someone is shaking me up from slumber. I wake up, sit down to write and feel someone guiding my pen". I'd heard of several inspirational highs for creativity, but this one set me thinking.

Mahabharat ruled the airwaves on Sunday mornings from January 1988. The first-week rating matched that of the *Ramayan*. By the third episode, it had Ramanand Sagar's pioneering mythology trailing. The mass adulation must have driven even the Gods crazy.

B R Chopra's yen for socially relevant subjects [films like *Gumraah, Kanoon, Dharamputra*] came into play during the making of *Mahabharat*. The ancient sage Ved Vyas had remarked "if it's not in the *Mahabaharat*, it's not in India". Which prompted the makers to give the epic a contemporary relevance, connect India's past with its present, a move that was misread by the powers in Parliament. The initial episodes of the series expounded a theory that a king does not become one merely by virtue of his birth [*janam*] but also by his deeds [*karam*]. It drew a political parallel in Delhi as a snooty aside on Prime Minister Rajiv Gandhi and his inheritance of the Nehru political legacy. The interpretation was censored for telecast, though it later found its way back into the digital video discs and repeat telecast copies. The series persisted with its modern interpretation, with the narrator *Samay* [Time] who spoke of the relevance of what happened five thousand years ago. The *Mahabharat* unlike the Bible, does not profess any commandments. It merely describes what transpired, leaving it to its audience to decipher what should have happened and what should not have.

'The hand of God' continued to reign over the series for two-and-a-half- years. [Jan 1988-May1990] During this marathon stint, no one fell ill, no unit member was hurt and no actor was replaced. The war sequence of Kurukshetra shot in the desert city of Jaipur in Rajasthan, packed in 500 horses, 5000 people, 100 pachyderms and 30 chariots. It was like an accident waiting to happen. More than hundred thousand spectators converged on the grounds from neighbouring Faridabad and Delhi on the weekend. They had to be kept at bay with elephants gently let loose on them.

One element about the series that riddled me as a practitioner was the casting exercise that the producers had undertaken. How valid was my theory that the look of the character gained precedence over histrionic ability? The bottom line for the Chopras was to adhere to a certain image of each character that people had pictured in their minds down the ages. Mukesh Khanna played musical chairs, from being cast as Duryodhana, then being considered for Dronacharya before settling down as Bhishma. "Pravin Kumar as Bheem, with his pronounced Punjabi twang did suffer a little', admits Chopra, 'but in the given scenario, his he-man looks did make a difference. It took him a while to come into his own, and by the Draupadi *vastraharan* [saree-disrobing] sequence, his involvement was total". Which set me pondering whether dubbing the voices would have helped smoothen some rough edges.

Leading Hindi film actors Raj Babbar and Juhi Chawla were part of the initial cast. While Babbar, a B R Films discovery [*Insaaf Ka Tarazu*, the Hindi take on the French film *Lipstick*] played a single episode character of Shantanu, Chawla was pencilled in for the part of Draupadi. Until a feature film break [*Qayamat Se Qayamat Tak*, the Aamir Khan family's version of *Romeo and Juliet*] came beckoning. Though they had a watertight contract with her, the Chopras did not deny her a career in the movies. They looked elsewhere for Draupadi and the choice narrowed down to Telugu actress Ramya Krishnan and Bengali rookie Roopa Ganguly. A screen test revealed that the latter had more 'fire" than the 'soft' South Indian lass and Ganguly stepped into Chawla's shoes.

Another grey area was regarding the special effects. The high-band tape recordings, the unavailability of high-end computer graphics and the restriction to a blue/green matte shoot, all threatened to deny the Gods the full glory of their divine acts. Movie special effects veteran Babubhai Mistry was initially hired. But his tendency to be content with any result irked the Chopras. "The sequence where the Ganga is stopped with arrows suffered, thanks to the old school approach," observed Ravi Chopra, 'that was when I took over despite my minimal special effects *gyaan* gathered from making commercials. A trial-and-error process was launched and I didn't let go till we got it right. I was determined to raise the bar for myself, go beyond the *Ramayan* and give the magical acts a real feel. So the *Brahmastra* had to assume the feel of a nuclear weapon, the *Virat Roop* had 18 layers of video to contend with and the Draupadi disrobing sequence took four days to match the sarees, the folds, and the cuts. So, despite working on a budget of six hundred thousand rupees [which, after the half-way mark rose to nearly nine], I ended up with a crore and a half rupees in the red. But as owner of the rights of the property, I managed a phenomenal recovery from dubbing, video and repeat telecast rights. The *Mahabharat's* turnover is more than the output of five of our hit films clubbed together, and as is known, we've had many a success in our company. In fact, its telecast on BBC 2 recorded 5 million viewers!"

It wasn't a simple task transcribing an epic that dealt in metaphors. Chopra often had to provide an explanation to the viewer about the unstated or the understated. *Guru* Dronacharya's act of cutting his disciple Eklavya's finger, thus, was seen in the light of the former's philosophy. "*All education is for me to give, but not yours for the taking. Which tantamounts to theft and hence the punishment.*" When Arjuna questions the perfect warrior Bhishma as to what stopped him from doing the right thing, the answer is traced back to Bhishma's promise to his father. He could not defy the dictates of the man who sat on the throne. But I feel that perhaps the biggest truth of the *Mahabharat* which could not be incorporated in the series, as it would defy norms, was the transmission of the *Gita*. It is an unexplainable theory that a verbal communication resulted in the 701 slokas that Dwayipayan represented through Sanjay and later came to us as the *Bhagavad Gita*. Given the perspective of the Kurus, Duryodhana sees Arjuna dispensing with his *gandeeva* and pleading to Krishna. A verbose *Gita* here would have enraged the Kurus and they would have intervened, to say the least. Moreover, it would have had the Kurus mistaking it as a plea from Arjuna to Krishna to reconsider his thoughts about not taking to arms in the battle to follow. And then the communication began through the guru, not from the guru to the seeker...the *Mouna Samvada*.

In modern times, a vast amount of research has been done in the area of mind exploration, particularly mental telepathy. Yogic philosophy, and now scientific experiments, have revealed that the mind is finer than electromagnetic waves, and more capable and far more subtle than the most powerful laser beams. Which brings one to the final sloka of the *Gita, "Yatra Yogeshwara Krishno Yatra Partho Dhanurdhara"* - Yogeshwara Krishna means 'beyond the subtle'. It needs to be read as the sublime mentor. Here He hones intrinsic qualities, thinking, emotional intelligence, attitudes, behaviours, habits and the mentee's personality and character. No space for lip service. Such an approach would, perhaps, have been abstract for audiences given to rituals in front of their television sets. Even Peter Brooks in his innovatively staged interpretation of *The Mahabharat* and its film version, did not dare.

My own run-in with the sanctimoniousness of the Gods happened during the filming of the series *The Sword Of Tipu Sultan*. Actor and director Sanjay Khan and I spoke about the possibility of doing a series on the monkey God Hanuman. "The Indian Superman", as Khan excitedly referred to him. I offered to write and direct the show and in the company of Gulzar's favourite writer Bhushan Banmali researched the subject. We came across some uncanny parallels with modern issues. The aspect of pollution for instance. Hanuman stayed healthy, breathing and flying through pure, unadulterated air. But it was the test tube baby theory that got everyone's goat. When molten gold was poured into Parvati's womb to stop Hanuman from being born, Bali came to the rescue and blew the seeds from Parvati into Anjaneya's womb. And Hanuman was born with Anjaneya as a surrogate mother. But a small portion of the molten gold too found its way into Anjaneya's womb and Hanuman was born with two tiny gold rings adorning his ears. Khan was insistent that this would rake up a controversy and decided to play safe, while I was looking to give mythology a contemporary connect. Eventually, the series materialised as *Jai Hanuman*, reaching out to its gallery of the faithful. The rancour from critics about the mythological shows not harbouring an IQ quotient met with the predictable refrain from producers. "The ability of the man in the streets to comprehend anything with depth is greatly lacking" Further the fear of losing ratings if the episodes weren't easily palatable, always played on their minds. Not comfortable with treading the beaten path, I had chosen to opt-out of the Hanuman epic, despite the extensive work that had gone into a heap of episodes.

The 'godman' crown then shifted heads to film actor-turned-software-producer Dheeraj Kumar. He gave the Gods and their disciples a run for their money and miracles. Almost every celestial form was a subject for his mega shows. *Om Namah Shivay. Shani Dev, Shree Ganesh, Santoshi Maa, Upanishad Ganga, Vaishno Devi, Suryaputra Karan*, the list is endless. It could well have led to a quaint scenario where there would be no more Gods left to film! Ravi Chopra, too, had his fill. In 2009, when the fledgling 9X channel offered him a whopping thirty-five lakhs per episode deal to film the *Mahabharat* all over again, he wasn't enticed, despite the possibility of a neat profit of fifteen lakh rupees an episode. 9X, subsequently wrapped up its entertainment channel. In 2008, the prolific software producer Ekta Kapoor, tempted and probably inspired by the ravaging warriors of the Hollywood blockbuster *300*, styled the actors in what appeared like Greek attire in her version of the epic. Additionally, she briefed her writing team to emulate the bigness of *Ben Hur*. It was an ambitious interpretation on paper, but looked 'greek' to the audience. The new-look *Kahaani Hamaare Mahabharat ki* failed to rekindle the craze and the experiment had to be dispensed with after 75 episodes.

Ravi Chopra was right. The Gods are more typecast in their image than most of our actors. As he proudly flashed a rare photograph of a 'curfew hit' Marine Drive on *Mahabharat*'s Sunday mornings in 1988, it set me pondering about how sacrosanct mythology is for the television viewer. Seriously allergic to both interpretation or a different conjugation.

DERAILED

Circa 1998. The security guard at the member-of-parliament Maneka Gandhi's gate in New Delhi signalled me in. I tip-toed all the way up to the main door, taking care to not step on any of the mongrels that paved the path. She had quite a pack of strays picked up from the streets of New Delhi. This was a kind deed. Not so her deed with me. I was being summoned to clarify the objections she had over a new children's series, *Chimpoo Shikari,* which I acted in and also directed. It had "talking" animals [a la Hollywood's *Babe*] and was set in a jungle. A comedy about a fumbling self-proclaimed hunter who couldn't hurt a fly. The 'animal welfare vigilante' in Gandhi had her radar turned on me. I couldn't figure out whether this was a privilege or admonition. She had approached Doordarshan and stalled the show, just hours before telecast. Now I waited in her lobby, my face pleading- "not guilty".

I wasn't the first victim of Doordarshan's touch-me-not policy. In 1985, Kundan Shah and Aziz Mirza's pet project, *Police Station,* underwent more interrogation than some criminals behind bars. Shah had set out to find an antidote to the soaps. A no-holds barred look at the police and their method of functioning. He spent several nights in torture chambers questioning their approach to crime. "Why are you breathing down *our* neck? We are a lowly 17 on the list of corrupt officials!" was the reply that greeted him. In the dingy back alleys of Princess Street in South Bombay, the cops had no qualms in accepting two thousand rupees to execute a bail order. "What's the big deal? Why shouldn't my inspector demand money? Don't you people grease others' palms? So why should we alone pay a price"?

They were looking down a barrel that was breeding corruption within. A *jari* worker awaiting an Eid visit home for three years, was prevented from doing so and locked up. The cops supported the owner and maimed the worker. At the milk stables, a union worker was silenced and the cops colluded with the accused. A mother's story about her missing son. A drunken husband who beat up his wife and had his own stand on it. So many of these stories that didn't find their way into an otherwise over-enthusiastic media network.

The 'biggest private limited office in Delhi-Doordarshan' promptly imposed a ban on the series. Shah felt that the ire was directed towards an initial episode that dealt with flesh trade. When *Police Station* was greenlit by the channel, Prime Minister Indira Gandhi had just been assassinated. The nation was undergoing a moral purge. But the euphoria barely lasted six months. After that it was "business as usual". Which explained the turnaround at Doordarshan. Eventually they offered to "help out". The three episodes of *Police Station* were condensed into a telefilm called *Dundhle Saaye* [Hazy Shadows]—a watered-down version of the original. Shah consoled himself with "at least we salvaged some of our monies".

Politically incorrect moments stir up a hornet's nest in Doordarshan. Basu Chatterjee had found India's answer to the popular British series, *Yes Prime Minister*, in Manohar Shyam Joshi's instalments of satire in a local newspaper. Om Puri was picked, and aptly so, to play the garrulous *paan-masticating* minister in *Netaji Kahen* [Spoke the Minister]. But the government's bark was worse than the serial's bite. Forced to rechristen it *Kakaji Kahen*, the series derailed in thirteen-episodes amidst bureaucratic wrangles and fickleness. I replayed Mirza's and Chatterjee's fate in my mind as I waited for Mrs Gandhi to emerge.

"*Shikari*" [hunter] is a banned word in Parliament". Gandhi spoke with clinical authority. I had a compelling urge to request her to ask Parliament to go beyond the 'word'. Come down on the illegal poaching, the camel and horse rides, elephants forced to beg on Bombay's streets, the horrific abattoirs and the inhumane animal trafficking, but please, oh please, go beyond "the word". But this wasn't the moment to win a debate. It was her word against mine. My financer's investment was at stake. He was a businessman who had unwittingly walked into the inviting trap of television. And I didn't want to be responsible for laying his investment waste. Gandhi began by objecting to the monkey in the serial with a chain around its neck. I defended the chain explaining that the monkey was domesticated and had to be protected from the wild ones in the jungle. She didn't appear too convinced. She then picked on an alligator being killed by a falling rock in the first episode. I said it was filmed with a rubber replica of the reptile and Chimpu was a hero by default. Hadn't she cheered Johny Weismuller as he flapped around with several rubber alligators in the Tarzan movies? I could see that she was in no mood for humour even if the Marx Brothers or Woody Allen turned up. The title was unacceptable and she asked me to send her a fax with the amendments to reconsider her decision.

I was in a dilemma. A premium amount had already been invested on the jungle adventure. I had taken great pains to dub the animal voices making it the first 'live' feature of its kind. I couldn't let all that go down the drain. I hired a typewriter in an office cabin in Doordarshan and banged away furiously. I made a short and quick title change. *Shikari* became *Safari*. My title designers needed to alter only three letters. And, then, I plunged into an outpouring of sentiment. I elaborated, not without reason, on how we were as concerned about animals and even stuck to vegetarian food on the sets. About how the animals were given a habitat conducive to them and how the 'talking' was done not by harming them but by feeding them, so they opened their mouths, as we slipped in the 'dialogue'. I faxed the voluminous rejoinder to her. After a while she called. Her voice struck a new tenor. "Ananth you have used up all my fax paper!" Well, she asked for it and got it. I smiled and disconnected. We had broken the ice. *Chimpoo Safari* was allotted a shallow evening slot at 7 PM, denying it publicity, exposure and subsequently sponsorship. At the end of it all, it was an out-of-the-box experience and good while it lasted. Besides, of course, the experience of meeting the country's most celebrated animal activist.

Kerala's whiz-kid Jijo, attired in a simple white dhoti and a bush shirt, camouflaged the enterprising brain behind the maker of India's first 3D film in Malayalam, *My Dear Kuttichhatan* [adapted in Hindi as *Chhota Chetan*]. When he chose to serialize *The Bible* for television, he chose me and my theatre colleague Meenakshi as casting directors, blissfully unaware as he was, of the talent on the Hindi scene. Actors like Kanwaljit Singh were appalled. He equated the thought of being auditioned to body frisking at the airports. I had to rid him of his apprehensions by passing the buck to the producers who weren't knowledgable about Hindi actors. Meenakshi had already been adept at the task while casting for *The Sword Of Tipu Sultan*. She roped in Raza Murad, Mona Ambegaonkar and other interesting faces to depict Biblical characters.

But, a couple of months into the project we found ourselves out of a job. Doordarshan, plagued by religious controversy over India's first Christian series, pussyfooted yet again and *Bible Ki Kahaniyan* ran into an unholy blockade. Following two court injunctions and opposition from groups in the troubled Muslim majority Kashmir state, telecast was called off in May 1993 after 15 episodes. Another stumbling block was the refusal of the sponsors to foot the tripled sponsorship fee after the series was given the highest - "Super A" status by Doordarshan. Doordarshan policies granted the producer three minutes of telecast time for commercials, which could be sold to advertisers who were given sponsorship billing.

After an interval of 3 years, *Bible Ki Kahaniyan* resumed telecast on June 16 1996 following a senior Doordarshan official John Churchill's declaration that the problem had been ironed out between the producer and sponsors. Churchill credited the Congress party that had been voted out of government in the previous general elections with the initiative for resuming the series, "as part of its strategy for minority support". The resumption had been delayed as Doordarshan had to wait for the end of another ongoing series to grant it a time slot. Welcoming the revival, the Catholic Bishop's Conference of India's (CBCI) deputy secretary general, Father George Pereira said, "It will help Christians feel they are not ignored in this country." He also claimed that CBCI had financially assisted Jijo, the Catholic producer of the serial and "would continue to support him." Politics, religion and every mentionable social element had craned their neck for attention with this series. I was however out of the loop by then, having moved on. The one bright spot was that the casting exercise had gifted me the knack to look for the right face for a character. An extremely useful tool as I undertake to cast for my films these days.

B R Chopra's filmmaker son, Ravi Chopra, found Doordarshan's "creativity" at derailing shows, amusing after the initial frustration. Despite the timeless Mahabaharat, the Chopras often ran into rough weather. The ambitious tracing of Delhi's history in *Main Dilli Hoon* found a spanner in the works after a year's run. The national broadcaster demanded a minimum guarantee of four hundred thousand rupees to grant an extended run. The Chopras did a quick calculation. Forty lakh rupees plus a neat sum as cost of production would put them in the lurch. So *Dilli* couldn't make it till Independence day. The series was aborted with Prithviraj Chauhan still astride his steed. Abortion of television shows has since become legal. It turned more rampant with the advent of satellite channels as rating points were factored in. 78 episodes into *Vishnu Puran* on the Zee network and Ravi Chopra felt the heat again. Creative head Sandeep Goyal, who had assumed charge, didn't subscribe to the *dasavatar* [The Ten Incarnations of Lord Vishnu] saga. Neither was a 7% viewership enough incentive. He pulled the plug half-way into the *Parashuram* era. Ravi Chopra desisted from directing television after that day.

2010. Facebook has taken over our lives. You find everyone you had given up for lost, here. I recently reconnected with Maneka Gandhi on her Facebook page. I renew my debate. I remind her about the continuing atrocities on the hopeless animals, whose cause she is championing. About how despite her efforts, elephants are Mumbai's biggest begging bowls and how horses still careen into speeding vehicles, have heart attacks on the racecourse and die. I remind her of how she was barking up the wrong tree in *Chimpu Shikari*. Either her memory failed her or she chose to ignore me. Then, out of the blue, her jungle tales were revived when a reality show *Mujhe Is Jungle se Bachao* was beamed in 2009 on Sony TV. She alleged that the unit was taking advantage of loopholes in the law by filming the show in Malaysian jungles. On another day, she whipped the authorities to wake up to the plight of sick steeds plying the Victorias in Mumbai. But her stoic stance on the issue of maneaters being shot down reflects the ambiguity of authority. Like television audiences, it has become selective.

CLASSICS ILLUSTRATED

My favourite comic book series during school days featured a roster of great writers. *Classics Illustrated* edited the works of Mark Twain, Robert Louis Stevenson, Charles Dickens, H G Wells, Jonathan Swift, Jules Verne and others within its covers. But *Treasure Island, David Copperfield, Tom Sawyer, Oliver Twist, Gulliver's Travels, Around the World in 80 Days, Twenty Thousand Leagues Under the Sea The Brass Bottle* and *Kidnapped* deserved much more than the condensed thirty-five odd pages of graphics. Classics exude a different texture and demeanour and that is probably what kept them alive for the medium of television to adapt them with unabridged affection. Indian literature was a cradle of such works and became inviting enough for an electronic medium to bring them to life. The Doordarshan granary gradually stocked many such shows and despite having a life span of twenty six episodes or less, they jog one's memory many years after telecast. Proof enough, that they are classics.

If R K Laxman had made the common man iconic in his political cartoon pockets in our morning coffee-mate *The Times of India,* his brother R K Narayan explored the ordinary man's capacity to absorb extraordinary events. R K Narayan was short for Rasipuram Krishnaswamiayyar Narayanaswami. The truncated name was suggested by author Graham Greene when his first book *'Swami and Friends'* was being published in 1935. Before authoring *Malgudi Days,* however, Narayan became known in show business as the author who had minced no words in his critique of filmmaker Vijay Anand's version of his novel *Guide.* But the bundle of fun and messages that life is, truly came across heartwarmingly in the Shankar Nag helmed *Malgudi Days* [1986], a series introduced with a lilting title theme and characters guided by their basic instincts, strong, hypocritical, and vulnerable. Yet, it was the optimism at the end of each fable that left you in good spirits. The search for perfection, the temptation to win a lottery, the cunning ways of astrology, and the folly of unconditional love were taken-for-granted traits that Narayan threw new light on. The school boy, a retired old man, a gardener, a maid, the village postman, a snake charmer, the cobbler, a gateman or even a dog, all had the reach-out-and-touch-me feel. Notable faces like Girish Karnad, Anant Nag, Harish Patel, Vishnuvardhan, Arundhati Nag and Dina Pathak featured in the one-off episodes. Nag followed it up with a companion piece *Swami and Friends*, that brought out the eternal fears and insecurities of adolescence. Shot on the outskirts of Bangalore, it was a refreshing detour from the other serials which leaned heavily on verbosity and visuals from the metropolis. Its naked innocence and simplicity of approach left an indelible mark on the viewer. Looking back, *this* was a series which I should have lobbied for a part in. Probably the distance and a long absence from the bay city that it called for, weighed on my mind.

Or was it the non-availability of Nag's communication details. Whatever the reason, I rue my laxity to this day.

Malgudi Days was a collection of some 30 odd short stories. If the creative order of today's television would permit, I would venture to do *Bachelor of Arts* as a follow-up to *Mithaiwala* [Vendor of Sweets] and *Swami and Friends*. While neo-youth films like *Jaane Tu Ya Jaane Na, Love Aaj Kal* and *Cocktail* have attempted to delve into the mind of "a confused generation", Narayan did it decades ago in *Bachelor of Arts* where the main character, Chandran, grapples with the idea of whether or not to go with the girl whom he professes to be in love with.

Narayan had created a 'once upon a time world' that often forced many enthusiasts to ask, '*Where* is this Malgudi?' To which he had replied, "It's imaginary and not to be looked for on any map. It may be a half-truth when I say that it represents a small town in South India but the characteristics of Malgudi seem universal to me". In the November of 2011, Narayan's home was granted heritage status and christened "Malgudi". The place finally came into existence. In these days of lost innocence, the reverb of "tana na tana na na na" capturing the rural serenity with a disarming charm would be just the right theme to get carried away.

It was an office chair I loved to lounge on. On the desk, in front of it, lay an early edition of *Forrest Gump* among other literary acquisitions in Urdu and English. The portrait of the late actress Meena Kumari on the wall appeared to peer serenely at the person seated below her. The flapping pages of *Forrest Gump* betrayed the signs of a book that signalled "read". Gulzar, the occupant of the chair below the portrait, along with his peers Hrishikesh Mukherjee and Basu Chatterjee were perennial favourites. Since college days they were the ones whose films spelt my initiation into the medium. A first-day first show screening was more or less mandatory. That class spilled over to the tube. By then, television had roped in the best of talent and it was difficult for a filmmaker like Gulzar to resist its advances. He was scripting the dance-based series *Noopur* for Hema Malini. However, his opening salvo [1988] when he took a brief sabbatical from films, was a tribute to the man about whom he confesses, "if it wasn't for him, I would not have been a poet". Mirza Asadullah Beg Khan —more famously known as Ghalib. *Mirza Ghalib* virtually became for Doordarshan what *Amadeus* was to Hollywood.

It was the Ghalib that Gulzar unearthed and interpreted after extensive research. Ghalib's original *takhallus* (pen-name) was *Asad* and he changed this to 'Ghalib', which literally translates as 'a conqueror'. Gulzar could pride himself on following the poet's footsteps. After all, he had traded his original name Sampoorna Singh for *Gulzar* [a full bloom]. The Thursday night prime time slot [on which I had made my debut with *Ados Pados* four years ago] assumed a glorious semantic air.

Following the series, the discerning viewer discovered the poet, Ghalib, who never cared to strive for a livelihood but scrounged on state patronage, credit or generosity of his friends. Around 1810, when he was all of thirteen, he was married into a family of nobles. As fate would have it, one of his seven children survived and this pain subsequently echoed in some of his *ghazals*. It is still difficult to picture anyone else but Naseeruddin Shah in the role of the zealous poet. Little wonder then, that the actor still rates it as one of his best works. Shafi Inamdar played his closest rival Zauq, tutor of Bahadur Shah Zafar II, then emperor of India entrenched in Delhi. There are some amusing anecdotes of the rivalry between Ghalib and Zauq and exchange of jibes between them. However, there was also a mutual respect for each other's talent. Both also admired and acknowledged the supremacy of Meer Taqi Meer, a towering figure of Urdu Poetry of the 18th century. Ghazal exponent Jagjit Singh's compositions for *Mirza Ghalib* evoked the Delhi of the 1800s and opened up avenues to delve deeper into the context of Ghalib's profound wordplay. It was a soundtrack that bettered those of the films made in that decade.

Despite Gulzar having displayed his finesse as a writer and director, *Mirza Ghalib* was not spared a few critical salvos. Ghalib afficionados recall Zauq's rather disconcerting facial gestures at the *mushaira* [a gathering of poets who recite their compositions]. Also, the ghazal that Ghalib recites there was deemed inappropriate. "It lacked the literary merit, by Ghalib's own standards, to be the first ghazal of his Diwan" wrote a critic. Fears were also expressed that Ghalib came across as crusty and cantankerous, displaying a morose and testy temperament, an erudite scholar, hospitable and the epitome of the genteel ways of the nobility, besides being gifted with a great sense of humour. Well, like its controversial subject, the series too expectedly had its share of raised eyebrows at the liberties taken, leading to what they claimed, a misleading portrait of the poet.

On February 15, 1869 Asadullah Khan Ghalib left behind a legacy extremely rich in its cultural and poetical values which will be read and sung for centuries. His fame came to him posthumously. He had prophesied, "although my time ignores me, it would be recognized by later generations." History has vindicated his claim. He is also arguably the most "recited and written about" among Urdu poets. A moved Gulzar quotes "*Kehte hein ke Ghalib ka hai andaze bayan aur*". It is this "*andaz-e-bayan*" [style of narration] that lends uniqueness to his works and enchants people even in this cyber age. "Remembering Mirza Ghalib on his birth anniversary is the least we can do." His house had been converted into a coal depot until a political figure and a poet himself, Atal Bihari Vajpayee, in 2001, stepped in to rescue the monument from doom. "It is now a museum and a shrine which we frequent on his birth anniversary. He was a great egotist, he knew that, perhaps revelled in it. One couldn't deny him that arrogance. He insisted on writing in Urdu, the people's language while other poets opted for Persian", observed Gulzar, disillusioned by the myopic attitude of a new generation to the greats.

As a tribute to Ghalib, Gulzar commissioned a bust of the poet to commemorate his 214th birth anniversary on December 27, 2010. It was installed at Ghalib's Gali Qasim Jaan home in Chandni Chowk. The bust was made on the basis of a portrait by former President Zakir Hussain as there are not many pictures of the poet for reference. Hussain had a photo of him, which he had purchased for Rs. 2, a huge amount at that time. "Ghalib is important for everyone. One should know about him even if you are not familiar with his language. I'm not averse to Shakespeare being mandatory in academic syllabi but Ghalib, Premchand, Tagore, Kalidas and Bashir too need to be introduced". In keeping with the poet's frugal existence, Gulzar too discounted his fees as director to maintain the budget of the series. "*Mirza Ghalib*" ended up looking more cinematic than most television shows with the director's passion playing a major contributor and Jagjit Singh rounding off the rest.

With *Mujrim Haazir*, producer and director Rakesh Chowdhary set two benchmarks for television. An eminently watchable adaptation of Bimal Mitra's classic *Aasami Haazir* [at your service], it succeeded in tempting the versatile actress Nutan from her film sabbatical to play the pivotal figure of '*kaliganj ki bahu*'. Bimal Mitra (1912–1991) wrote several novels in Bengali, but he was adept in Hindi as well. Guru Dutt's celebrated film *Sahib Biwi aur Ghulam* was his first foray into Hindi cinema. *Mujrim Haazir* was based on the true story of Sadanand, who in order to repent for the sins of his father and grandfather takes on a society filled with corruption, anger, and injustice. But the series doesn't paint just a grim picture all round. Everything beautiful and innocent about human nature has its say too.

One particular sequence I still recall is an Eid celebration at a villager's house. A five-year-old, seeing his parents savouring 'sewaiyan' [pudding], asked his mother to feed some of it to his pet goat. The mother said, "*Bete, bakri sewaiyan nahi, ghas khati hai* (Goats don't eat pudding, they eat grass)". To which, the child naively asked, "Even on Eid?"

Chowdhary resurrected the old Calcutta ambience remarkably. For viewers like me in the late 1980s, this was a window to a world we hadn't explored yet. Another instance of television throwing up so many variables at an early stage. Navni Parihar made her debut in the series as the docile, demure bride in a decaying aristocratic set-up. She was to share screen space with me later in *Prehari*, the serial on the Border Security force. Then, many years later in 2008, she played one of the pivotal characters in my first experimental film *Staying Alive*. The sound of the *kahaars* "*Hun Huna Re Hun Huna, Hun Huna Re Hun*" was a refrain that was exclusive to *Mujrim Haazir*. I had often wished that Choudhary would break the barrier again. Mitra's other classic *Begum Mary Biswas,* a telling account of 18th century Bengal overridden by the British, was a potential blockbuster that surprisingly wasn't in the purview of any television producer.

The success of *Mujrim Haazir,* spurred other directors to dabble in more literary works. Rangeya Raghav [born Tirumalla Nambakkam Viraraghava Acharya], was a prominent Hindi writer of the 20th century. He started writing at the age of 13, and during his short life of only about 40 years, he was endowed with a number of literary citations. *Kab Tak Pukaroon* (Till when shall I call out?), one of his most acclaimed novels, fitted adroitly into a television scenario. Dealing with the conflicts between the nomadic Nats (a la Romas of Europe) and the Thakurs [a high caste community] - both groups placed at different hierarchical social levels in the Indian traditional society of yesteryears, this series featured theatre guru Habib Tanvir with Delhi actor Pankaj Kapoor and gave Friday prime time viewers some serious material to chew on. This was director Sudhir Mishra's initial foray into television production and quite clearly the forerunner of the kind of films he was to attempt later [*Is Raat Ki Subah Nahin, Dharavi, Hazaron Khwaishein Aisi*].

Followed Amol Palekar with *Mrignayanee*. The "middle-class" hero of *Rajnigandha, Chhoti Si Baat, Golmaal* and other rom-coms had flirted with television in *Kachchi Dhoop*, a children's series that introduced Bhagyashree Patwardhan who was to later star in *Maine Pyar Kiya*, the film that made Salman Khan a star. But *Mrignayanee* [1991], the story of a king, Man Singh, [played by Mohan Bhandari] attracted to a beautiful tribal girl [Pallavi Joshi] saw him create an ethos and display a directorial skill, which like Mishra was to diversify into films. *Raag Darbari* [1986-87], based on Srilal Shukla's book of the same name, on the crumbling bureaucratic system [featuring Om Puri, Zarina Wahab] and *Srikant* based on Sarat Chandra Chatterjee's novel *Srikanta* which saw the charismatic Farouque Shaikh's debut on television, rounded off the literary adaptations. *Srikant* directed by actor Navin Nischol's brother Pravin Nischol, also had rising stars Sujata Mehta, Mrinal Kulkarni, Irfan Khan and Naresh Suri in its cast. It was filmed on 16mm instead of the standard low-band video format. The series wasn't concluded in its first year [1985-86] as the makers preferred to pick up the thread later in a second season.

One name that had deeply influenced me with films like *Kanneshwara Rama, Bara* [The Famine] and the simmering account of Muslims in Uttar Pradesh *Garam Hawa* [Scorching Winds] was Mysore Srinivas Sathyu. The art director of Chetan Anand's *Haqeeqat* [his debut film] and several theatre productions [predominantly those of the Indian People's Theatre association] had a sensibility refreshingly removed from the mainstream claptrap. So, in 1992, when he decided to film Thakazi Sivasankaran Pillai's Jnanpith award-winning Malayalam epic *Kayar* [Rope of Coir], as a television series, I didn't want a replay of the Malgudi miss-the-bus incident. I promptly sought an appointment with Sathyu at his Santacruz residence. I had no qualms in admitting to him that a part in *Kayar* would do a great deal of good for the actor in me. I hadn't worked with Sathyu before, so the hard sell was needed. As he regarded me, I could feel he was trying to slot the face in a character. My Kerala roots could have aided his decision too. The role of the avaricious high priest, Sheshayan who manipulated his way through situations and paid a price for it, was a mirror of a society at the orthodox level and the decadence that had set in. The multi-dimensional character was probably just the rigorous honing I was looking for. Not even the now-meager-sounding fee of two thousand rupees an episode, in fact a come down from *Ados Pados*, was going to demoralize me. I was here for a long term creative pact.

Sathyu had invested an initial Rs. 20 lakh in canning seven episodes of the 26-episode serial in the sensuous, lush rice bowl of Kuttanad in Kerala, when the moral police reared its head at Mandi House, New Delhi. Thakazhi's exploration of the evolution of key aspects of Kerala society, especially the impact of land legislations on the matriarchal system of the Nair caste, was allotted an odd late-night slot [9:50 PM] because the review committee found certain episodes "desirable only for adult viewing". Strangely enough, the committee had seemingly progressive authors and editors Khushwant Singh, Amita Malik, R P Singh, Madhu Jain, Anil Saari and Prabhat Joshi. A visibly upset Thakazhi declared in the media that the reviewers ought to be whipped for daring to suggest that the serial was 'too bold'. "What do these people understand about Kerala's culture especially the matriarchal system of the past which gave Nair women tremendous freedom in marital relationships? In such a system, the father was not the looming figure but it was the uncle. Divorce was very simple, the woman merely had to put her man's things — a mat and pillow outside her door. As for the man, he could find another woman willing to accept him if he so wished. These are socio-cultural facts which the north Indian psyche cannot comprehend. And how could journalists, as most of the committee members are, judge the literary, sociological, historical and aesthetic value of a work like this?" he argued. He questioned the review committee's remark of 'sex' in an episode where a pregnant woman, carrying an illegitimate child, sheds her dhoti out of fear and panic as her uncle thrashes her. "The incident depicts the autocratic and fearsome figure that an uncle was in a matriarchal system."

The tirade had little impact on the Mandi House mandarins who mumbled illegibly in reply and stuck to their decision of a late-night slot. It was to be expected in a world which was still on a censor spree. Like with Mark Twain's *Huckleberry Finn*, one of the classics we were brought up on, which had the word "nigger" replaced by slave. So what if the "n" word was in vogue at the time Twain wrote it! Despite *Kayar* being discontinued [the novel encompasses a 250 year span of Kerala history upto 1970], it was enriching while it lasted. The filming in my homeland was an eye-opener in several ways. In streets lined with temples, rich paddy fields and humble mud abodes close to the sanctum sanctorum of the deities, Sathyu adorned television with new locations. He steered clear of loud, unreal emoting. "I want real characters, looking natural. It is a thin line that divides the real from the unreal". I warmed up to the fine art of an understated performance and could immediately feel the difference between "acting" and just being the character. If audiences today feel my performances are "real", I owe a lot to Sathyu for instilling the discipline in me. It was a rewarding moment when the frail and ailing Thakazhi who visited us on location, himself corroborated it with a pat on the back. "You made my Seshayan come alive!"

Sathyu's body of work may not fill up reams of filmography, but his place is special. In his patent understated way. He restricted himself to telefilms for a while before returning to feature film making in 2010 with *Ijjodu*, based on the age-old Devdasi system. It was in the fitness of things that his *Garam Hawa* actor Farouque Shaikh flagged off the film's release. To this day, unfamiliar viewers pronounce *Kayar* as *kaayar* [coward]. Its maker is amused because he is anything but that.

In the shadows of M S Sathyu those days, was Prakash Jha who may have begun with a rip-roaring football film *Hip Hip Hooray*!, but soon took on the grime with *Damul*. For television, he toed the Malgudi line with his endearing *Mungerilal Ke Haseen Sapne* [1989-90], about the doomed hopes of an archetype middle-class Mungeri, who finds daydreaming the perfect antidote to his woes at home and the workplace. Everything from bossing around, to dating a beautiful colleague and forcing his wife to obey his orders is the stuff that his dreams are made of. Of course, his castles in the air come crashing down like Humpty Dumpty, but that doesn't deter him from building them again. Raghuvir Yadav played Mungeri with just the right mix of disdain and humour. The supposed sequel, *Mungerilal ka Bhai Naurangi*, the wisdom of the satirical Sufi figure *Mulla Nasriddin* and the wit of *Tenali Rama*, the Birbal of the South [played by Vijay Kashyap], were probably the last of the "classics". The likes of Gulzar, Sathyu, Jha, Nag, Palekar and Mishra created a studious aura for television. There was this urge to emulate them. On one of my later visits to a channel head, I casually broached the genre and the scope for exploring a rich heritage of literature. He regretted that it did not fit into their "current creative scheme of things".

The classics live in fear of being abandoned.

ELEMENTARY, MY DEAR WATSON

Imagine Sherlock Holmes and Dr Watson having this conversation

Holmes: "It's elementary, my dear Watson. There *is* no God, and life *was not* created. The god hypothesis is rather discredited".

Watson: "Yes, Holmes, such religious beliefs are just myths from the past. Every time you understand something, religion becomes less likely. Only with the discovery of the double helix and the ensuing genetic revolution, have we had grounds for thinking that the powers held traditionally to be the exclusive property of the gods might one day be ours".

This was indeed a verbal exchange in April 2003 by a real Dr Watson and his former research colleague, Dr Crick, according to a report in the *London Daily Telegraph*.

Well, it wasn't as elementary as the legendary Holmes and Watson made it out to be. The comprehension of the real detective genre and its religious implementation on Indian television appeared to be as complicated as the discovery of the double Helix. The genetic revolution in scriptwriters wasn't a tradition and God couldn't care less.

So *who* would break the myth? Heads turned when our best bet, the redoubtable, Satyajit Ray decided to televise his own creation, the private detective Feluda. In 1985, when *Satyajit Ray Presents* was first announced, we film buffs braced ourselves for a master class. After all, it wasn't often that the acclaimed director who had ensconced himself in Bengali cinema with child-like stubbornness, decided to speak a universal language. But it was just what the doctor ordered for the small screen. It wasn't Ray's first television foray though. Earlier, in 1981, he had made Premchand's *Sadgati* [Salvation] a telefilm that starred Om Puri and Smita Patil and premiered on a Saturday evening. Connoisseurs like me lapped up the story of an outcaste cobbler exploited by a village priest.

Pradosh Chandra Mitter, more commonly known as Feluda, a thirty-plus private eye, first appeared in the widely read Bengali children's magazine *Sandesh* [1965] that Ray edited, and was a regular in novellas and short stories until his demise. Feluda's calling card read– Private Detective, 27, Rajani Sen Road, [a middle-class suburb], South Calcutta. Playing Watson to Feluda's Holmes, was his teenage cousin, Topshe, and the two were usually accompanied on their cases by their older friend, a pulp-fiction writer Lalmohan Ganguli, who besides the comic relief, pitched in with occasional logistical backup. Although the influence of Doyle's Holmes is apparent, the stories were coined for children, and therefore went easy on the sex quotient (in fact, there were hardly any female characters other than aunts and grandmothers) and violence [a pointed Colt was adequate to threaten a bad character]. Like Hrishikesh Mukherjee used to jest, "the maximum violence in a Bengali film is the blood that is seen when the hero cuts himself while shaving".

Satyajit Ray Presents on Tuesday prime time nights was reminiscent of the *Alfred Hitchcock Presents* series. Though not written or directed by him, his mere recommendation meant credibility. Ray's series was directed by his son Sandip Ray. The casting coup was Shashi Kapoor who had made concerted attempts to wean away from the beaten path with films like *Shakespearewallah, Utsav, Vijeta* and *New Delhi Times*. Theatre actor and practising psychiatrist Mohan Agashe played *Jatayu* [the Indian counterpart to Watson] and the series raised the bar on Doordarshan with tense understated moments and mood lighting. Kapoor joined the ranks of such celebrated Bengali thespians like Soumitra Chatterjee [and later Sabyaschi Chakraborty] in portraying the detective who depended more on his grey cells than gun-powder. Feluda continued to live on. In 2010, the Hollywood-based Disney Channel acquired the rights of *Feluda-The Kathmandu Caper* for an animation movie on India's best-loved private eye. At the beginning of the millennium, I had sent feelers to Sandip Ray for the adaptation rights of a Feluda story for a Hindi film. His messenger replied that Sandip wasn't keen to part with it as he contemplated doing a film on the character, himself. Ten years down the line, as Ray readied another Feluda film, and I thought that my dream of paying tribute to the venerable senior Ray, would remain just that, a marvellous turnaround happened. In 2016, Sandip Ray graciously wrote me the rights of his *baba's* short story *Golpo Boliye Tarini Khuro* for a feature in Hindi. My opportunity for a tribute!

Detectives operate late nights. Or so Doordarshan believed. So one of the earliest series in the genre *Karamchand* (1985) was allotted the 10 PM slot, inadvertently opening up a time-band that had remained inert till then. Its maker, Pankaj Parashar, when he was but thirteen, had been hooked on to a popular radio detective series called *Inspector Eagle*. On one occasion he told its producer, Vishwamitter Adil, that the last episode lacked mystery. He could easily guess who the killer was. Adil challenged him to write a better episode and *Inspector Eagle* ended up with five episodes being credited to Parashar.

Post his Film Institute of India stint in Pune, Parashar cajoled the Lintas advertising agency chief, Alyque Padamsee, to produce a detective series for television. Though Padamsee did not believe that Parashar could write *Inspector Eagle* episodes at that age, he relented. Armed with a budget of Rs 20,000, a camera and two lights, Parashar set out to shoot a 15-minute pilot. He hated the title *Rajesh Bond* that was initially mooted. It was after some deliberation that Pankaj conjured up the name *Karamchand* and christened the series. Alok Nath, the actor fresh from the National School of Drama, was spotted at the Prithvi Theatre and cast as Karamchand. His sidekick Kitty, however, wasn't part of the pilot. Sudhir Mishra was asked to write the pilot for peanuts. Anand [of the Anand Milind composer duo] worked on the title track and a struggling Nepali boy sang the brooding number. The boy was to later become popular as Udit Narayan.

Padamsee was kicked with the results and so was Doordarshan. But a spat over salaries forced Parashar to drop Alok Nath and go for a loner called Pankaj Kapur. Kapur, who was banking on *Ek Ruka Hua Faisla*, Basu Chatterjee's film version of *Twelve Angry Men*, was reluctant to step into television. It was left to Sudhir Mishra to convince him that some extra income would only give him a healthier bank balance. Of course, Mishra quietly claimed his pound of flesh by having his actress-wife Sushmita Mukherjee cast as Kitty.

Karamchand, however, ran into some clueless mysteries. The sponsors Hindustan Lever backed out stating that the protagonist was too untidy and laidback. Padamsee then got Ulka advertising onboard and the first episode came on, only to be roundly criticized. The series found its footing only from its third instalment. By the tenth, it had garnered 40 commercials and was being talked about for its chutzpah. The slithering camerawork stumped even veteran actor Manoj Kumar who wanted to know how the shot was executed. The handheld cameras, a generous dash of comedy and the protagonist's munching away like Bugs Bunny on a carrot while solving cases, made him an amusing cavalier. A constant, cursory wave of his hand, donning dark glasses that eventually became a style icon and signing off with a "shut-up Kitty" to his bimbo assistant, were some of the other irreverent gestures that stood out as birthmarks for an Indian tribute to, amongst others, Inspector Closseau and the *Pink Panther* series. Kapur's mannerisms and

Parashar's panache sowed the seeds for the detective genre on Indian television. Monday nights provided the much needed fizz to television viewing. Parashar quit the series after 26 episodes to film his whacky Goan drug mafia caper *Jalwa*, but the flood of nearly 50,000 requests a day at Doordarshan saw him return six months later for another round of 13 episodes.

A second coming, years later in 2006 on Sony's satellite entertainment channel was seen as a welcome revival. By then however, quite a few private eyes had entered the playing field, denting *Karamchand*'s novelty. The work atmosphere, too, had undergone a sea change. Parashar wasn't as enthused as he was in the beginning. As for the price of carrots, which was a mere two rupees a kilo when Karamchand made his debut, it had shot up to more than twenty over the years. Parashar and team could only wistfully munch away.

The general observation, that except perhaps for Arthur Conan Doyle detective stories did not get bracketed with literature, was debatable. The lone Indian exception was Saradhindhu Bandyopadhyay and director Basu Chatterjee was quick to home in on this. Bandyopadhyay, an advocate-turned-littérateur, had 'Holmes flowing in his ink', his Byomkesh Bakshi and Ajit having characteristics similar to the Sherlock-Watson marriage. Other obvious influences were Agatha Christie's brainchild Hercule Poirot, G K Chesterton's creation, Father Brown and American writer and literary critic Edgar Allen Poe's "tales of ratiocination" involving Auguste Dupin. Sardindu's main concern was about how the Indian and Bengali fictional detectives created between 1890 and 1930 were reduced to being mere clones of the English detectives. In what could be assumed to be a postcolonial response, he introduced the Bengali '*bhadrolok*', the gentleman sleuth Byomkesh Bakshi and his Watson, Ajit Bandhopadhyay in "*Pather Kanta*" in 1932, investigating cases in an Indian metropolis. Initially serialized in the literary magazine *Basumati*, the stories and novels were all eventually published in hardcover editions, beginning with *Byomkesh-er Diary*. In all, Sharadindu put together 33 stories about Byomkesh, capturing the customs and manners of the City of Joy during the East India company rule. Chatterjee adapted 32 of them into television episodes that necessitated a forty-five-minute slot instead of the regular 25 minutes. Rajit Kapoor, my brother-in-law from *Ghar Jamai*, portrayed Bakshi. His performance was a radical, confident leap from where he started out as a rather reticent actor. For Chatterjee, the series marked yet another departure from the comic tag that his films gave him.

Post *Ghar Jamai* [1986], Sridhar Kshirsagar was on an experimenting spree. For logistical reasons, the serialization of novelist Gurcharan Das' *A Fine Family* that he so looked forward to, was aborted and Sridhar's gaze fell on the whodunit. Drawing inspiration from *The Thin Man* series, a comic mystery starring William Powell and Myrna Loy, he concocted the Radha Seth-Tom Alter detective pair of *Jugalbandi*. It was Benjamin Gilani who started off with Seth in the lead, but due to his prior commitments had to be bumped off in the second episode and his deputy Alter took over. The finesse of *Khandaan* was mirrored again in *Jugalbandi*, though on hindsight Mohena Singh who later helmed the series, felt that "despite the fact that Sridhar had raised the bar for himself as a director-writer and producer, the concept was a tad alien. Too western in thoughts, despite its lovely settings and good drama. Maybe it was ahead of its time, one would never know now." But it offered me my first variation as an actor. From the lovable *ghar jamai*, it transformed me into a slimy blackmailer in the second episode of the series. A paradigm shift, it was a character that pitted me against the likes of Tinnu Anand, who had struck a purple patch those days directing Amitabh Bachchan in *Main Azad Hoon*, the Indian version of Frank Capra's *Meet John Doe*. It also earned me a special mention in film critic Khalid Mohammed's television review in *The Times of India*. A minor achievement I would say, considering how stringent Mohammed was known to be with praise. Besides being an early grounding for the psycho uncle's part in *Khiladi*, the Abbas-Mustan film that gave a fillip to my big screen career. *Jugalbandi* opened another door for me, that of the writer. An episode set in a circus saw me pushing the pen as Sridhar took a backseat and approved. The circus as an espionage setting offered immense scope for concocting twists and turns and the result was a colourful mélange.

Until Shekhar Kapur, basking in the success of his films *Masoom* [his take on the novel *Man, Woman and Child*] and *Mr India*, [*The Invisible Man*] landed on the scene of the crime in 1994. With the swashbuckling Vijay Anand in tow. He titled it *Tehkikaat* [*The Investigation*]. Once again with my theatre associate Meenakshi as casting director. Naturally, I couldn't let go of an opportunity to watch Kapur at work. The first day's shoot in the lobby of the Sea Princess Hotel in Juhu was meticulous and laidback. All the compromise of television filming was replaced with a candour that paid little heed to economics. Anand, a stalwart who had directed some of Hindi cinema's finest entertainers [*Teesri Manzil, Jewel Thief, Guide, Tere Mere Sapne, Johnny Mera Naam*] was taking a bow on the small screen and Kapur remained steadfast to the technique of the big screen. It was a learning process to watch them work in tandem in a 'new' medium. As expected, the series exuded a slickness that made it eminently watchable. Even though *Tehkikaat* couldn't do without the usual suspects of the game-the Holmes and Watson syndrome. Saurabh Shukla's Gopi played Watson to Anand's Sam D'Silva as they engaged in solving murder mysteries in each episode.

More smoke flowed from the barrel of the gun. The Adhikari Brothers, Markand and Gautam, created *Commander* for the first satellite network, Zee in the mid 1990s. Ramesh Bhatkar, the Marathi stage actor and son of the acclaimed composer Snehal Bhatkar, played the part and director Gautam Adhikari with the camera attempted to replicate Parashar's *Karamchand* style. *Commander* was the detective who unfailingly resolved baffling crimes both with calculation and action. I was assigned multiple characters in the series, but one particular role of a schizophrenic flautist who victimized Rama Vij, caught the eye of Mani Ratnam, the celebrated South Indian filmmaker [*Nayakan*], who was making a caper in Tamil called *Thiruda Thiruda* [Thief-Thief]. I received a call from his assistant that I had been pencilled in for the part of a crime branch officer who is hot on the trail of the thieves. A costume measurement plan was in place too. Then after a few weeks, Ratnam and his office went incommunicado.

The next thing I knew was that the South Indian singer S P Balasubramaniam had shot for my character. My heart sank. After a couple of years when I ran into Ratnam in Bombay, I made no attempt to hide my disappointment. His "oh really?" nonchalant smile may have had a hidden reply, it also gave me a taste of film politics that could reverse your fortunes overnight. The Adhikaris continued to conjugate the genre turning the Commander into a *Marshall* [Played by Mukesh Khanna]. More swanky locations. More intriguing cases to solve. For me donning different faces in varying episodes meant more meat than an on-going title role that could risk getting repetitive. Specially as the suspects had more at stake than the detective himself.

Most of the films that veteran B R Chopra had produced, credited the writing to B R Films' Story Department. I often tried to picture what this outfit would be like. I got my answer when Ravi Chopra cast me in the Perry Mason inspired series *Kanoon* on the newly launched Metro channel of Doordarshan. The Metro channel was an offshoot of the national network and was initially launched in 1984 in New Delhi and then extended to the metro cities of (then) Bombay, Calcutta, Madras and Bangalore. B R Chopra was entertained by my suggestions for my character in *Kanoon*, named Pasha which was more of a comic take on Watson. He urged me to join the script team. So, there I was in his sprawling office seated in front of a long concave wooden desk amidst well-known writers like Satish Bhatnagar, Hasan Kamal, Ranjan Bose, Ram Govind, and Ravi Chopra himself. The famous B R Films Story Department was at work, moderated by Senior Chopra. I took a deep breath and looked around. These were the chairs which the likes of Dr Rahi Masoom Reza and other writers of those times would have warmed. I was like a beginner being inducted into a post-graduates class.

Incidentally, *Kanoon* was the title of one of the most popular films of the B R banner. It had dispensed with the mandatory songs and yet, gone on to be a box-office success. So, in a way, it was nostalgic to produce a series with the same name. Pankaj Dheer, the rebellious Karna of *Mahabharat* played the detective lawyer. Life on the sets was unlike anything I had experienced before. The actors never ceased to revel in their 'glorious past' - the *Mahabharat*. Sometimes the acting mannerisms would seep into the courtroom drama [1998] and Ravi Chopra would snap them out of their past-times. I was the odd one out and realised how much of the fun I had missed out on. Although it was amusing when on many an occasion, viewers commended me on my portrayal of Dhritarashtra in the epic. I wondered why, until someone played Holmes and said "elementary my dear Ananth, your features vaguely resemble actor Girija Shankar who played Dhritarashtra." A thought I amusedly distanced myself from.

Kanoon completed 150 episodes, a healthy number in those days of weekly shows. Of course, I was the subject of ridicule when it came to my dear *maasi*. Most of the time my character Pasha merely sat through the court proceedings and observed. "What are you doing just sitting there, she often asked, 'you need to get going, argue like that lawyer". I wish lengthier roles were written, I moaned. But despite her reservations, it was an enjoyable exercise performing and contributing to the scripts. I haven't experienced such writing camaraderie ever since. But with most of the names no longer in our midst [Chopra, Bhatnagar, Reza], the possibilities of an encore are extinguished.

The detective was first sighted on Indian television during the black-and-white days. *The Old Fox* [*Der Alte, German*] played by Erin Koster took age and obesity in his stride to crack crime puzzles. Though dubbed in English, he had us watch in rapt attention. Jump cut to the present. With the advent of daily soaps, the detective is fighting a losing case. One of them managed to cling on for 15 long years. B P Singh with his crime buster show *C. I. D.* on Sony Television. The face with the scowl [the towering Shivaji Satam] and his band of boys and girls had no dearth of cases to crack. Singh attributed it to the mushrooming crime scene in the city that incessantly threw up socially relevant plots. In fact Singh had become so proficient in the genre, that he turned tail at attempting anything else, a comedy, for instance. C. I. D. could well be 'the last of the Mohicans'. Why? Elementary, my dear Watson!

THE TELEVISION INFERNO

When your second name is Sippy and you have behind you an 'Eastern Spaghetti' money spinner called *Sholay*, you have a task at hand. Ramesh Sippy found the inferno of the 70mm screen spectacle a hot benchmark. Every time he embarked on a film, audiences braced for an encore. Hence, when he found the small screen inviting, his viewership was more or less firmly in place.

Sippy didn't take long to discover that the medium was far removed from his big screen technique, besides demanding another discipline. Two episodes every week was akin to just less than half a film. For a filmmaker used to deliberation and thoughtful execution, the pace of television could have played on the nerves. So, I wasn't surprised when Basu Chatterjee confided that an initial phone call from Sippy offered him the director's chair for the latter's ambitious *Buniyaad* [*The Foundation*] in 1986. Sippy was excited about the script by Manohar Shyam Joshi, a saga of the pre- and post-Independence days. He called it *Buniyaad* and wanted Basu*da* to direct it. "But there was a catch', recollects Basu*da*, "Doordarshan wanted to emulate the success of *Hum Log*.

Perhaps bring back its joint family audiences. *Buniyaad* was to be aired twice a week a la *Hum Log*. Sippy being a businessman must have felt "the more the merrier". Basu*da's* plate was full with *Rajni* and *Darpan* which he used to conceptualise, write, direct and edit. Television was the new dinosaur gobbling up time and episodes. He had no option but to turn down the offer. The message was loud and clear–television wasn't going to be an ancillary detour for filmmakers.

Buniyaad wasn't Sippy's first brush with television, though. In 1985, he formed a software division of Sippy Films that began with a comedy caper *Chapte Chapte* [Stop Press], a drama revolving around an investigative journalist [Kanwaljeet] and the characters in his newspaper office that included actors Alok Nath and Anuradha Patel. Sudhir Mishra, who had teamed up with Vinod Chopra in his impressive debut feature *Sazaa-e-Maut,* [The Death Sentence], was director on the series. In a khaki outfit, I took on the mantle of the not-so-humble office peon Kamble who prefers to play house detective himself. It wasn't entirely my fault if, after *Ados Pados*, I found the part seldom demanding or galvanizing the actor in me. An off-the-cuff remark, "On one occasion I had to wait all day merely to hand over a glass of water to the boss" found its way into *Filmfare*, a popular film monthly. Mishra stumbled on it and made a mental note. I found myself out of favour in his subsequent projects. Moral of the story learnt. This was my first lesson on 'being politically correct.'

Sippy's inspiration to make *Buniyaad* stemmed from his father G P Sippy having lived through the partition and witnessed the politically motivated carnage that was to remain a permanent blot on the conscience of two countries. When Manohar Shyam Joshi, who had also penned *Hum Log* turned up with a story of the destinies of two families, who despite being devastated by communal riots, still managed to live with their principles intact in an era of violence, it was the perfect blueprint for a mega-series. The embers of *Sholay* hadn't died yet. Ramesh Sippy debuting on television was nothing short of an event.

It wasn't easy shaking off the film module and habits. Sippy took over the reins of the partition saga like a movie. *Buniyaad* made news "because it was being shot on film", while lesser mortals had nothing but a low band recorder at their disposal or the just introduced, high-band video tape to boast of. The Film City at Goregaon was turned into pre-partition India and it looked anything but a television show scenario. But regardless of the economics, Sippy had a go at it. Initially, it called for nothing short of nine takes for a shot to be canned. Sippy preferred to warm up his actors in this fashion. The exodus scenes of the partition raised the bar for television and the recreation of the strife-torn land and homes had even hardcore critics raising *Buniyaad* to the status of a *Sholay* of television. *Hum Log* loyals who missed their twice-a-week dosage of soap got a far better and bigger replacement offer. The cast of Anita Kanwar, Alok Nath, Kanwaljeet, Dalip Tahil, Asha Sachdev, Kulbhushan Kharbanda, Mazhar Khan, Vijayendra Ghatge, Krutika Desai Abhinav Chaturvedi, and Vinod Nagpal [after *Hum Log*] became overnight household favourites. Their presence not only bolstered the acting department but narrowed the line between cinema and television. The cross-over was seamless.

Maybe it was too good to be practical. It spiralled out of control by the time the show's twenty-sixth episode was being shot. Visions of India's first television series shot entirely on film died a premature death. The budgets shot through the roof. Sippy's film-like approach wasn't exactly the prescription for viable television. So the video recorder and tapes sprung up and the film camera made a quiet exit. Additionally, Sippy chose to hire another director to step on the gas.

The mantle fell on rookie Jyoti Sarup who had hoped to make it as an actor, but eventually assisted directors like Ramanand Sagar, Shakti Samanta and Atma Ram in their films. For Sarup, the crown came with a heavy reputation. Expectedly, the episodes drew comparison with Sippy's touch. But despite the trepidation, *Buniyaad* retained its popularity and erased the red line that was looming large on its makers' balance sheets. When Alok Nath's Haveliram went missing, it raised some kind of mass hysteria that was doused only on his return. Sippy had playfully toyed with the sentiments of the viewers and in the process discovered how to manipulate a show's popularity. It was a ploy that most soaps, after the turn of the millennium, deployed to refurbish viewership. Sippy meanwhile, also discovered love. In Kiran Juneja, who played Haveliram's sister Veerawali. Of course the strict workhorse that he is, Sippy kept the romance under wraps. They tied the knot only after the series had wrapped.

Sippy applied for an extension of 104 episodes from Doordarshan which was turned down citing "policy matters". So the finale had the characters suddenly aging and ready for the curtain call. The final episode had been earmarked in our diaries. But just as it was slated to go on air, the city of Mumbai suffered a power outage. Cruel irony of timing. Audiences cursed and the sponsors cried blue-murder. Doordarshan was left with no choice but to arrange a repeat telecast. There was probably less furore when a wrong question paper was distributed in an exam hall!

A prequel to *Buniyaad* was burgeoning in Sippy's mind. He wanted to catch up with the missing years in between. But it wasn't to be. He had to bide his time for the satellite generation to play the *Buniyaad* card again. *Gaatha* [The Saga] for Star Plus, was designed to be a long-running show on fifty years of the independence struggle. But the hour long episodes fell short of becoming another *Buniyaad* and the series was terminated by the channel even before its contracted run of 26 weeks. If Sippy was disappointed, he didn't show it. He attributed the stop to accommodate the election-specific programmes that Star Plus concentrated on during the polls. He repackaged *Gaatha* shifting the focus from the battle for India's freedom to a woman's odyssey titled *Virudh* [Against Each Other]. But despite a new garb and name, neither Joshi nor Sippy could replicate the *Buniyaad* appeal. Almost like *Sholay's* success proving too demanding to live up to.

Even after four decades, *Sholay* and *Buniyaad* continue to remain benchmarks for Ramesh Sippy. Sarup, meanwhile, went on to win an Indian National film award for *Bub*, the first ever Kashmiri film made after 38 years in the disturbed valley. He then edited Al Gore's two-Academy Award-winning film, *An Inconvenient Truth*, from 96 to 36 minutes, for Indian audiences, besides directing the dubbing of the Hindi version. After *Buniyaad*, he moved on to a show titled *Guldasta*, a bouquet of episodic short stories. I featured in one of them and would never tire of listening to *Buniyaad* anecdotes between shots.

After *Chapte Chapte*, I was hoping to connect with Sippy again. A theatre adaptation of Ray Cooney's comic farce, *One for the Dot*, threw up the opportunity. I enacted four roles in the play [titled *Four at a Time*, for Indian viewers] and Sippy and Juneja in the audience admitted to be awestruck by the pace of one character transforming into another, costume, attitude and all, at the blink of an eye. I was called in to play a prototype of then Assistant Commissioner of Police, Shivanandan, in his new soap *Kismat* [on Doordarshan's Metro Channel, Tuesday nights]. Mercifully, I wasn't typecast as the South Indian prototype. Shivanandan, whom I had got to know personally, was a suave cop who would think on his feet. Sippy saddled him with a quirk. He would break into a Malayalam proverb to add a philosophical touch to a situation. He entrusted the writing of the regional dialogue to me and it was quite an experience blending my views with his. I also witnessed his meticulous execution, never perturbed by a production manager's 'behind-schedule' warnings. There was no compromise when it came to filming a scene.

During a shooting break, I mooted the idea of a two- or even three- camera set-up that could speed up work and enhance match-cuts. Sippy smiled wryly. He admitted his utter discomfort with a multi-camera set-up. A single camera and a chronological shot breakdown of scenes was his cup of tea. That's how he had shot all his life. Soon enough, the deadlines cropped up, and Sippy did the next best thing. Hire another director. Enter, who else, but Sudhir Mishra. Our eyes met, but spoke nothing. This time, I had far more than the "they also serve who only stand and wait" part.

DOUBLE-EDGED SWORD

In 1989, I finally quit my job at the agency. No employer would tolerate a two-year absence even if he was as benevolent as my boss, V P Sathe. Besides, I often felt a nag that it was grossly unfair on my part to pursue my artistic endeavours at the expense of the agency. Moreover, it was a decision I had to take sooner or later, if I had to make a career in acting. The character of *Purnaiya Pandit* in the mega historical *The Sword Of Tipu Sultan* demanded investment of time and attention. It was a mammoth production based on Bhagwan Gidwani's best selling book and would bring to Indian television a visual sweep not attempted before. And to think that I almost did not get cast!

When I visited Sanjay Khan's office for an audition, the veteran stage, television and film actor Dr Sreeram Lagoo was already slotted in the part. However, they were looking for an actor to portray the younger years of the political confidante of Tipu Sultan. Providentially, the onus fell on me. It was an exciting moment. A major role hadn't come my way since *Ghar Jamai* and I knew it would be great as long as it lasted. Little did I know that fate had a few tricks up its sleeve in toying with the longevity factor.

February 8th 1989. The early morning flight to Bangalore was at seven. A three-hour drive from there to Mysore would take me to my home away from home for the next two years till the show wrapped. It was five in the morning and the driver hadn't turned up. Fearing that I would be late, I sprinted the ten-minute distance from my apartment to the Wadala railway station and managed to hire a cab. I just about made it on time for the flight. At Bangalore, there was no placard with my name, let alone a reception committee. I looked around frantically and after a while, chanced on a cabbie who was willing to ply me to Mysore. During the three hour journey, the cab broke down twice. This just didn't seem to be my day. Of course, I had not perceived all this as a portent of things to come. In hindsight, it all appeared to be some divine force trying to stop me from getting to my destination. Only, divinity hadn't reckoned with my indefatigable will.

The cab spluttered into the Premier studios at Mysore around five in the evening. The shadows had already started gathering. It was exactly twelve hours since I had left home. Exhausted, would be an understatement. The odours that smelt of "work", however, pumped the adrenalin back. I walked onto the stage where Khan was filming a scene set in a thatched village house. The roof was low and stitched together with hay. Raj Kapoor's audiographer of many years, Allaudin Khan, greeted me. I had briefly met him at R K Studios which I used to frequent with my boss Sathe. Sanjay Khan was in the middle of improvising an additional bit of dialogue for a character. I instinctively wondered why he had come all the way to

Mysore to film on a set such as this. This could have been achieved more conveniently at Mumbai's Film City. But Khan's disarming smile welcomed me as he urged me to check out 'Purnaiya's palace' on the adjoining floor. "That's where we are tomorrow", he remarked with the confidence of a man who had the next two years of his life sorted out.

Unlit and sans any decor, the palace walls lamely tried to impress. I decided to wait until the morrow and perched on the lawns of the studio, acquainting myself with the rest of the cast and unit members. Actress Neena Gupta was there too with her baby, Masaba. Frantic activity was afoot as the crew kept springing out and returning to the set through a four feet door that seemed more like a prison entrance. It was turning dark and my strength was ebbing. I decided to retire to the apartments that were hired for the artistes. The car drew alongside and I pulled myself in urging a few other cast members to accompany me. We bundled ourselves inside the vehicle and drove out of the studio gates.

The conflagration must have occured around the time we hit the road. Ten minutes later as we reached the apartments, an alarmed messenger told us that something terrible had happened and the set had gone up in flames. We wasted no time in rushing back to the scene only to be greeted by an ominous darkness and the wailing of ambulances. The studio lights were out, and in the ink-black night, I could just about register a silhouette of bodies that appeared to have been hurriedly piled on each other. A hundred voices were trying to make sense in the chaotic atmosphere. We instinctively looked for Neena and her baby and were relieved to know that she wasn't on the sets when the fire broke out. Apparently a celebration scene called for crackers and fireworks. The flames licked the low thatched roof resulting in a short circuit that engulfed the set without giving a chance to the unit to escape. The tiny door that could let out only one person at a time was another impediment. The young cameraman was charred holding on to the camera. Allauddin Khan didn't live to do another Raj Kapoor film. We asked for Sanjay Khan. Someone mentioned that he had been badly injured while trying to push others out and had been rushed to a hospital. Meanwhile a hostile crowd of those who appeared to be relatives of the local unit members who were charred, was gathering outside the studio gates. A voice in the darkness barked a word of warning asking us to leave before the situation got out of hand. There was nothing we could do to help. It was all over in a flash. We obeyed the voice and drove back to the apartment. Drained, starved and in a state of shock, this was as close to numbness I had ever been. The night was spent discussing the inferno, the possible causes and consequences. Police sirens howled outside sending the night into an eerie spin. But my twenty-four hours without food and rest were inconsequential as images of the tragedy ravaged our minds. The morning after would be one to reckon with.

The headlines were full of it. They dubbed it as the worst tragedy ever in show business. Non-availability of firefighting equipment and ignorance of fire safety norms were quoted as major reasons. Loose wiring and absence of ventilation were further causes for the fire to spread. Instead of fire-proofing material, the walls had gunny bags and the temperature rose to around 120 degrees centigrade (248 degrees Fahrenheit) thanks to the powerful lights being used for the scene. The final death toll was pegged at 62, making it the highest number of fatalities on a film set.

It was only then that the full impact of the tragedy hit us. We had had a narrow escape, leaving the studio in the nick of time. Suddenly, my actor colleagues seemed grateful that I had forced them to accompany me in the car. Sanjay Khan, we learned, was transferred to a Bangalore hospital. We were given train tickets to Bangalore and flight tickets for the evening to Mumbai. I accompanied Neena Gupta and her baby Masaba to the railway station. On the way, she got off at a local post office and booked a 'lightning' call. I overheard her trying to reach the operator on the other side. Assurances of her and the baby being safe must have been exchanged. We drove, lost in silent thought, till we reached Mysore station. We boarded the train to Bangalore, mentally bruised and shaken.

The taste of curd rice and *sambar* [South Indian lentil gravy garnished with vegetables] at Kannada actor and director Shankar Nag's house in Bangalore still lingers on my tongue after all these years. I had eaten after 48 hours. Gupta knew the Nags well and Arundhati and Shankar made sure we were comfortable, even as we tried to come to terms with the trauma. Frantic phone calls to family members followed. The news had spread as fast as the fire itself. At the hospital in Bangalore, where Khan was admitted, I met his wife Zarine who was shaken but put up a stoic front. She guided me to the intensive care unit where we could get a glimpse of Khan through a spherical glass window. Khan himself suffered major burns and had to spend 13 months in hospital to undergo

72 surgeries.

I was back home that evening. The "tomorrow on the sets" that Khan had excitedly spoken of, tragically, never came. Back home in the madness of everyday existence–the hum of the refrigerator, the ticking clock, the routine doorbell ring, the silent phone – reality struck. All my scheduling for two years of work was in shambles. I had quit my job, the series "would never be made" declared trade pundits and even my theatre producers had found replacements for my parts. I had managed to shut all doors in one go! *Ghar Jamai* director and friend Mohena Singh, sensing my despair, offered to take me out for lunch at the Taj and cheer me up. She gifted me a copy of Ingmar Bergman's autobiography, *The Magic Lantern*, a gesture I appreciate to this day. I had to gather the scattered pieces and not let what had happened scar me forever. I began seriously toying with the idea of a company to produce shows for television. But, funding wasn't easy to come by. It was tough being on one's own. This was probably why most people like me opted for the security of a nine-to-five drill.

Six months down that line I ran into a colleague who told me that *The Sword of Tipu Sultan* was being revived and that they were casting all over again. I had not visited their production office for quite a while now. When I landed up, I was greeted by a pin-up board that had photographs of actors with the character names scrawled below in sketch pen ink. Purnaiya was taken by a bald actor who glared into the camera. I further learnt that Akbar Khan, Sanjay's younger brother would be director on the series till the latter recovered. I couldn't resist breaking the queue and barging into Akbar's room. His reaction to my claim for Purnaiya is something I will never forget, "Oh my brother cast you, did he? We didn't hear about you after Mysore, so we looked for another actor". The look on my face must have spoken volumes. Khan didn't waste any time in reversing his decision, and my mug went up on the board with the title "Purnaiya Pandit". The bald actor was shifted to play a lieutenant, Khanderao.

It was a hot, sultry, dusty afternoon when the train pulled into the Sawai Madhavpur station. We were now headed to Jaipur for the series. Mysore remained a bad memory and no one wanted to return. Not that the locals would have taken kindly to it either. A newspaper report that only five thousand rupees was paid as compensation to those who lost their lives, had sparked off angry protests. Khan had decided that Jaipur and its palatial surroundings would be the ideal cover-up for Seringapatnam and other locations in the story. Huddled amidst the stuntmen, with a thin layer of sand on my hand, I survived an overnight ordeal. That left even the stunt team wondering why a lead actor was travelling in a third class compartment. This has been a mental block I have been trying to negotiate all my life. I lived with this fear that it would displease the authorities if I asked for conveniences. And the insecurity manifested itself largely on this schedule.

The outskirts of Jaipur, I realised, was a great place to be if you were a cactus or a camel. The historic Samode palace, a two-hour drive from Jaipur was chosen as base. It had glittering interiors, huge lawns and open spaces a few kilometers away that served as battlegrounds. The first month at Samode was like a war plan gone awry. The scheduling went so haywire, that I did not face the camera for nearly thirty days. That period could have fetched me some useful work in Bombay. Being kept on stand-by endlessly withered my patience. The food that the unit cooks served was a far cry from what my palates were attuned to. The ghost of the routine, spice-laden shooting unit food had followed me all the way to Samode. I couldn't stomach it beyond a week. A kindly chef at the palace restaurant obliged by cooking some excellent roti, dal and vegetables for me at a subsidised rate of Rs 75. So my dinners were taken care of. The only moments of solace were the evenings besides the bonfire. Akbar Khan would ask me to sing Jagjit Singh. "*Tum ko dekha to yeh khayal aaya*" was amongst his favourites. Singing was a hobby that I got very few opportunities to pursue.

Samode Palace was, I discovered, a fortress turned into a wedding destination, besides being a tourist's favourite hideout. So every time a group of fair-skinned visitors spilled out of a bus or a wedding party with a decorated elephant sashayed in accompanied by blaring music, we were given an eviction notice. So the unit drove two hours to Jaipur each time and returned after the palace fell silent again. Eventually, the long, empty days drove me to the verge of deciding to quit the show. I confided in Manju Mishra, a co-actress, who quietly but firmly discouraged me. "It's too good a role to quit, hang on patiently" she urged. And am I glad I obeyed. When work began, it did in right earnest. The initial rushes of Purnaiya, so impressed preview audiences and Khan, that they decided I would stay put for the entire series. I knew it meant disrespect to Dr Lagoo, but at that moment, like the classic situation "my need seemed greater than his". The acclaim also meant that, first Akbar Khan and then Sanjay Khan graciously invited me to share their special meals putting an end to my culinary woes. Purnaiya eventually had the longest span in the series, a three-generation character who lived through Hyder Ali, Tipu Sultan and his children's times. The Chanakya-like demeanour that the character exuded, caught the fancy of audiences and was to become for me, what the paparazzi pompously declare as "the role of a lifetime".

But Tipu's woes hadn't ended. Petitions were filed in the Supreme Court of India against the telecast of this serial. The petitioners argued that the serial was not based on the real-life and deeds of Tipu Sultan. After hearing the arguments, the Supreme Court gave a judgment that the serial could be telecast only with the disclaimer *"No claim is made for the accuracy or authenticity of any episode being depicted in the serial. This serial is a work of fiction and has nothing to do either with the life or rule of Tipu Sultan. The serial is a dramatised presentation of Bhagwan Gidwani's novel".* It is amusing how a mere statement like this, irrespective of its authenticity, can douse the flames of protest. Nevertheless, till the night of the scheduled telecast on a Saturday at quarter-to-ten, we were unaware whether it would come on. But when the rousing Naushad signature tune did seep in eventually, everyone heaved a sigh of relief. A year and a half of mishap and toil had drawn blood. The splendour of the battle sequences and the palace settings hit a new benchmark for television shows in India. The success must have spurred Sanjay Khan's recovery. He was battle-scarred but pulled himself up to take on the title role in the twenty-fifth episode. Like a wounded tiger bouncing back, Khan showed admirable tenacity in braving the heat and dust of Rajasthan and enacting Tipu, a role that called for physical and mental faculties being pushed beyond the point of endurance. The series had become a heroic triumph in more ways than one. It fetched television rating points in the region of 70 and remains the only historical series to be shot entirely in real palaces and locations, unlike the Plaster of Paris sets that took over this genre.

The Sword of Tipu Sultan [along with Hema Malini's directorial debut *Noopur*] fetched me the most coveted citation those days, the Uptron Award for Great Television Performances in the Best Supporting Actor Category in 1990. Looking back, it hadn't come easy. Purnaiya was pushing my limits and going for broke. The extreme Rajasthan weather kept posing challenges for me. Accoutered in sparse clothing in the biting cold of the winter and the heavy ornate wear in sweltering heat, certainly did not make it easy. It set me thinking as to how those towering figures from history would have negotiated such cumbersome wardrobes. Then came the steeds. The horses used for the battle sequences weren't the film-friendly, trained-for-camera breed housed at the Varma brothers' stables in Goregaon's Film City. The thoroughbreds with rippling muscles reminiscent of well-built wrestlers, were hired from the Jaipur Police Academy. In one particular battle sequence, I was astride a coffee brown mare, sword raised high on one hand and the other gripping the reins as tightly as possible. The animals took off like bullets when a dummy gun was fired to spur them into 'action'. I felt I had been propelled from a cannon. Flaying the sword to simulate a charge, I held on for sheer life, trying to control the animal from galloping into nowhere. When I finally managed with all my strength to rein those hoofs to a screeching halt, I could feel the gush of air from the other horses thundering past me. One slip and it would have been those hoofs trampling me into the sand.

Yet, at the end, it all seemed worth the trouble. The intermittent two-year stint had its moments of bonus too. The British film, stage and television actress Helena Bonham Carter [*Room with a View, Fight Club*] and her psychotherapist mother, Elena, were holidaying in Jaipur. Elena came across as a warm person who was pleasantly surprised about her daughter's popularity in India. Also, the replay of history concerning the British in *The Sword of Tipu Sultan* caught her fancy. "When you come to London, do call on us", she said. When I queried, "Will you remember us?", she shot back with a confident and inviting, "Of course, try me!" Well, I can't wager if she would have remembered, but I sure forgot to call on her!

The filming of the series and the socio-political activities around it had their share of interesting contradictions. It was a near-magical moment when Purnaiya had to render *"Bismillah ir Rahman ir Rahim...."*. I took two days and special care to imbibe the entire prayer and render it with reverence and as flawlessly as possible. Sanjay Khan and his coterie were suitably impressed. This was a fine salvo for secularism. But one knowledgeable Doordarshan censor thought otherwise. They "couldn't risk a Hindu priest mouthing lines from another belief". The portion was edited out of the final telecast tape. The hurt from the hypocrisy is still to heal.

During the general elections next summer, I had my first taste of politics at the highest level. I partnered with Khan in campaigning for prime ministerial candidate Rajiv Gandhi in the dust lands of Uttar Pradesh. Braving near-collapsing stages, bulls running amuck in the crowd and the sweltering April heat, I belted out my favourite line "History has it that Tipu Sultan and Purnaiya Pandit walked hand in hand. And even today, right here, the Sultan and the Pandit are together". The crowds roared in approval. They had had enough of divisive politics. If only those policing censors could have witnessed such unbridled secularism!

Purnaiya will remain a defining moment in my television career. Frankly, I had underestimated the audience. I couldn't envisage the viewer taking fancy to a wisdom spewing Pandit with machiavellian traits. But they proved me wrong. Purnaiya's Chanakya demeanour made him as popular as the titular character. During a break in filming, when we were back in Bombay, Khan called up to say that a friend of his from London, Firdous Ali, a media person wished to meet 'Purnaiya'. I landed up at his office the next day, and walked into his cabin. An affable, silver-haired Ali looked through me and walked away. When Khan told him that I was the Purnaiya he was looking for, he looked at me totally unconvinced, "I was under the impression that Purnaiya was an old man!" he uttered in a clipped British accent. Well, these are moments actors live for. Firdous became a close friend and kept in touch for a long while. He couldn't pull off one trick for me, though. A foot in the door on British television. "Too few parts for Asians", he bemoaned. The scene, of course changed a decade later. Dalip Tahil, Harish Patel [my portly co-actor from the series *Hum Hindustani*] and Ayesha Dharker, all Indian actors, did manage to feature in popular soaps there. Aggressive networking with agents was the key, I learnt.

Tipu Sultan on television evoked nostalgia for veteran actor P Jairaj. We were seeing less of him those days on screen, but Purnaiya made him reach out to me. I gladly accepted the invitation. I walked into another classic chapter of Hindi film history. At Jairaj's house in Bandra, he let me into his archives and the ways of filming during the silent era and later, when sound made its appearance. He had put a board outside his study room which said "My Room". He conspiratorially and authoritatively, at the same time remarked, "I let only select people enter this room. But, I felt you *must* see the memorabilia on display". These were unsolicited lessons of life and work. I grieved silently when the aging actor departed. I was grateful to him for sharing his priceless insights and precious memories with me in his final years.

Spurred by the success of *The Sword of Tipu Sultan*, Sanjay Khan decided to delve into the Maratha kingdom and unearth some more warriors. *The Great Maratha*, was designed to match the double cutting edge of Tipu. It even featured Shabaaz Khan, the son of Hindustani music virtuoso Ustad Amir Khan, who had made an impressive debut as Hyder Ali in *Tipu Sultan*. As the next big production after *The Sword of Tipu Sultan*, it got eyeballs though not the excitement and awe that the Sultan aroused.

April 2010, London. Winter was on its last throes: Sotheby's, the well-known auctioneers brought down the hammer on "a very rare sword with a tiger-form hilt, from the palace armoury of Tipu Sultan, circa 1782-99, with a 19th century silver-mounted Scabbard". The price matched the majesty. A record bid of GBP 5,05,250 pounds, mocking its initial estimate of a modest 50000 to

70000. Incidentally, in 2003, the 200-year-old sword was bought with much fanfare by liquor baron Vijay Mallya. The weapon finally found its resting place amongst Mallya's other memorabilia. Presumably, the last episode in its historical journey appears to have been scripted.

Years later, I wandered again around the precincts of the ill-fated Premier Studios in Mysore. I requested the sentry to let me take a walk down memory lane. He refused. The place had been sold to a corporate firm for a possible industrial complex. Old players were no longer welcome. The history of the studio was done and dusted.

HISTORY
REPEATS

The book was right on top of the shelf, out of hand's reach.

"But I took a liking to its title *Tamas*". Govind Nihalani was relishing a rare break from his hectic schedule of Richard Attenborough's *Gandhi* which was filming in Delhi in the winter of 1980. He was manning the second unit of the epic that would go on to repeat a momentous chapter of Indian history. At the Sriram Centre bookshop near Mandi House in New Delhi, the Bhisham Sahni [thespian Balraj Sahni's brother] novel perhaps fell into the right hands. "Sometimes things happen inexplicably. I discovered that *Tamas* was about the great Indian partition, a subject after my heart, as I was a product of those times. I had read Yashpal's book on the period, but this one rung a bell."

Tamas, however, lay untouched in Nihalani's room for more than a week. He preferred to read it when he had sufficient time out from filming. When he did get down to reading it, every sentence struck him not as words, but images. Something told him 'this is it'. He decided that he wanted to do it, but didn't have a clue how to go about it. It was around that time that Nihalani's searing human drama, his first film, *Aakrosh* [The Cry of the Wounded] was selected in the Indian Panorama section of the International Film Festival of India, held that year in Delhi. The directors of the films screened were invited for a tete'-a-tete' with then Prime Minister Indira Gandhi. An evening with Gandhi however turned into a rationed two minutes with each person. Nihalani who was deeply under the influence of the book came straight to the point. "Madam, if a serious film were to be made on the partition, would the government extend support?" "What do you mean by government support?", she enquired. "The National Film Development Corporation, for instance. Regular producers do not fund this kind of film". Gandhi instantly asked him when he wanted to make it. "It is a sensitive film. It will all depend on the political situation at that time". Nihalani realised that her sharp mind had taken cognizance of the Hindu-Muslim elements in the film. The communalism in the film and the country would not be without repercussions. "I realised I was sitting on a potent subject. I was certain as hell that I wanted to make the film. While filming with Attenborough, I mentioned *Tamas*, and a British character which I wanted him to play. He was absolutely forthcoming and said he would do it without charging a pie."

Attenborough never got down to playing it though. Barry John, the theatre person did. That was because *Tamas* was not made into a film as originally intended. Nihalani could not muster the funds required for a full-length feature. So he settled for television instead. Not the mandatory half-hour episodes, but a eight-part, mini-series of one-hour each.. The mini-series was a tad alien to the broadcasting industry in India. Of course, American networks like ABC had produced a twelve-part, one-hour series of Irwin Shaw's novel *Rich Man Poor Man* back in 1976. 1977 saw Alex Haley's critically acclaimed slavery drama, *Roots*, attain television blockbuster status, as an 8 episode mini-series.

Shot on 16mm, *Tamas* began filming in 1986, on sprawling sets that recreated Punjab at Mumbai's Film City Studios. Nihalani with his art director Nitish Roy, did a recce of the state of Punjab and shot images. "We just couldn't afford to film something like this on outdoor locations. Doordarshan hadn't commissioned it, so the expenses had to be borne by us. Lalit Bijlani of Blaze Enterprises managed to rope in the fabric giant Raymonds as sponsor. And the entire series cost us just under a crore of rupees to complete. It was an absolute act of madness on my part. I had never envisaged what I was getting into."

Before filming, Nihalani met the author, Bhisham Sahni, whose earlier work had been filmed by Saeed Mirza as *Mohan Joshi Haazir Ho*! Sahni himself played an important part along with Om Puri, Nihalani's regular from *Aakrosh* and the gut-wrenching cop drama *Ardh Satya*. The casting for *Tamas*, though a cakewalk ["I didn't need to do any auditions", declared Nihalani] wasn't without its share of detractors. It had displeased a section of the cast members from Nihalani's first film *Shantata! Court Chalu Aahe* [in Marathi, based on Vijay Tendulkar's successful theatre production]. Satyadev Dubey, the theatre veteran and his friends wondered how Nihalani could ditch them in an important project like this. But Nihalani was adamant that he preferred actors who spoke the Punjabi native language correctly. The only exception he made was for Uttara Baokar, who despite having Maharashtrian roots was a trained actor from the National School of Drama, and whose accent didn't betray her origins.

"*Tamas* became a milestone because the book did not get bogged down by the politics of partition", observed Nihalani. "It brought into focus the extreme elements from both communities, who, with their muscle power and rhetoric, influenced and exploited the common man. When they talk about their religion being endangered, they actually have an agenda that goes beyond religion. The gullible fell for it, resulting in an apocalypse. It was Sahni's humanistic, yet non-judgemental vision of the grassroots of India's most forgettable political upheaval that obsessed me throughout".

Nihalani hadn't given up his dream of *Tamas* as a film. He did edit the material into a four-hour film and had it censored to garner 3 Indian National Film Awards. Of course it wasn't feasible for a theatrical release. Not just the length but the sensitive issues at stake. Besides, an individual backed by vested political interests had already raised objections during the telecast of the series and Nihalani and Doordarshan found themselves as defendants. The huge battle culminated in the Supreme Court. "Thank God, we won!"

Tamas, the mini-series, thankfully and luckily got made with due credit to Nihalani's forte of making films with shoe-string budgets. The National Film Development Corporation [NFDC] was the lone backer. Yet Nihalani's innovative thoughts failed to dispel the myopic ways of the system. Though *Drohkal, Hazaar Chaurasi ki*

Maa and *Party* satiated his hunger, several other films he wanted to make, had been confined to his head due to producers enquiring about recovery. "I don't look at them as frustrations. They are not happening probably because the time hasn't come for them yet." The thought made me despondent. With time fleeting mercilessly, Indian cinema could ill afford to lose out on those plots swimming in his restless mind.

Before *Tamas*, there was a more comprehensive look at history that worked its way towards becoming television memorabilia. Independent India's first Prime Minister, Jawaharlal Nehru's searing travelogue through various periods of Indian history, *The Discovery of India*, was probably the only subject that could tempt filmmaker Shyam Benegal to do a detour after acclaimed films like *Ankur, Mandi, Manthan* and *Bhumika*. The series, *Bharat Ek Khoj*, that explored the 5000 year history of India, from its roots, through its turbulent heritage to the Declaration of Independence from British rule in 1947, became a Sunday morning textbook broadcast on Doordarshan in 1988. Benegal had a trying time condensing the voluminous work into 53 episodes, but the docu-drama approach with Om Puri as the sheet anchor was the mainstay. The versatile actor donned as many characters, besides voicing the essential commentary. Naseeruddin Shah's amazing resemblance to the Maratha king Shivaji landed him the part while Om Puri donned Aurangzeb's robes. Ratna Pathak Shah was cast as the queen Lakshmibai. Understandably, Puri rated *Bharat Ek Khoj* [along with *Tamas*] as his most satisfying work on television. Pandit Jawaharlal Nehru was played by 'usual suspect' Roshan Seth for whom it was a reprise after Richard Attenborough's epic *Gandhi*

[1982]. Benegal did tend to sprinkle a few fictional elements to dramatise the journey, but it didn't take away from the impact of his work. *Bharat Ek Khoj,* like Puri rightly stated, deserved a re-run at regular intervals. It could serve as a constant reminder of Indian history for the new generations.

Dr Chandraprakash Dwivedi, then a comparatively new player on the television scene, decided to lock horns with Indian history's great proponent of politics, economics and diplomacy. But *Chanakya*, his first ever attempt at a series was fraught with pitfalls. He faced initial rejection from Doordarshan. But unlike other producers who walked away crestfallen after a thumbs down from Mandi House, Dwivedi followed up with missionary zeal because he wouldn't take "no" for an answer. His well -researched letters must have made a strong impact in the corridors of Doordarshan which finally surrendered in 1988 and flagged off a pilot episode ahead of several others who had submitted proposals on the same subject. The 1990 Doordarshan Sunday morning prime hour show, *Chanakya*, took liberties in grinding fact with fiction to tell the 340 BC to 320 BC account of the strategist who prioritized honour and ethics above wealth and power. Set in medieval India [then, Bharat], *Chanakya* picked up cudgels for Chandragupta Maurya whilst plotting to dethrone the reigning king, the murderer of his father. Shades of Hamlet! The sets and costumes were recreated with great care in the open spaces of the Film City. Dwivedi's command over the language stood him in good stead as he did a studied pontification of the role of the *Acharya*. The 47 part series remains his best work to date. Dwivedi, in subsequent years, dabbled in different departments of television production, including heading the satellite channel Zee's programming section. His rather rigorous methods [prospective serial makers were asked to read extensively, and rightly so] didn't gel with people used to a conventional routine, and a disillusioned Dwivedi put in his papers. His film *Pinjar*, another tale set during the partition, reinstated his standing as a person who abhorred anything formulaic. Of course, he continues to discover to his dismay that his *"chanakya-neeti"* isn't compatible with today's rather regressive creative systems.

Circa 2011: I browse through the DVD section at a bookstore in a mall. *Tamas* finally is out on this format. *Chanakya, Mirza Ghalib* and *The Sword of Tipu Sultan* were made available a while ago. They glare from the display stands. As though nursing a grouse against television's utter disregard for history today. *Chandragupta Maurya* on NDTV's channel Imagine, *Rani Laxmibai* [Zee] Mahmud Ghazni's appearance in *Somnath* and regional versions of *Shivaji* occasionally surface. All of them appear driven more by production demands than seeking a depth in the characters and their doctrine.

History is yearning for another interpretative repeat.

STAR TREK

At first, I dismissed it as some prank. The voice on the other end said, "I am calling from Hema Malini's house. She'd like to see you". Why would a big star like her want to meet me? Doubting the credentials, I called back on the number they left and it was indeed the star actress's residence. After a roster of star directors in Sai Paranjpye, Yash Chopra, Basu Chatterjee, Hrishikesh Mukherjee, Aziz Mirza-Kundan Shah and Sridhar Kshirsagar, was it another kind of star turn? The actors themselves? Was I finally getting a foot in the wedge? I had never met Hema Malini, the star, before. She was the actress nicknamed 'dream girl' and had virtually lived up to the tag. The reigning queen for more than two decades, she still commanded a loyal following and a persona that exuded the sheen of a glorious career. As I proceeded towards her Juhu bungalow, I decided to meet her on home ground, our mother-tongue, Tamil. We exchanged the customary "*namaskaram*". Ms. Malini instantly likened me to one of her brothers ["you resemble him so much"]. The ice was broken and we hit the ground running. The danseuse in her had targeted the small screen. She had conjured up the concept of *Noopur* [Anklets], a series that would feature her both as an actress and director. The journey of a girl who was an exponent of the dance forms, gave her ample scope to display her dancing talent. I was to play a writer who kept pace with her to pen a book on her life. And Kabir Bedi was the man in her life.

But, she revealed that *Noopur* was conceived on a different note. When she shot the pilot in 1989, it was titled *Nritya Yatra* and featured Alok Nath. The episode, however, met with creative differences at Mandi House and Malini sought out the maverick Sridhar Kshirsagar to doctor the project. I realised the common factor now. Did Kshirsagar recommend me? I would never know. But he struck down Alok Nath and most of the script, preferring a major re-write. The revised version didn't meet with her vision, prompting her to don the mantle of the director to tell her story in her own words.

In 1990, the homework began in right earnest. Gulzar, with whom Ms. Malini had done some critically acclaimed films, was an obvious choice for scripting the show. At her behest, I met up with Gulzar to discuss background and characterization. Sure enough, as Gulzar revealed, the series to a large extent, was autobiographical. She had entrusted the job to a director who had drawn out the best in her. *Kinara*, *Khushboo* and *Meera* had seen Ms. Malini shed the star tag and emerge a mature performer. Besides, all those years of experience in front of the camera must have instilled the confidence to act and direct. She knew she was on a niche wicket. The series was designed to showcase a different form of dance in each of the thirteen episodes. Connoisseurs would dig that. A regular audience would need time to connect. But, enforced by her star image, the experimentation succeeded. We travelled from the city to Madras and other locations for the backdrops of her dances. Shuttling breathlessly between *The Sword of Tipu Sultan* and *Noopur* schedules took its toll on me. But I had no complaints. Filming with Ms. Malini was a pleasurable experience. She goaded me on to 'copy' her, particularly the classic Shiv dance pose. "You should do it gracefully" she urged. The part of her jovial conscience keeper let me break new ground. Until the inevitable final episode.

As I read the script of the thirteenth episode, I realised that for some inexplicable reason, my character was missing! Normally I wouldn't indulge in protests, but I found myself uninhibitedly debating the issue with Ms. Malini. The character needed to complete its arc-the book on her life had to be published! I must have put up a pretty sincere show, because she seemed to be convinced. There was one hitch though. She couldn't go back to Gulzar for a rewrite. I quietly offered to chip in with the additional scenes. She looked at me askance. My eyes said, "try me". It was my attempt at 'professional' scripting after *Jugalbandi*. The episode was shot just like I wrote it. Later, I heard her exclaiming to her mother and brothers, "Can you believe it? This man wrote himself into the script!"

Noopur was the beginning of an enduring friendship with Hema Malini. When she learnt of the fatal night of the fire on the sets of *The Sword Of Tipu Sultan*, she had set her office machinery working to somehow connect to me to assure her of my well-being. It was a touching gesture coming from a big star to a junior colleague. She didn't restrict the work front either. In *Women of India*, another ambitious series she produced, she cast me as *Narad* in the *Draupadi* episode. This ambassador of the Gods was the only mythological character I played. Madhoo, her niece, fresh from her debut film *Phool aur Kaante*'s success with Ajay Devgan, played Draupadi. She graduated to making a movie [*Dil Aashna Hai*] whilst commissioning me to direct a pilot episode of a new series called *Hulchul*. It was to be the first thriller-adventure series on Indian television a la *Master of the Game*, a Sidney Sheldon novel and starred today's popular actor Sumeet Raghavan in his first lead part. By then the satellite channels had descended on the scene and the economics dithered in different directions. Despite her best efforts she couldn't strike a workable deal. *Hulchul* stayed in the beta tape boxes, but remains one of my best efforts. I had broken away from the set television grammar. In hindsight, the seeds of cinematic visualization must have germinated during its filming.

2009. Almost two decades since *Noopur*. The girl child syndrome had captured the fancy of the general entertainment channels and Ms. Malini set out to enlighten urban audiences on the hardships a girl faces and her fightback. She confessed that she had entertained thoughts of a dance reality show in keeping with her bent of mind. "But no one wants to watch classical dance shows these days. Hence, I opted for social issues. *Maati Ki Banno* [A Girl of the Soil] is the story of a girl forced to live as a housemaid at her aunt's place in Mauritius and is married off to a boy in Bihar. It is a show with a message that all obstacles can be overcome if you have the will". The story of Banno didn't go as far as Ms. Malini would have wished. I thank my stars that she made *Noopur* at the right time. With the trend that satellite channels had created, it may well have never been made!

The Deol family packed in a bundle of energy. Before you knew it, her daughters, Ahaana and Esha, blossomed from school kids to performing artistes. Her house reverberated with the sound of anklets and the music of her ballet rehearsals. Papa Dharmendra's visits recharged the atmosphere. Each time I shook his hand I felt my palms disappear in his giant grasp. Ms. Malini often tempted me with an offer to direct Esha with a script that would suit her best. Whilst I was still fishing for the right one, she called one day and announced with a great sense of pride that Esha was getting married. She made certain that everything from the wedding card to the three-day ceremonial programme was as big as weddings could get.

The tryst with the stars assumed another dimension with the popular comedian Mehmood Ali deciding to have a go at television. Delhi based producer Gurbir Singh Grewal decided to make a twosome of Mehmood and me in a family sitcom *Basera*. [The Abode] He was an actor whom, even leading men held in high esteem. A permanent fixture in the movies of the sixties and early seventies, Mehmood was the proverbial laugh raiser and hence, scene stealer. His musical showdown with the genial Kishore Kumar in the 1968 film *Padosan* had turned into cult comedy. It would be an experience to rub shoulders with him. The film industry had a peculiar way of getting familiar with stars. Most of them were addressed by nicknames. Mehmood was called *Bhaijaan*. Though it was my first tryst with him, I ended up addressing him by the latter.

The Delhi winter was inviting. It would be foolish to turn it down and be ensconced within the four walls of a location. But I had gone there on a job, not to "sit back and enjoy the weather" like the Afghanistan rebels claim when they are not on 'duty'. Maybe it was sheer force of habit, but *Bhaijaan* retained the same tenor of his big screen performances on television. The approach to my character '*Idea*' Raman as a casual, ideal foil to him, didn't seem to gel. Raman was this wise guy who cooked up ideas to extricate the main character from ticklish situations only to drag him into a bigger mess. I chose to play it on a casual easy-go-lucky note. The contrast in pitch irked. Grewal was at a loss how to play one down or play up the other to rectify the imbalance. "You won't even register" warned Grewal. Under the circumstances, I thought it wise to temporarily discard subtlety and scale up my performance, much to his relief. This was a retreat to theatre, kind of playing to the gallery. *Bhaijaan* carried on regardless. This was the Mehmood that a generation had loved. This was what they expected him to do. Sure enough, he delivered.

That those who laugh the most do so to hide their sorrows, was true of *Bhaijaan*. After a daily wrap, he would drive down to the hotel ["I love driving"] and would let me hop on. He would speak of the tumultuous life he had led. As he did a rewind, his voice resonated with a nostalgic tenor. He spoke of his father Ali who was a celebrated dancer. Of his indulgence in romance and the resulting heartbreaks. Of the good old days when rising star Amitabh Bachchan was courting Jaya Bhaduri and how the two would meet up every evening at his brother Anwar Ali's house in the, then, relatively quieter Juhu suburb of Bombay. Of his sons Macky and Lucky, and how *Kunwara Baap* and *Ginny aur Johnny*, the films he made were semi-autobiographical. But the most tragi-comic one still plays on my mind. In the early sixties, when he hadn't yet become Mehmood the comic star, a fan ran up to him for an autograph. Pleased as punch, he flaunted his signature proudly on the paper and handed it back. The fan took a while to examine the autograph. He then looked quizzically at Mehmood and exclaimed, "*Oye tussi Premnath nahi ho?*" [Damnit, you aren't Premnath!?] The man tore up the autograph without an iota of shame and disappeared into the crowd. Mehmood's partial resemblance to the popular actor Premnath had resulted in his undoing. He laughed it off, as he had done with so many other turbulent moments in his life.

Circa 2003. I was in Malaysia filming my second feature *Dil Maange More*, when I heard of Bhaijaan's moving on. He had been courting ill health for quite a while and was confined to a wheel chair for a few years. For a man who had entertained millions over two decades, very few people turned up to pay homage. The funny man had died unsung. It is what we have come to expect of a world that rushes past – with no time to squander over people who don't matter anymore.

Delhi-based producer Dinesh Babbar, a nephew of filmmaker B Subhash, was instrumental in my brush with another star, Sharmila Tagore. Babbar had produced my directorial debut, a feature for television called *Sambandh*. At the fag end of the 1980s, there was a spate of films and television serials on the seemingly unending Punjab State insurgency. I wondered if there was any point of view left for me to explore. That was when writer Dr Rahi Masoom Reza, basking in the success of *Mahabharat*, pulled one from out of his hat. Not many filmmakers were fortunate to have Reza pen their first script. The sessions at his Hill Road residence were educative exercises in scripting. *Sambandh* told the story of an entrepreneur in Punjab who wanted to quit the ravaged land and migrate to New Delhi, following the killings of his servant and maid which he considered as ominous portents. Reza raised a provoking query here-why are *we* running away? Shouldn't those cowards with their faces covered, racing across on their bikes and spraying bullets into innocents, be on the run? His no-holds-barred approach to the terrorist plague rattled me a bit. I feared Doordarshan would raise its by-now notorious fangs and end up diluting the impact. But Reza egged me on to film it exactly as it was written. *Sambandh* was telecast on a Sunday morning prime time and received rave reviews. The point of not deserting one's soil was well taken, though my boss V P Sathe felt that the end was utopian. Punjab had showed no inclination of dousing the unrest. But I wanted the film to end on a ray of hope irrespective of the truth that stared us in the face. Just as well. For, a few years later the film turned almost portentous. Peace returned to the region and gradually eclipsed memories of a tormented past.

Sambandh fetched me a fair share of credibility at Mandi House, the "market" that caters to television production houses, a place where angels fear to tread. My guess was that Babbar didn't have to encounter bureaucratic red tape for his second project. This time he was being ambitious. He had contacted the stunningly pretty star of the 1960s and 1970s, Sharmila Tagore. Her base in New Delhi made her accessible to him. It must have taken some persuasion on his part to get her consent to feature in his telefilm *Mrigtrishna* [The

Mirage]. It was to be her first full-fledged television appearance. The plot was loosely based on maverick footballer Maradona's flirtation with drugs. When the addict [played by television actor Pankaj Berry] is wheeled into the hospital, the doctor [Sharmila Tagore] is reminded of her own son whom she had lost to the world of drug abuse. She sets out to rehabilitate the boy only to come up against a wall of stubborn defiance. The film ends on a tragic note but not before dropping a stern warning to the characters, and thereby the audience, to lay off the pernicious powder.

I realised I was in the portals of royalty as I arrived to meet Tagore. As she walked in bereft of make–up, she still looked a diva. Like in *Devi* of Satyajit Ray's classic and Pushpa of *Amar Prem*. It was a new director and the new environment of television staring at her. Understandably, she looked for a certain degree of assurance. Even as I narrated the story, I could see a filament of doubt running through her mind. Perhaps it had to do with the rather demanding hours of television and the lack of the comfort zone she had enjoyed in the movies. She gracefully offered to introduce the film and be done with it. For a moment my senses froze. I needed to gather my wits. I hadn't expected her to turn it down on the eve of the shoot. Then, as calm and composed as I could get, I spoke. "Sharmila*ji*, you are the star. You've seen it all with the best of them. You really don't need to do this film, I understand. But I need to. And I need you. Even as I am aware that I must not let you down, it is far more important that I do not let myself down." She looked at me silently. Had I overstepped? Then without a trace of emotion she asked, "Which scene do we begin with tomorrow?" That moment underlined a dictum for me as a director–know your job and carry your conviction. It can help negotiate any unexpected blind turn.

Mrigtrishna was filmed in an actual sanatorium in Delhi. Permission was granted only after official hospital hours when the inmates would be calm. The young victims of drug abuse chained to their beds and tiny rooms were a pathetic sight. The film crew was instructed to maintain a silent mode during work so that the patients were not perturbed. As we went along, I learnt that Ms. Tagore appeared to have an aversion towards her left profile being exposed on camera. She defined the parameters to me. I made every effort to frame the shots accordingly. But in one sequence where she had to turn, the camera caught her left profile. I approved the shot but the video assist was a dead giveaway. Film stars often found the monitor and instant playback a novelty that did not exist in their time. Now glued to the set, she raised the profile matter again. "I asked you not to shoot from this side". I played back the shot and frankly found no reason for alarm. Once again I found myself telling her "Sharmila*ji*, it looks perfectly fine. And has someone ever told you how lovely your left profile is?" She never brought it up after that. Either she must have bought my theory or considered it a waste of time to argue with a stubborn new director. The 90-minute film was complete and telecast on World Anti-Drugs day, once again on Sunday morning prime time hour. Ms. Tagore's presence lent the film dignity and credence.

A time leap occurred. In 2003, when I was casting for my feature *Dil Maange More* and approached Soha Ali Khan, Ms. Tagore's daughter as one of the leading girls with the young Shahid Kapoor, the clock had come full circle. Soha debuted in the film and I met up with Ms. Tagore again. Strangely, she had only faint memories of *Mrigtrishna*. She thought *Dil Maange More* was an endearing film and we have stayed connected ever since. In 2009, we shot as co-actors in Nagesh Kukunoor's thriller *8 X 10 Tasveer*. Both in Calgary and Cape Town, we took in the natural sights. Particularly the Kirstenbosch Botanical Garden in Cape Town which takes your breath away and soothes the senses. When I had first watched Tagore in a racy thriller called *Aamne Saamne*, during my school days, I could never have guessed that I would one day end up talking about the peacocks in her Pataudi estate or the kind of flowers she'd like to carry home all the way from Capetown. The *Mrigtrishna* was no longer one.

Though stars who were past their prime took to the medium of television, the major stars of the 1990s and the new millennium still looked upon it as a poor country cousin. It suited the television brigade of actors like me, who had painstakingly created a little world of our own. But the colour of money and the reach was too good to resist. In the next two decades, the reigning film stars [Amitabh Bachchan, Shah Rukh Khan, Salman Khan among others in Mumbai, besides many more in South India] discovered the new lucrative medium.

No screen too small, where the future is big and inviting!

On location for Vinay Dhumale's *Avsesh* with the late Tom Alter.

Purnaiya Pandit in *The Sword of Tipu Sultan*

On location for the telefilm *Mrigtrishna*

With Mohan Gokhale in the episode
Mr Bhatia from *Mitte Ke Rang*

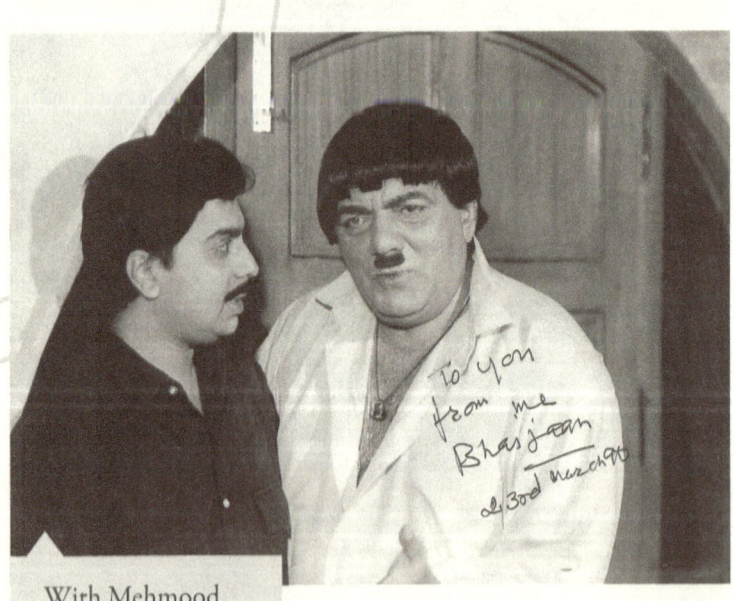

With Mehmood
in *Basera*

V P Sathe, Writer and Director of *Bombay Publicity Service*

Thakazhi Sivasankaran Pillai author of M S Sathyu's *Kayar*

Vishal Singh and Joy Sengupta in *Ghunghat Ke Pat Khol*

Hema Malini in *Yug*

Sharmila Tagore in telefilm *Mrigtrishna*

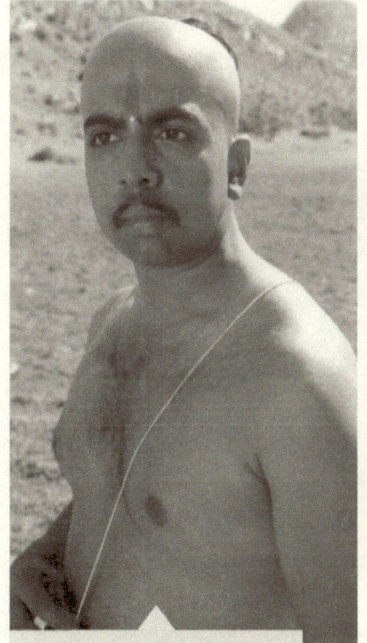

As Purnaiya Pandit in
The Sword of Tipu Sultan

The polaroid snap
Sir Peter O'Toole in
Jodhpur for *Kim* – the film
on Rudyard Kipling's novel

Viveck Vaswani with Abhinav Chaturvedi, Sulbha Deshpande and others on the sets of *Nayi Dishayen*

As a 90-year-old estate agent in the theatre production of Arthur Miller's *The Price*

In Hema Malini's *Women Of India* as Naarad

Soni Razdan, Kanwaljeet, Dalip Tahil in Ramesh Sippy's *Buniyaad*

With Actor-Director Ravi Baswani on location for *Kisse Miya Biwi Ke*

In Hrishikesh Mukherjee's
Hum Hindustani with
Sheela David Sharma

In *Peele Pattey*, an episode
of the series *Tane Bane*,
with Meeta Vashisht

With Sreela Majumdar in M S Sathyu's *Kayar*
based on Thakazhi Sivasankaran Pillai's epic Novel

EPISODE

2

THE MIDDLE

Even as terrestrial television in the form of the national broadcaster Doordarshan stretched its legs and yawned, taking its monopoly as a given, licences were granted to private broadcasters in the early 1990s. The age of satellite television was ushered in amidst great anticipation. Better clarity, high definition telecast facilities.... the possibilities exciting and endless. If the sleeping giant was shaken out of its complacency, all it had to show for, initially, were a few additional metro channels. For Doordarshan, it was a virtual playback of the famous Aesop fable, The Hare and the Tortoise.

OH, WHAT A LOVELY WAR!

"Times have not become more violent,
they have just become more televised"
— Marlyn Manson [American singer, actor, author]

Circa 1995. A tide in the time of television turned its future on its head. A Supreme Court ruling put paid to the "unconstitutional" airwave monopoly of Doordarshan, opening the floodgates to private broadcasters. With that one stroke, it also set the stage for India to gradually balloon into one of the world's largest and most competitive television playing fields. It was time to relegate those paltry twelve-channel television sets to the 'Relics' category. The same brands now touted a hundred-plus channel display operated with a remote control gadget.

But the initiation for us viewers had happened four years earlier. International satellite television sneaked into India through CNN's coverage of the Gulf War in 1991. CNN perched on a Baghdad-hotel terrace, captured the American bombarding of the city in retaliation to Iraq's invasion of Kuwait. I recollect how the war entered our living rooms after a mad scramble for cable networks. The excitement of finally acquiring the international channel hitherto restricted to overseas jaunts, coupled with the "live" war opera, eclipsed an important factor. CNN couldn't have timed it better to open a subscriber base in India. This was despite the reception of its signals falling outside legal purview in the country. The satellite technology, took the Delhi corridors of power unawares. It was unstoppable. CNN, ITN and BBC arrived to an overtly curious reception by Indian viewers.

This 'invasion' was the forerunner of what news channels would eventually peddle, with taglines proclaiming "Breaking News" "Exclusive" and the customary, "here's a flash". The American onslaught to ward off Iraq from Kuwait was just the invitation that television journalism needed to take on a dramatic *avatar*. We sat intrigued, watching the coalition forming, vital, if the war was to be seen as not merely an offensive by the policing USA against an Arab state.

August 1991: the Hong Kong based Satellite Television Asian Region [popularly known by the acronym, 'StarTV'], later merging with Rupert Murdoch's News Corp, launched five channels in India on the ASIASAT-1 satellite. By early 1992, nearly half a million Indian households were tuned in to the predominantly English language StarTV telecasts. A year later the figure rose to 2 million. As local cable system operators mushroomed across the country [pegged at 60,000], the autumn of 1994 recorded an estimated 12 million households (accounting for a little less than one-fourth of all television owners) as satellite channel subscribers. These systems redistributed the satellite channels to their customers at rates as low as Rs 155 [USD 5] a month. The huge potential of the satellite television audience was the key to STAR entering into an alliance with an Indian company, Essel Packaging-owned by Subhash Chandra Goel, who had come a long way from his roots as a rice trader in Haryana. Zee TV became the first privately owned Hindi satellite channel of India. I was among the early birds at their offices. Karuna Samtani, creative head, found my concept of an Indian *Dennis the Menace*, fascinating. I had christened it *Dumpy* and even identified a mischievous kid in Delhi to play the brat. Teething troubles delayed Samtani's decision. The kid grew up and with that, like Mr Wilson, I showed Dennis the door.

The Star-Zee marriage however did not last long. Rumours were afloat that Murdoch had bought a stake in Zee only to dissolve the company and rid himself of the competition. Subhash Chandra Goyal did a U-turn and launched a full scale operation to rescue his brain-child at a reportedly whopping buy-back price. By the end of 1994 there were 12 satellite-linked channels available in India, all of them beaming from a handful of satellites. This number shot up by the end of 1996, with Indian programmers and international media players like Turner Broadcasting, Time-Warner, ESPN, CANAL 5 and Pearsons PLC, seriously considering the introduction of new satellite television services for India. Some stayed, others aborted. Several regional channels, too, came into being during this period. Sun TV (Tamil), Asianet (Malayalam) and Eenadu TV [Telugu] amongst them. Today, television channels and complementary off-shoots have opened up in nearly all major Indian languages.

Doordarshan felt like Robinson Crusoe, stranded on a lonely island after the satellite ships set sail. The blame was laid at the government's door for an archaic style of news dissemination that made Doordarshan's rendition of news bulletins dreary. They were caught in the act of playing up to the guidelines of the ruling party. "Brush all controversial issues under the already dusty studio carpet". That was the signal for private television broadcasters to step on it and bridge the gap for a more spunky presentation. Not surprisingly, BBC's model was the one they yearned to emulate.

The promoters of TV Today Network's business launched their own news segment *Aaj Tak* by leasing a daily night slot on the government's own DD Metro network. Characterised by the popular sign-off line "*Ye Thi Khabar Aaj Tak, Intezar Kijiye Kal Tak*" [That's all the news for today, await the morrow], the slot gave Doordarshan a run for its money, yet the latter chose to avoid the warning bells. News programmer Nalini Singh's five-minute daily news capsule, *Ankhon Dekhi*, and *Newstrack* [both on DD Metro], initiated inroads into a hitherto untapped viewership. Television Eighteen India Limited (TV18) broadened the playing field when they produced *The India Show* [1993, Star Plus], and a weekly business news programme, *India Business Report,* for BBC World.

News presentation has come a long way since the evenings with Dolly Thakore and Pankaj Mohan. When the latter once appeared to snooze off, he had to be woken up with a gentle "hey Pankaj". From those days of a lonely channel, today it fans out to an overpopulated scenario. News presenters who had become as familiar as television actors for over a decade were the first to be challenged by the boom. Charusheela Patwardhan, Dolly Thakore, Sarita Sethi, Luku Sanyal, Salma Sultan, Smita Talwalkar, Bhakti Barve, Pankaj Mohan, all faces of the small screen's early years and their ilk were relegated to file pictures. Incidentally, even the late Smita Patil had tried her hand at regional news in Bombay before her stint as one of the most sensitive actors in Indian cinema. Patil was the first television personality to predict that a new breed of stars would be born....the television star! It went on record in journalist Chaitanya Padukone's column. It turned out to be true in her case too. Shyam Benegal who knew her as a newscaster, was the first to recruit her into films. And indeed, a star was born! The presentation of news had assumed a dramatic cloak, dismantling Doordarshan's memories. In the middle of 2010, at a special preview of my Marathi film *Mee Sindhutai Sapkal* in Pune, I met Patwardhan after what seemed ages. She was still the affable face of television and had quietly reconciled to the new phase and face of news broadcasts. Six months later, a common friend informed me that a sudden heart attack had claimed her. Barve too, had crossed over many years prior, following a horrendous car crash on the Mumbai-Pune highway. This early tribe of newscasters seldom had the back-up of visuals and the manipulated music score to fortify their broadcasts. But pioneers, they will always be.

United Television [UTV], founded by Ronnie Screwala and a man to admire for his accomplishments, Sameer Nair of Star Plus, hit on a bright idea to get a pie of the news scramble to produce a half-hour programme that would be a spoof of the news. I was commissioned to make it and went about it with the eagerness of an Art Buchwald and Bob Hope rolled into one. I cast actor Ranvir Shorey as a Japanese nerd who saunters into a fuel pump to purchase fodder for his vehicle...a bullock car(t). We had foreseen the petrol price crisis nearly twenty years ago long before cartoonists had a field day with similar caricatures. Many such anecdotes that mocked the prevailing socio-political system revved up the pilot episode. I awaited Sameer Nair's feedback with much optimism as he watched it with a straight face. "So, it isn't the greatest show on earth", he reverted point-blank, 'and whoever heard of background music while the news is being telecast?", he added, ridiculing the concept of a score we had incorporated to underline the essence of each situation. Nair may have quite forgotten this arbitrary judgement, even as he watches the news segments today, garnished by dramatic rhythms, graphics and other cacophonic effects. My show did not come on, relegated to the bin with other innumerable 'pilot' episodes, but a few years later a spoof on similar lines "*The World is Weak*" [a take-off on *The World This Week*], began telecast and has had a popular run with Cyrus Broacha and Kunal Vijaykar, both accomplished funsters. Nair had narrowly missed the rush-hour bus.

Gloss and drama became the passwords for news presentations. 24×7 news channels have a voracious appetite. News-gathering was a task cut out for the heads of these channels. Formats underwent re-development. The liberalized zone, freed from the fetters of government control, worked overtime to rake in eyeballs even as they peppered prime time with the unavoidable film-based programmes, and occasional sting operations on corrupt bureaucrats and morally suspect film stars. On the flip side, the Jessica Lal murder case that shook the ramparts of the Capital, was pursued relentlessly bringing to book a politician's kin who threatened to go scott free. However, in an attempt to ape its western counterparts, channels cling on to innovative backdrops, frenzied cutting and sensational headlines that often look ripped off from pulp Hindi fiction titles on sale at Higginbothams or AH Wheeler outlets on railway stations.

Desperate to woo the viewer, the channels collided, and continue to do so, in a melange of violent visuals, grating music and outlandish descriptions. What else can one make of *"khooni panja"* [Bloodied hands] to describe a macabre murder or *"maut ka saudagar"* [Traders of death] as a headline for a food adulteration bust?

Satellite channels that were propelled by a war, were now, ironically at war with each other. The one-upmanship trend continues to be in overdrive. Whilst news channels thrive on the "breaking news hysteria syndrome" that could include a day-long rescue operation of a kid who has fallen into a well, astrologers belt out predictions for the country and film-folk tweet blasphemously. News and fiction now vie for the tag of soap operas with political conflicts and terrorist attacks assuming a sentiment-soaked narrative to give viewers the feel of watching a reality show. A "good dramatic story" is what the news channel doctor has prescribed.

Many years after that doomed invasion, along with a shaken world I hung on to every word and visual of the destruction of New York's twin towers as the horrors kept unfolding for a week on CNN and BBC. The impact of such frenzied coverage of this monumental tragedy on the new breed of Indian television journalists is often debated. Less than a decade after 9/11, a go-getter journalist like Barkha Dutt [NDTV] would prostrate on the pavement outside the Taj Mahal Hotel in Mumbai ducking shrapnel to cover the 26/11 siege of the city by terrorists. Or report from behind enemy lines in Egypt as the country wrought a revolution for democracy. Respect for the art of telecast restraint seemed to have retracted. Filtering of news instead of the blow-by-blow account of the Mumbai attacks, would have kept the terrorists (holed up in the Taj's hotel rooms) in the dark about the commando operations. Winning eyeballs was, however, the priority, resulting in playing straight into the arms of the perpetrators of the horror.

Sure, we had come a long way from the fly-infested studio of Doordarshan. The studio fly, incidentally qualifies to be the first television star with its ubiquitous buzz in front of the newsreader's face. As we all watched, and probably got more annoyed than the newsreader on whose nose it was attempting a landing, it wasn't camera-conscious at all. Today, despite the occasional fumble, newsreaders are a hyper-energetic and, [might I add, a violently angry] lot shielded by visuals that take you into the thick of the action. And if you are not amused by the linguistically-challenged small-town stringer who has turned "our man on the spot", then the mythology parables and ghost story theories will definitely stalk you.

It wasn't just the gold rush of channels featuring Zee News, Star News, Sahara, and regional language stations. International channels too found more footprints in the Asian region. Business channels have found faithful eyeballs glued to the stock exchange ticker. Prannoy Roy, Barkha Dutt, Rajat Sharma, Arnab Goswami, Vinod Dua, Pankaj Pachauri and Prabhu Chawla were the faces in place of our black-and-white icons. Each of them in search of the Holy Grail–*voicing* concern, influenced by political leanings and making a die-hard effort to contribute to the magic numbers of television rating points. Heated arguments on topical issues in shows like *The Buck Stops Here* or *Face the Nation* often end up conclusion-less. One sees the palpable wind-up mode on the anchor's face as the hour draws to a close. "You have anything to say in ten seconds?" asks Dutt of a participant in *The Buck Stops Here*. He rattles off a possible answer. Dutt signs off with a time-out factor. Pushed back to the drawing board of the issue, again.

Having said all that, there is no denying the enormous impact of television news. In a nation like India, it is not surprising that Hindi news channels hold the edge over their English counterparts with the regional ones too eating into the pie. However, PN Vasanti, director of the Centre for Media Studies, observed that despite the number of news channels being on the rise, their credibility was not. Viewers often cross-check information with the newspapers the following day. Which brings me back to CNN, BBC, Sky News and other international media. The tendency is to flip between Indian and 'imported' channels so as to catch the news in a more sober perspective. I watched the 26/11 Mumbai Taj carnage on BBC and CNN, simply to experience a different media culture. I compared the raving and ranting over the Maria Susairaj crime of passion [she and a paramour killed her suitor], with the American and British reporting of Frenchman Strauss-

Kahn's involvement in a sex scandal. These are two different mirrors of society. For obvious reasons, the reflection on the Indian channels is somewhat akin to the distorted images you see of yourself at the mirrors placed in village fairs. Not to mention the conspiracy theory which gave one the creepy feeling that 9/11 and 26/11 had more to it than meets the eye. Television news channels have yet to delve into this matrix of investigative expose. Not quite off the cuff, a thought creeps in. Are we not in a world where the media is being politically exploited? A platform for world leaders to even woo the electorate?

Pre 1994: Bombay Doordarshan invited me to read the news one evening-live! I had never tried *this* stunt before. Live theatre performance is one thing, here you are dispensing facts to the world without a rehearsal. I simply could not digest the fear of stumbling my way through. Taking a deep breath, I focused and went through the twenty-minute exercise. I came away unscathed, savouring the experience. It was also a first-hand experience of what goes on in the newsreader's mind. A few years later I watch actor Amitabh Bachchan read the news as a promotional strategy for his film *Rann*.

I wonder if they take on guest readers like guest-editors in dailies. Wouldn't mind having another go at it!

THE NEW WAVE

The time had come to step out of the cocoon. Expand horizons. Seek new audiences. Breakaway from a decorum that Doordarshan was habituated to. The officials at Doordarshan, who had overlooked their self-aggrandisement, also felt the new winds blowing. The footprints of Zee and Star [1992], followed later by Sony [1995], with their liberal approach and secure policies succeeded in making the queues outside Mandi House, Delhi, dwindle a bit. The producer's neck was no longer on the line, at least as far as finances were concerned. The risk of attracting sponsors on Doordarshan was replaced with the "commissioning of programmes" wherein the production house was assigned a budget to complete an episode. The rider, however, was that the channel retained all rights to the series, unlike Doordarshan where the producer-owned the market exploitation rights of the show. It also triggered another paper chase—the art of saving as big a sum as possible from the commissioned budget to add to the producer's kitty. When a certain episode yielded less than the average calculations, it resulted in the ingeniously coined term *"profit mein loss"* [taking a hit in the profits]. Along with producers, channels began to mushroom.

Soon, there was Business India TV [Bi TV], NEPC, Channel 9 [9 Gold] and Home TV–all of whom needed some time to discover that the new fad wasn't a cakewalk. They were obsolete a year after coming on air, resulting in financial setbacks to enterprising rookie producers, including me, who had invested in a bank of episodes.

The Adhikari brothers, Gautam and Markand, had spent a great deal of time in the wings of Doordarshan in Mumbai eyeing prime slots. But they hadn't made much headway beyond a few Marathi shows. Zee changed all that. They were among the early birds to catch the worm. One evening the phone rang. It was Markand Adhikari seeking me out for a new series he was producing. Even as I wondered aloud if it was another Marathi venture, he revealed with a proud tenor in his voice that it was in Hindi. "*Commander*" on Zee [1992], was an offshoot of the detective series, *Tiger*, that the Adhikaris had brandished on the regional Mumbai DD channel. Ramesh Bhatkar, son of the accomplished music composer Snehal Bhatkar [the evergreen number "*kabhi tanhayion mein, hamari yaad aayegi*" from the film *Hamari Yaad Aayegi*, 1961], played the detective while I took on different characters in one-off episodes. The opening night episode had me playing a murder suspect. Gautam Adhikari, who directed the series, was toying with audience recollect. *Khiladi*, the Abbas-Mustan film that sprung a surprise on the audience by casting me as a killer, had just been a success. Adhikari was sure that viewers would make me out to be the usual suspect, while he waylaid them with another actor. A psychotic character in another episode [co-starring Rama Vij, the teacher from *Nukkad*] was my purported ticket to Mani Ratnam, which like I shared earlier, was not to be.

The Adhikaris steadily cemented their position as a software producing major. *Waqt* [Zee, again], a mega soap featuring veteran actors from screen and television got me going yet again with them. As a political fixer who plotted the fortunes of the characters, I tried my hand at subtle play while exuding the cunning. The portrayal also won me the admiration of Gautam Adhikari who was at once amused and amazed at the accuracy with which I maintained action continuity even as shots were cut for different magnifications. When he made his first feature film *Bhookamp* [The earthquake], he didn't leave me behind. A small, yet key, role of an informer who dies a gory death, assured me that my ties with the big screen weren't compromised.

The casting bubble burst on me yet again. Despite being considered for one of the lead roles in *Shriman Shrimati* [a comedy that went on to have a prolonged run on Doordarshan Metro], the show went on air with Rakesh Bedi and the late Jatin Kanakia. It was my first disillusionment with the Adhikari brothers but I didn't make it evident. After the fire on the sets of *The Sword of Tipu Sultan*, I had braced myself for all eventualities. It was also a period that tempted me to delve into production. I had shot the pilot of a sitcom titled *Memsaab* [Woman of the house]. I screened it for Markand Adhikari. He turned up his nose and remarked, "You shouldn't be indulging in production, you are better off as an actor". I still haven't figured whether he was being concerned or sarcastic.

At the turn of the millennium, their software company grew into an independent channel, SAB TV. Veteran actor Jeetendra, whose Balaji Telefilms was well entrenched by then, had stakes in the company. *Dial 100*, a cop drama I directed for actor Deepak Tijori's production house was commissioned by SAB in 2003. The show featured names like Abhimanyu Singh and Murli Sharma who would go on to make a mark in films. Fortunately, the brothers didn't replay old apprehensions again. But the channel showed up red on the television rating points chart. The Sony Entertainment channel business team sensing a meal, moved in for the kill and took over. Not to be undone, the Adhikaris launched another channel *Mee Marathi* [2005]. Followed five years later by *Masti*. They seem to have struck on a new formula for gold. Launch a channel, run it for a while and sell it as a brand! In hindsight, Markand regrets selling SAB, which has since then made a fair turn -around in its fortunes in the Sony bouquet. "The circumstances at the time forced us to sell. We have learnt from the sour experience and this has made us more mature in our approach. With SAB TV we pulled off a sort of 'mini-revolution' on Indian TV".

While Star grappled with an identity crisis, deciding whether to be an English or Hindi channel, Zee found its way. The vision of Subhash Chandra Goel was taking shape. A fledgling Balaji Telefilms which Ekta Kapoor, Jeetendra's (Ravi Kapoor) daughter, assimilated from her basement at her Juhu bungalow, found a platform on Zee. *Mano Ya Na Mano* [1995], a series directed by Rajesh Ranasinghe, based on supernatural happenings launched her company. That was the first time I met up with television's young future diva. She had produced the pilot of a serial called *Captain House*, and sought my services as a director. But the writing found itself in a blind alley. Kapoor's reference material was VHS cassettes of American television shows, and it didn't quite gel with me. The thought of borrowing or even being inspired from another person's work, wasn't the way I wanted to kick-start a directorial career. After much deliberation and discussion, I preferred to step out. Kapoor handed over the reins to another director. It was *Hum Paanch* [1995], a comedy of a father [Marathi actor Ashok Saraf] and his five incorrigible daughters, that etched the Balaji label. Eyebrows were raised on the father being rudely heckled by the girls, but that didn't stop the series from turning Tuesday nights into Zee's most-watched slot. The *enfant terribles* had landed. It also left a mark for a bespectacled, virtually unrecognizable Vidya Balan, who more than a decade later, surfaced in ad filmmaker Pradeep Sarkar's remake of Bimal Roy's *Parineeta* [2005]. Though the boisterous Rakhi Vijan and the raucous Bairavi Raichuria trumpeted for attention, Balan was the hidden star in *Hum Paanch*. It did a long 9-year run. In the second season, I confronted the family as a corporate boss in a couple of episodes, enjoying the effort to retain my sanity amidst their mayhem. Balan had quit the show by then.

Zee continued to defy the orthodox mould of Doordarshan's television. With *Tara*, the quintessential soap opera came into being. Obviously inspired by the lifestyles of characters in *Santa Barbara*, *The Bold and the Beautiful* and other American soaps, writer Vinta Nanda's contemporary take on Indian women was wrought with complexities that may not have found acceptance during television's infant days. *Tara's* trials and tribulations, did play on for five years, making it the first modern feminist series. A liplock [Alok Nath-Navneet Nishan] heralded the "bold, new" stance of *desi* television. Deeya and Tony Singh could well be television's first professional couple. In 1993, the accent shifted to youth and *Banegi Apni Baat* was their first vehicle on the Zee network. Probably, when they cast the ensemble of Aly Khan, Surekha Sikri, Irrfan Khan, R Madhavan and Shefali Chhaya, the couple didn't realise that they were looking at future stars. The plot of youth, transitioning from campus challenges to career pressures resonated with a generation on the cusp and opened opportunities for the producers to go on to bigger shows like *Just Mohabbat, Left Right Left* and *Jassi Jaisi Koi Nahin*.

The series didn't fight shy of taboo elements like condoms and sexuality. The new school of youth was the concept and the target. Deeya Singh, the director, in an interview admitted that, "the brief issued to us by the channel was that everything from pimples to condoms and pre-marital sex was to have a say in the serial." R Madhavan, a big screen candidate, began his toddler steps in *Banegi Apni Baat* before making it as a star prospect in the second season of *Ghar Jamai.*

As I fastened my seat belt for the rapid transition, it struck me that television in India was steadfastly attaining a magnitude we had heard of and glimpsed in North and West America. Directors had to quickly adapt to changing trends, policies and attitudes. Doordarshan desperately sought to reinvent. The first make-over happened in 1993 with the DD Metro channel telecast in prime cities. It was a concept that should have been initiated much earlier. With improved transmission quality, the Metro channels wooed a young breed of content makers. Names like Rajeev Mehra (*Zabaan Sambhal Ke*), Imtiaz Ali (*Imtehaan*), Aanand Mahendroo (*Dekh Bhai Dekh*) who had made his bow on the main channel,

Anubhav Sinha (*Sea Hawks*) and others found extra bandwidth for their products. Being metro-centric, the focus remained on youth and the log lines were distinctly different from those on the National channel.

As STAR shed its international garb and transformed itself into a full-fledged Hindi language channel Star Plus, I felt it hit the right audience pockets to provide Zee a run for its money. But despite its English content being shunted on to a subsidiary, Star World, Star Plus was finding it tough to fully shake off its "alien" tag. The 1960s star Asha Parekh with *Kora Kagaz* [1998] and actress Neena Gupta with *Saans* in the same year, were brought on board to woo prime time soap addicts. Renuka Shahane and ex-cricketer Salil Ankola in the former and Kanwaljeet and Gupta in *Saans* brought in the ingredient of face-value.

Around that period, Naved Antulay [son of the former Maharashtra chief minister A R Antulay] floated a production company that debuted with a thriller titled *Saraab* [Illusion]. He looked for a nation-wide reach and hence, preferred good old Doordarshan. *Saraab* comprised of episodic suspense stories. Antulay had a penchant for Hollywood thrillers and he picked one of my favourites for an adaptation. Alfred Hitchcock's *Strangers on a Train*, the Farley Granger-Robert Walker starrer about two men who decide to bump off each others' wives. Playing Robert Walker's part was one of those moments where I felt extremely flattered. It was the next best exercise for actors like me, who wouldn't ever experience the company of the great Hitchcock.

Following *Saraab*'s commendable viewership and critical acclaim,

Antulay was now keen on exploring the newly created satellite viewer base. He tied up with Star Plus to produce another thriller series *Kohraa*. One of the episodes was another Hitchcock spellbinder "*I Confess*". Thrilled at landing the part, I shared the moment with actor Farouque Shaikh, whom I was directing in *Chamatkar*, produced by Partho Ghosh for Sony. He delved into a eulogy about me playing Montgomery Clift's role. I realised the need to skillfully negotiate the part or else the eulogy could well turn into an elegy!

In 1996, Kant Kumar, a producer who had made a comedy called *Professor Ki Padosan,* a film that was stalled after the untimely death of the thespian Sanjeev Kumar, was looking for some respite to channelize his production machinery. A mini-series of 20 episodes on Zee titled *Jaal,* with Shekhar Suman and Sujata Mehta playing the protagonists, opened up avenues, but the initial four episodes shot with another director were bounced by the channel. I was hired to do some damage control and see the rest of the series through. The thriller genre has always fascinated me and I applied all the slick tricks in the book to resurrect the show. Antulay watched the climactic episodes of *Jaal* and hired me to direct the rest of the *Kohraa* stories.

The first of them was an adaptation of the Hollywood money-spinner *Ransom*. It found myself fighting my demons again–of not wanting to remake or be influenced by a published work. It made me more than determined to apply my mind-space to the execution and to steer clear from replication. The episode had an interesting cast. Sudesh Berry, Pallavi Joshi and Raj Kiran. Kiran had just migrated to television after starring roles in films like Rajshri Productions' *Shiksha*, Mahesh Bhatt's *Arth* and Prakash Jha's *Hip Hip Hurray* [in which I essayed a cameo]. He came across as enthusiastic and hard working. Though he often connected with me to consider him for suitable parts, he never betrayed signs of the terrible aftermath that was to befall him. We first heard of his unexplained absence from the scene after the telecast of the *Kohraa* series. Then a report surfaced that he had been confined to a remand home. He was again reported missing and was believed to be convalescing at a sanatorium in Atlanta, America. His daughter, Rishika however denied this in the media and claimed that his whereabouts were unknown. Had we seen through his demeanour and read his depression, would we have managed to avert his fate? What was the fountainhead of insecurity weighing him down? These are tough questions that may or may not be answered. But as a witness to a charming actor who simply faded away from public gaze, it makes me more fearful of the frailty of a profession, which besides the requisite skill, calls for a demanding test of character and not just a sound and attractive mind and body.

Long before Star Plus became a bone of contention for Zee and Sony, my fortunes were closely entwined with its programming. After *Kohraa*, the association was renewed for three of the biggest shows on the channel. However, not everybody there sounded chirpy. While Deepak Saigal, the late filmmaker Mohan Seghal's son lent me a patient ear, programming executive Tarun Katiyal cheekily suggested to his team that they reserve a cabin for me in the office. Nevertheless, I carried on gamely. Sattee Shourie, a doughty lady, was the producer of the comic series *Hera Pheri* [1997], which could boast of the biggest roster of names assembled for a comedy to date. Given her film making background with multi-starrers like *Farishtey*, Shourie insisted on making *Hera Pheri* top-heavy.

The cast read like a who's who of television. Shekhar Suman, Mandira Bedi, Rakhi Vijan, Tanaaz Currim, Rohit Roy, Asrani, Bhavna Balsaver, Amit Behl, Mahesh Thakur and Rajesh Puri were amongst them. The late Anant Balani who debuted as director with the Salman Khan-Raveena Tandon starrer *Patthar Ke Phool*, co-wrote most of the episodes with me. Infused with a whacky sense of humour, *Hera Pheri* was the kind of show that should have logically fetched the channel high rating points. Despite being the top show on Star Plus, it had to live with the channel's modest general viewership. I sat with the show's executive producer Shailaja Kejriwal after a script reading. "Everything is sounding good, but, sadly we don't seem to be getting the numbers". It was then that I said something which I little realised would turn prophetic. "Keep that chin up and keep going. The ratings *will* come and you will be on top one day". Star's dramatic turn of fortune that followed around the millennium is, of course, an interesting case study.

Handling a cast as big and riotous as this, needed oodles of tact and patience. When Tanaaz Currim was required for an urgent shoot in an episode to be telecast the following week, she expressed her inability to leave Ichalkaranji, a location far-flung from Bombay, where she was engaged with another series. I spent a sleepless night clueless as to how to handle the shoot. The telephone ring pierced the still of the night. It was Madame Shourie calling at 3 AM. Her voice had a confident ring about it.

"You begin the shoot *beta*, you will have your actress on the set by 10 AM". I was genuinely concerned. The lady had driven out of the city before dawn all on her own, landed up at the hotel in the distant district of Ichalkaranji, bundled a baffled Currim into her car and delivered her like a courier shipment on my sets. The actress did not know what hit her but she simply had to comply. Currim hadn't got out of her delirium, "I heard this knock on my door, I was all groggy when I opened it, so it took me a while to realise it was her. She didn't give me a chance to talk. I just changed and sat in the car". Stories floated in the film industry about Madame Shourie's stern demeanour. About how she was a difficult proposition to work with. The *Hera Pheri* situation called for just that iron-lady approach. Shekhar Suman's rationed availability, a paucity of locations and other occasional jitters were surmounted with her gallant calm. Until Star Plus arbitrarily downed the shutters on *Hera Pheri* after a year of telecast. Shourie felt there was potential for another fifty two episodes and was disappointed with the channel's decision. She preferred to migrate to studio-building rather than play up to channel dictats. Future Studios at Goregaon manned by her daughters Mona and Archana, turned into television's busiest hub. "You always moaned about the lack of proper locations and facilities," Shourie told me, "the idea for this studio germinated from your complaint". I was touched when she attributed the earnings from *Hera Pheri* as the seed capital for the studio. For the first time in nearly two decades of work, I witnessed a rare display of humility and acknowledgement. Madame Shourie was an exception to almost every rule. Tough exterior, soft at heart. She remained as stoic as ever when Mona's life was cruelly cut short by cancer, ten years after she had made a success story of the studio.

Appearances can be deceptive. In the case of Shekhar Suman the comic outward garb could have been a facade. On the sets of *Hera Pheri*, I could often sense the actor within him cry out in despair. Playing the funny man wasn't a challenge anymore. It took him an entire new series to prove it. *Main* [1977], produced by Amar Bhutala who went on to etching a successful route in film production, told the rare story of a failing star who reflects on the stiff upper lip attitude which resulted in his fall from grace. Loosely inspired by the Rajesh Khanna odyssey, the character in *Main* sets about on a trail of reconciliation, when he learns of his impending fate. Though Suman initially fought shy of scenes where he is humiliated by his first wife, he rallied around to give, in my opinion, the best performance of his career, breaking the comic shackles. Yet again, Star attributed the not-so-high rating to the "serious nature" of the soap. But it helped me vary my deliveries with the same actor. On one hand a farcical comedy, and on the other a deeply introspective look at life. Then, one day after *Main* completed its run, Suman instinctively switched off acting. He moved on to doing a Jay Leno styled talk-show, *Movers and Shakers,* on Sony Television later that year. Judging a stand-up comedy or exercising his vocal cords in dance and music shows was probably a more lucrative route for Suman who must have badly missed featured roles in the age of daily soaps. But, I'm sure, he holds *Main* close to his heart till date.

I daresay, *Cincinnati Bublaboo* was the last of the big comedies on the small screen in India. It was set in an environment that hadn't yet hit the shores of this country in 1999 - the mall syndrome. I relished the thought of expanding the concept of the popular British series

Are You Being Served and widening its scope in a sprawling mall where characters, consumers and cultures collide. Actor Rakhi Vijan and her then husband Rajiv Tandon [director Ravi Tandon's son] subscribed to the zany idea and title. The creative heads at Star Plus perceived it as one of their most ambitious ventures. The show still holds the record of a channel attracting as much as two crore rupees in its kitty even *before* filming commenced. For the first time, the Indian television industry witnessed in-show branding. Brands which were [and still are] deviously hidden from camera had their moment of pride, displayed at the various outlets in the mall. Among the big consumer brands were McDonalds, LG, Lakme and other assorted labels. All of whom willingly loosened their publicity purse strings to be on a television dramedy. Much later in the day, reality shows like *Big Boss* and *Kaun Banega Crorepati* and even news channel desks toed the line that *Cincinnati Bublaboo* had flagged off. Laptops, detergents and every consumer item flashes a label in the new in-your-face marketing. Of course it is with a tinge of regret that I read "researched reports" of in-show branding by columnists of today's times who seem to be blissfully unaware of its genesis.

Cincinnati Bublaboo was also a joy ride of names. Suresh Menon, Joy Fernandes, Rajesh Puri, Smita Bansal, Rakhi Tandon, Bharat Dabholkar, Meenakshi Thakur, Atul Parchurey and Shoma Anand were star tickets of the comic genre. A plush, gigantic set of a mall at the Kamal Amrohi-owned Kamalistan Studios in Jogeshwari had turned into some kind of a tourist attraction. But then, just as we sailed into the twenty-sixth episode, curtains fell without warning. Star Plus CEO, Sameer Nair, had pulled a rabbit out of his hat by roping in Indian cinema's biggest name, Amitabh Bachchan, to anchor the Indian version of *Who Wants To Be A Millionaire*. *Cincinnati Bublaboo* had to be prematurely withdrawn. Shailaja Kejriwal, showrunner, offered a line of consolation. "The show was four years ahead of its time, viewers are yet to relate to mall culture". Everyone made way for *Kaun Banega Crorepati*. I sat in Sameer Nair's cabin that displayed a picture of Steven Spielberg, strategically placed, on his television set. Nair continued with his spiel of why he had to axe several shows. I was not listening anymore. I was staring at Spielberg and wondering how he would have dealt with such a turn of fortunes. A few weeks after *Kaun Banega Crorepati* went on air, Star Plus' ratings flaunted double digits. My prediction had come true. Uncanny. Only, I wasn't part of it.

Satellite television had taken over my life replete with all the twists and turns of a soap opera. But there was a brighter side, literally. The telecast quality. It had been heartbreaking for me to see the lush green spinach of *Ados Pados* turn into desaturated moss on Doordarshan's screens.

To my great relief [and the camera person's], greens would be greens from now on.

THE LAST METRO

Earth, wind, rain and fire
Wealth, power, blood, desire
One goal to live for before we die
One taste of glory
A mouthful of sky.

The theme number of the first ever series in the English language in India was, for sure, catchy. Five post graduates have a reunion after 13 years, only to confront some ugly secrets of their past and contend with forces that threaten them into submission. The contrasting Indian and Western cultures grappled with each other, as *A Mouthful Of Sky* delved into the aspirations of independent India's generation battling personal demons.

Filmmaker, analyst and a consultant on the business of cinema, Amit Khanna, one of the directors of Plus Channel, a software company, which had filmmaker Mahesh Bhatt on its board, had indeed thought out of the box. A series in the language that we think in, even as we speak in Hindi. As expected, the idea was met with much scepticism. English would limit its audience. But it also doubled the curiosity factor. Doordarshan's Metro channel was an ideal vehicle for this urban culture. Whatever the trends said, a series in the Queen's language excited me. I played an investigating police officer in the customary *khaki* uniform, but desisted from turning it into a familiar local Maharashtrian caricature. The other actors too adapted to the format admirably. It helped that quite a few had English theatre roots. Rahul Bose, Milind Soman, Sameer Soni, Ayesha Dharker, Simone Singh [her debut], Krutika Desai, Bharat Dabholkar, Ranjeev Mulchandani, Parvin Dabbas and Neesha Singh made up the enterprising roster of names. Bhatt, this time, had decided to give novelists a look-in for the script. So Ashok Banker, popular for his novel *Byculla Boy*, provided fodder to *A Mouthful of Sky*, while the erstwhile editor of *Stardust*, turned columnist and author Shobha De graduated to scripting for television. She had opened her account with one of the early daily soaps, *Swabhimaan* also produced by Bhatt.

A Mouthful Of Sky, opened to a lukewarm response from audiences and critics. The latter, predictably, dismissed the models in the show as "wooden". The obvious mirror of American and British soaps was held up to reflect where the series lagged behind. Yet, it was granted brownie points for the sheer effort. For one, the cast wasn't the regular tube faces. And the multi-camera unit ensured longer takes and interesting match cuts. The show, however, remained a one-time experiment. The only attempt at an English series in India. But, it was a good day at work and enjoyable even in its limited run.

The English language as a serial medium, found itself gloriously lampooned in the British series *Mind Your Language*. It was amongst the early British comedies that raised a constant chuckle. Whether the British were laughing at themselves or at the world didn't matter. The piquant humour was confined to a classroom where Professor Higgins from Bernard Shaw's play, *Pygmalion,* was turned on his head amidst a dozen Elizas, both female and male, from all parts of the world. Even the 'His' and 'Hers' signs outside the toilets had the King and Queen's mugs respectively. It was a series too tempting not to be lifted. And what better platform to adapt it than in India where the national language, Hindi, is spoken with varying conjugations in different regions! During the 1980s, the thought of concocting an Indian version did cross my mind. It excited a wannabe producer to fish for funds and I merrily got down to scripting the first four episodes. They even managed to shoot the four pilot episodes. I, once again went back to playing in home territory, the South Indian, with shades of *Ghar Jamai*. But the producer lacked the clout to wrangle an approval from the channel and despite all his efforts, the tapes remained confined to his cupboard.

Years later, it caught up with me again. *Zabaan Sambhal Ke* was a transliteration of the original English title. Veteran filmmaker F C Mehra's son Rajiv Mehra picked a Tamilian, Parsi, Punjabi, Maharashtrian, Sindhi, Bengali, Sardar, Englishman, Arab and even an African to populate a classroom filled with Hindi bashing specimens. The teacher hired was film and theatre actor Pankaj Kapoor who would attempt to instill pride within the prejudiced, for Hindi.

As far as comedies go, *Zabaan Sambhal Ke* [1997], followed Aanand Mahendroo's *Dekh Bhai Dekh* and steadied the Metro channel's ratings. The play of words lifted the scripts beyond the mundane and the actors had a go at it with unbridled enthusiasm. When I was signed on for the show it was well into its seventh episode and the "class" had bonded well. I was the new boy in school trying to find my "seat". The students were my scoundrel colleagues from stage. English theatre regulars Hosi Vasunia, Keith Stevenson, Tanaaz Currim, Dinyar Tirandaz and Tom Alter shared the Hindi blues with 'vernacular stars' Shobha Khote, Viju Khote, her daughter Bhavana Balsaver [Yes, the whole family had moved in!], Viveck Vaswani, and Rajinder Mehra. Besides this melange, an African lad, Simon Asoyo also grappled with the tongue twisters of the language. Pankaj Kapur, as the teacher lost in translation, wasn't a replica of Jeremy Brown of *Mind your Language*, but brought to his character, Mohan Bharati, his trademark conviction. It was my first shot at playing a Bengali. An opportunity to shed the South Indian 'Subbu' tag. I was determined to go beyond the routine rolling of the Bengali tongue. Fortunately, the company of Bengali co-actors in theatre helped to polish my rough edges. So the *babumoshai* magician didn't stick out like a sore thumb. In fact, the *"gulla gulla rasgolla"* gibberish, which I had conjured up as the 'magic words' before an act, turned out to be quite popular.

Guest actors spruced up the episodes. To have Deven Varma, the actor who infused subtlety into comedy, was a delightful experience. Tiku Talsania, Johnny Lever, Tinnu Anand and Javed Jaffrey dropped in too. The series went on to have a successful run. Even a second season, on a channel called Home TV in 1998. By then, I had forayed into direction and commitments kept me from joining the gang again.

A decade later, in May 2010, Shemaroo, the software production major, released the video discs of *Zabaan Sambhal Ke*. The gang had a joyous reunion. But, the infectious rabble of the late Hosi Vasunia and Keith Stevenson, now an American citizen, was missing. "Let's do it again," was the password, but the unwilling smile on Mehra's face said it all. The plate tectonics of television had made it rather out of reach.

Saraswati Audiovisuals was the serene name that actor Jaya Bachchan chose for her software production house. Her first show, *Dekh Bhai Dekh* [DD Metro, 1993], was a comedy revolving around three generations of the Diwan family in their ancestral home. Aanand Mahendroo rented the defunct Savera cinema in Malad, a Mumbai suburb, and turned it into a sound stage for the multi-camera recording. An on-line edit console didn't exactly speed up post production, thanks to Mahendroo's penchant to re-edit until there were no optional takes left.

I was amused by Mahendroo's persistence while filming *Dekh Bhai Dekh*. In the two episodes I featured in, retakes kept touching figures above twenty as he relentlessly pursued certain evasive high notes of comedy. Scripts would be improvised on the spot by him and actor-writer Lilliput. All of which was very well, except that it stretched shoots beyond schedule. Reports had it that the four hundred thousand rupees allocated for each episode was found inadequate and Mahendroo often ended up doling out his own extra bucks. But that was the director in him. A cool-as-acucumber, live-life-king-size, approach. Twenty-six episodes down the line, Mahendroo invited me to consider directing the show. It was a tempting offer, considering the viewership the series had registered. But a few issues nagged me. Mahendroo had given the show a style that viewers had accepted. Also crowded frames with characters standing in a line and delivering dialogue wasn't up my street. I figured there was no option with so many characters in a scene, but I had another take on it. Which would call for a redesign of the blocking. I brought myself to politely turn down an assignment any director would have gratefully grabbed.

Towards the concluding session of the series, Mahendroo and his team of actors and technicians were all set to film a few episodes in London, but the spiralling budgets put paid to their ambitions. Quite naturally, the actors and director were peeved over their London dreams being aborted. Mahendroo rallied to fly down a small unit to fulfil the commitment. What ensued was a delightful ramble on the streets of London. The artistes were let loose to mouth their own lines, which were then dubbed with scripted words on return to India. It could rate as the most improvised exercise on television. The long-running weekly series ensured television stardom for Navin Nischol and Shekhar Suman who played the brothers. Veteran Shubha Khote's daughter, Bhavana Balsaver, wasn't far behind. Khote had foreseen a career for Balsaver as a leading lady in films. She had some impressive portraits of her daughter circulated too. For some strange reason, it did not materialize, despite the girl being more hardworking and intelligent than her peers. It must have been heartening for her then to see her daughter finally taste popularity, albeit on a smaller screen.

"*Kisiko mohabbat ka hai junoon, kisiko adavat ka hai junoon, koi muflasi ka mara hua, kisiko daulat ka hai junoon*"-Sunil Mehta and Prem Kishan, who put together the five year long saga on DD Metro, aren't too off the mark with their claim to *Junoon* [1997] having the most celebrated names assembled for a single show on television. Navin Nischol, Anita Kanwar, Parikshit Sahni, Tom Alter, Benjamin Gilani, Tanuja, Saeed Jaffrey, Farida Jalal, Archana Puran Singh and Mangal Dhillon were among the stars who dotted the *Junoon* landscape. The story of a showdown between the Dhanraj and Rajvansh clans had every ingredient that a viewer fished for in a soap. The 520-episode series helped the Metro channel effectively quell satellite competition. *Junoon* netted Rs 50 lakhs a week for the national broadcaster on the Metro channel before being shifted to the National Network late-night slot at 10:30 PM where it fetched Rs 36 lakhs a month (9 episodes) from additional spot buys alone. The late-night, non-performing slot was elevated from a two percent viewership to twenty-five percent. The simultaneous telecast in a dubbed Tamil version was a trendsetting move.

Junoon made me take a definitive step forward as an actor. Sharing screen space with the magical Tanuja, one of my favourite actresses, was a moment to cherish. As the man in her life in a crisis-ridden relationship, the scenes held scope to ponder and perform. Perhaps it was her sheer presence that put me on guard. I often got down to talking about her films. Particularly the time when leading man Sanjeev Kumar, after watching Basu Bhattacharya's film *Anubhav*, suggested it should be called '*Tanubhav*', to toast her performance. She merely smiled and took another puff from her cigarette.

To my utter surprise, the feedback for my part in the series came from the least expected quarters, when I met the acclaimed Bengali master Mrinal Sen a year after completing the show. As a keen student of his cinema, I got down to drawing him into a master class. It was during the course of that conversation, that he recalled "the series you did with Tanuja" and billed it as one of the most sensitive portrayals he had seen. That coming from Sen, the maker of *Akaler Sandhane, Mrigayya, Parshuram* and *Chorus*, I didn't grudge myself the feeling of being on cloud nine. It was a prized moment.

The channel continued to attract big names. Ramesh Sippy [*Kismat*, a soap garnished with thriller ingredients], Ravi Chopra [*Kanoon*, a Perry Mason inspiration] and UTV [*Sea Hawks*, a maritime drama]. In the first week of September 2000, the Kerry Packer-backed HFCL 9 Broadcasting India Ltd, decided to test Indian waters. In place of a full-fledged channel, they struck a deal with the Metro network, with a three hour prime time slot [evenings 7 to 10]. The terrestrial channel was named 9 Gold. The programming targeted family audiences with genres including drama, comedy, horror, and live events. Shows like *Kundali, Kavita, Kabhii Sautan Kabhii Sahelii,* and *Chonch Ladi Re Chonch* had a sizeable viewership. The channel was spearheaded by Ravina Raj Kohli who had relinquished her post as creative head at Sony Entertainment to independently drive a channel.

Kohli had a brainwave. Films for television, on the lines of HBO.

Called *Director's Cut*, these two-hour features premiered on Saturday nights and sought out names like Pankaj Parashar and Saurabh Shukla to direct. After *Sambandh* and *Mrigtrishna*, both television films, I now had an opportunity to film my first full-length feature.

The concept for the film was planted in my mind by the veteran actor Satyen Kappu during the picturisation of a series called *Alvida Darling*. Kapoo was on a trip down memory lane, when he was getting married to a small-town girl who had her face hidden behind the traditional *ghunghat* [a veil]. The newly married couple were at the bus station heading for Mumbai. He seated her down with the luggage, while he walked away to enquire about the bus timings. When he returned he was aghast to see his wife missing! Then in a flash, he spotted her. In the distance, she was following a porter who had picked up her luggage. Not wanting to lift her *ghunghat*, she had assumed that the porter was the husband. Actor Farouque Shaikh wondered aloud, what if she had walked away with the wrong man? That set the premise for a film. A comedy of errors turned inside out. Two boys get married to traditional village belles on the same day and their *ghunghat-clad* brides get mixed up with the wrong husbands in a railway station melee. When the boys discover the truth in the city, its too late. They are saddled with someone else's wife. The search begins for the right match, but the intervening period has a surprise in store. The girls discover that two perfect strangers had treated them with care and dignity. A new relationship, that defies tradition, blossoms.

Ghunghat Ke Pat Khol produced by Dinesh Bansal, was the second film in the Director's Cut series and evoked a heartwarming response. Joy Sengupta, Neha Pendse, Vishal Varma and Sucheta Paushe played the couples while 'storyteller' Satyen Kappu and veteran actress of the 1960s Shashikala brought up the senior brigade. I was very keen that filmmaker Hrishikesh Mukherjee, with whom I had struck a healthy camaraderie, watch the film on telecast. Of course, my anxiety got the better of me. But needn't have palpitated, though. After watching it twice in back-to-back viewings, *Dada* approved. He advised me to continue with such films that advocate social values, though he felt that the resolution to the mix-up in the film was unorthodox, even controversial. His words were silent propellers. *The Times of India* reviewer saw a theatrical feature film potential in *Ghunghat Ke Pat Khol*. My film making ambitions had got off to a clinical start.

Towards its ninth month, 9 Gold took stock of its achievements and claimed an increase in the viewership base of DD Metro from 15.6 million to 25.6 million in the 7-10 PM band. The time spent by viewers for the 7-10 PM block had increased by 89%. Yet, when it came to renewing the contract with Doordarshan, HFCL-9 closed the door on what had been an acrimonious relationship and declared it would not bid for the prime time slot on the Metro channel "due to the unrealistic non-financial terms of the contractual arrangements proposed by DD." The company announced that the television business of HNBIL on Metro would cease to exist from 10 September 2001. After that date, HNBIL would downsize its operations and a core team would remain to explore further opportunities. However, all the staff related to the DD Metro business were told to look for jobs elsewhere. HFCL 9 wrote off what industry sources estimated to be Rs 1,500 million in accumulated losses. After going off-air, it signed a contract with Star Plus and traded the entire library of programmes. DD found itself going it alone after its call for bids from private broadcasters was greeted with a lacklustre response. The three-hour band was fuelled with re-runs of popular shows *Yeh Jo Hai Zindagi, The Big Picture, Nukkad* and *Udaan*.

In January 2002, we heard the last of Metro. Prasar Bharati chose "low visibility" as the reason. Doordarshan's valued tributary, that could have given the private channels a run for their money, became obsolete. Directionless policies led to the amputation of its own arm. A handicap that worked to the advantage of the competition.

SHAIKH, RATTLE AND ROLL

My patience was wearing thin as the engine idled in yet another bumper-to-bumper wait. Lining the sidewalk, or whatever was left of it, two trees craned their necks towards each other engaged in discreet conversation. Yet another spread its tentacles across the grey sky like a mutant spider. Mumbai, with its concrete towers, had telescoped into the celestial ceiling. The man I was heading to in the congested complex of Andheri's Adarsh Nagar, Partho Ghosh, was basking in the success of two feature films, *100 Days*, a generous helping of *The Eyes of Laura Mars* and *Agnisakshi*, inspired by *Sleeping with the Enemy*. Television, in the latter half of the 1990s, had opened up a new avenue of additional income for filmmakers. Ghosh had wasted no time. In fact, he had a delightful concoction going. Titled *Chamatkar* [A Magical Occurrence], it had an unusual lead character. A family man who had an ability to pick up long-distance conversations. A trait that would later extend to infiltrating people's minds.

Farouque Shaikh, the charming star of films like *Garam Hava, Chashme Buddoor, Katha, Umrao Jaan, Bazaar, Shatranj Ke Khilari* and several Hrishikesh Mukherjee films played the inflicted chap Prem, infusing the happenings with his brand of comic timing. The catch was that the channel [Sony] had already begun airing the series, but apparently conveyed their dissatisfaction to Ghosh over its execution. A change in guard was what they prescribed after twenty-five episodes.

Ghosh and his executive producer had no qualms about a replacement but my heart went out to the director who was being shown the door. This was *déjà vu*. During the *Kohraa* series on Star Plus, Naved Antulay had replaced the director after two stories. I could be looked upon as some kind of usurper. Even as I tried to comprehend the situation, Ghosh's executive producer Raja delivered his no-exit verdict. If I was battling pangs of conscience, they would find someone else. It was a catch-22 between ethics and career. As I reluctantly opted for the latter, my mind tried to bury the guilt in a quiet corner. Ghosh then said that he would take the credit of "producer and director", leaving me with the crumbs of "episode director". Pragmatism got the better of me. I did not protest. Of course, Shaikh was apprehensive and rightly so. He didn't want the show to plummet further with this kneejerk decision by the channel. I applied myself to the task at hand. Preparation was, and still is, one of my strong points. The tradition of plunging into homework after returning from school had finally found its practical applications. The first day's shoot at the late filmmaker Devendra Goel's bungalow went off without a hitch. After the wrap that night, the executive producer called to say that

Shaikh was very satisfied with the day's work. "Ananth knows his job" was the solemn verdict. That, like they say, was the beginning of a beautiful friendship.

Farouque Shaikh was the first of the stars I rubbed shoulders with, after turning director. *Chamatkar* found him enmeshed in a whole lot of insane situations thanks to the chaos created by his super-acoustic abilities. The criss-crossing of voices his character heard, led to a merry comedy of errors. In the midst of the mayhem, Shaikh and I took great delight in taking on the establishment and several social deterrents. The end product was a result of several improvisations. The day's headlines would invariably find tongue-in-cheek references in the script. Of course, unlike John Cassavetes did, the creative producer didn't think that an "Improvised by Ananth Mahadevan" billing would have made sense here. The feedback from the channel executives was thankfully, positive and the ratings, smile-inducing. After five episodes, Partho Ghosh relented. He relinquished the Director's tag and stayed content as Producer.

The best episodes of *Chamatkar*, and Shaikh wholeheartedly agreed with me on this, were the pre-election episodes. With Parliament polls round the corner, we played national-lampoon with the contesting parties and their candidates. No one was spared. The episodes were deliberately shot just a couple of days before telecast so that they were headline fresh. Bihar Chief Minister Laloo Prasad Yadav's white hair being attributed to the flour in a grinding mill found immediate connect with the fodder scam he was allegedly involved in. Shaikh reveled in the expose' and had a field day. Until, alarm bells were sounded. After the third episode was telecast, apparently an unruly mob had gathered outside the Sony television office premises protesting against the caricatures. That night, phone calls about the unrest kept coming fast and furious. We wondered whether we had pushed the envelope beyond repair. But then, no party was in power and that insured us from any chance of being sued or picked up by the law.

For the 'centenary' episodes of the series, the channel suggested that we recruit special guest stars to make an appearance. Producer Ghosh's proximity to the film folk made this easy. Actor Aditya Panscholi, cricketer Vinod Kambli and the maverick composer-singer-actor-filmmaker Kishore Kumar's son, Amit Kumar. Kambli had just broken a leg. He was recovering, and ambled on to a location full of fanboys who had just one query – when would he get back to playing for India? The episode revolved around a plot to sabotage Kambli's cricket career by some ugly bodyline bowling. Shaikh premeditates the plan and foils it in the nick of time. Kambli's famous sixes were what we were eager to feast our eyes on. His partnership of 664 in a junior league with Sachin Tendulkar, of which he had scored 349, was the kind of stuff prodigies were made of. Kambli limped, asked us to bowl short and dispatched it promptly behind the ropes. Uncannily, the plot from the series in which someone attempts to put a spoke in his game, seemed to have a phantom-like grip on his career. It wasn't quite the Kambli of yore we witnessed after that. The losing semi-final against Sri Lanka in the World Cup match at Calcutta saw tears escape him. To worsen matters, the case of a possible match-fixing in 2011, witnessed the cricket fraternity come down on him like a ton of bricks. His heart surgery, in 2012, was the nadir of his career. That's when he would have hoped for a *chamatkar*.

The Amit Kumar episode saw me enter the portals of the hallowed Kishore Kumar bungalow [*Gauri Kunj*] at Juhu Tara Road after a long time. It was in 1982 when I had first set foot there. Kishore Kumar in one of his famous moods, had 'banished' the press and refused to meet journalists for a long while. One day at the advertising agency, his public relations officer R R Pathak, called to tell me that Kishore*da* would relax the ban for me and give me an audience for *The Daily*. In the fashion of a disciple, I sat in front of him, taking in the magic air of his sprawling living room. He spoke to me for over two hours, displaying rare candour and wit, and even showed off his stub of a toe that was severed when, as a child, his foot grazed against a sharp vegetable cutter in the kitchen. At the end of it all, came a question that was brand Kishore Kumar. *"Ananth tum mere saath abhi teen ghante tak baithe ho, tumhe kabhi laga ki main pagal hoon?"* ["You have been with me for nearly three hours now, did you ever get the feeling that I was a mad man?"] It was a remark that wasn't to be sullied by an answer. I merely smiled. He continued, "You are a theatre person, call me over sometime for a performance, even I would like to be entertained". A statement so poignant, said under the garb of nonchalance, with an ever so fleeting wistful catch, it makes me sad even today as I recall it. The interview that appeared in the tabloid, *The Daily*, was pruned due to want of space, but delighted him. When his son, Sumit, was born after his marriage to actress Leena Chandavarkar, he called on me to design the baby's first birthday card. The evening he succumbed to a heart attack, I was performing a play titled *"Jaane*

Na Doongi" at the Prithvi theatre. The team and the audience paid a two minute homage to one of the greatest entertainers of the country. The show went on. It was a comedy. Yet, so sombre was the mood, that no one even sniggered for the full two hours. They felt it would be disrespectful to the departed soul.

Amit listened in rapt attention as I recalled those moments nearly a decade later. At the window above, I caught a glimpse of a silent and lonely Leena Chandavarkar, almost symbolically silhouetted against the setting sun. She looked down at the ruckus below. Her late husband may not have taken lightly to a film crew entering his house. We carried on quietly, shooting the episode that featured Amit Kumar losing his voice, as someone spiked his drink, before Shaikh stepped in to weave his rescue act. Today, in his mid-sixties, Amit Kumar's voice resembles his '*baba's*'. Of course I could never muster enough courage to invite his *baba* to a performance. No show could ever have been worthy of his wizardry.

Outstation shoots for situational comedies like *Chamatkar* were a rarity, but the channel suddenly decided to loosen its purse strings for a two-episode stint in Calcutta. This was what I had eagerly been angling for some time now, because television I felt, had stagnated indoors for a long time. Calcutta has always had a character unlike any other city. I found myself looking for elements quintessentially Calcutta or, at best, something unusual.

I found it while on a pavement, facing the new Howrah Bridge, I spotted an unusual meeting of rail, road and sea. This was where I would begin the episode. I would then move on to the sprawling Howrah Bridge and film in a boat that wound its way under it. It was a visual that played in my mind ever since I watched *Khamoshi*, the Asit Sen film with Rajesh Khanna and Waheeda Rehman. Hemant Kumar's "*Woh shaam kuch ajeeb thi*" was a number that haunted me both for its composition and the way it was filmed - with the bridge adding to the mesmerizingly romantic atmosphere. Shooting there was my little tribute to Calcutta and its cinema. The next stop was the iconic tram, threatened with extinction. It was a prop that you could hop on and off while the actors improvised.

Those were the days when programme executives were instructed to attend script readings of each episode before they were filmed. Suggestions poured in at every opportunity, as the overseeing process turned, occasionally, into an ego assuaging exercise. When I shot the ending of a *Chamatkar* episode differently from what was written, Anupama Mandloi, the Sony creative head, probably driven by protocol, promptly shot out a protest memo to the producer. When I argued that the revised end had more punch than the original, I was told that changes could be implemented only after a prior notice. The "suggestion box brigade" at the channels, over the years, has demonstrated frenetic activity. The flip-side to this was when the executives approved the draft of a *Chamatkar* episode which I rated as sub-standard writing. I insisted on it being re-scripted and surprisingly, they agreed. I hoped that my move conveyed the other side of the coin. That a director's reputation was as much at stake as the executives' accountability.

Somewhere around the 125th episode, voices of dissent reverberated in Ghosh's office. An erratic payment schedule was the cause. Ghosh sprung an amusingly nasty one on me. He lamented that the series was exceeding its budgets and he wasn't saving anything on the project. This was in direct contrast to the channel maintaining that the ratings were good enough for their chief operating officer, Kunal Dasgupta, to "finally erase the red mark off my balance sheet". I figured that Ghosh was planning to milk the cash cow. If I quit in disgust, he could get to recruit a director at half the salary. The series was anyway merrily cruising along and could be set to auto-pilot. Ghosh's intentions received an unexpected thrust, when a bizarre twist in fortunes [*see next chapter*] made me fall out of favour with the channel creative heads, Kunal Dasgupta and Raveena Raj Kohli. Ghosh pleaded helplessness and said it was a channel decision not to continue with me. I was forced to withdraw from the show. Ghosh, still citing a financial loss, got away by depriving me of the remuneration of the last two episodes. Trapped between channel politics and an unrelenting producer, I had to draw heavily from my resource of mental strength and patience to see those days through. *Chamatkar* stuttered along with a new director and wound up after completing another forty-odd episodes. I couldn't help feeling that if they had only let things be, the show had the potential to go on uninterrupted.

Despite the break, the 'honeymoon' with Farouque Shaikh continued, albeit a couple of years later. Shaikh, the ever encouraging friend, was waiting for the right opportunity to bond again. If he had a grouse against me, it was my tearing hurry to get somewhere. And in the process taking on too much work. His handwritten letters to this effect are something I reflect on, in hindsight. He had a valid point, only it took me a few years to realise the gravity of his words.

For the second coming, it was a marital comedy produced by Dinesh Bansal. A warring couple knocking on the domestic court's door for a divorce is asked by the marriage counsellor to spend a year together to renew compatibility. While the husband and wife are hell-bent on proving they are not, their children invent ploys to keep them together. Titled *Alvida Darling* [Goodbye Darling], it had Varsha Usgaonkar, another popular big screen actress, making her debut on television. What could have been a perfect antidote to domestic blues on a weekday evening, was allotted a Sunday morning slot by Zee Television. It was an hour when even real-life couples, who were in the middle of a marital discord, took a well-deserved break from their partner. Often, channel chiefs dismiss fears of an unorthodox slot with "a good show works on any slot" or "we are building this bandwidth with a high profile show" theory. But in most cases it's the product that becomes the sacrificial goat. *Alvida Darling* drew acclaim from its faithful audience and ran its distance of 52 episodes, but I couldn't help voicing my protest. A refreshingly different concept and product had been robbed of a sizeable viewership thanks to indifferent programming.

Tailpiece: One hot afternoon, on the sets of *Chamatkar*, I had decided to do away with the mandatory lunch break to accommodate an overload of scenes. Farouque Shaikh, sensing my discomfort said, "It isn't some masterpiece that will fetch us the Oscar. It's merely another episode that will be forgotten after telecast. So, let's eat". I kept pondering about his statement for a long while. This was a lesson in pragmatism. It also fuelled my urge to break-away from the 'mortality' of television to the posterity of cinema. I did not fancy being trapped, a la Chaplin's *Modern Times*, in factory-mode for life.

THE INVASION
OF THE SERIAL
SNATCHERS

America's radio, Broadway and film star Billie Burke once said of Hollywood, "To survive there, you need the ambition of a Latin American revolutionary, the ego of a grand opera tenor and the physical stamina of a cow pony". I was soon to discover that though Burke may have said this in the early 1900s, she could well have licensed the description to cover the burgeoning Indian television arena.

Dinesh Bansal was an entrepreneur who set his first footprints on television soil with a series called *Kurukshetra* [Zee TV, 1995], helmed by the veteran film director Lekh Tandon. The series was remarkable for the discovery of a promising new actor Ashish Vidyarthi, who later went on to win national laurels in Govind Nihalani's dark film on terrorism, *Drohkaal*. It was writer Sujit Sen who initiated a dialogue with Bansal. I got talking about the possibility of a second season of Sridhar Kshirsagar's comedy

Ghar Jamai. The 'north-is-north and south-is-south and the twain *shall* meet' concept held a pan-India appeal. The new South Indian boy on television, R Madhavan, could play the title role and Satish Shah could be called on to pick up where he had left off as the nagging Punjabi father-in-law. With satellite television making in-roads, the accusation that derailed the original series–of precipitating communal differences, was old hat. Like I had shared earlier, Kshirsagar found the offer a godsend and relinquished the rights for a fee as meagre as twenty thousand rupees. That included the catchy title score, a fusion of North and South arrangements. Sadhana Singh, the leading lady of Rajshri's sleeper hit, *Nadiya Ke Paar,* was pencilled in for the mother-in-law and Mandira Bedi, now popular for her *Shanti* avatar in India's first daily soap by the same name, was brought on board to play the daughter. With Gracy Singh [who would later be picked to play Aamir Khan's leading lady in the Asterix-versus-the-Romans style film *Lagaan*], as Mandira's sister, the casting was as good as it gets.

The pilot episode took all of three days to film. Then popular, now extinct, Naaz Café atop Malabar Hill in South Bombay, featured as a key location. This was amongst the last few shoots held there. Shah was excited about the witty script and the meticulous shot break -up. "You are shooting this like a film" he exclaimed. Armed with a first episode of considerable merit, I offered to make a presentation to the Sony channel heads, where *Chamatkar* was having a good run. The proposal caught Bansal's fancy. Though he was known as a Zee channel loyalist he was eager to expand his footprints to other platforms too.

Kunal Dasgupta had a permanent smile pasted on his face as he watched the pilot. I didn't take my eyes off him. His reaction was an instantaneous "we'll take it", unmindful of displaying the enthusiasm of a child who had acquired a new toy. Bansal was granted three hundred and fifty thousand rupees for an episode, a handsome budget for its time. A contract was drawn up, a set erected and a filming schedule set in place. The mandatory bank of the first four episodes was canned. *Ghar Jamai* was ready for a comeback in a new avatar.

Looking back, I wonder whether I should *not* have taken a break at that point. How was one to foresee what would transpire the moment I turned my back? Besides, I had earned it. A holiday was the least I deserved for a successful show on air [*Chamatkar*] and a brand new one set for telecast. The far East, Thailand, was a good choice for a brief vacation. The reclining Buddha did a lot to soothe my senses. But in less than a week, my enlightenment was to be rattled by topsy- turvy ways of the world.

On the evening of my return to the city, I was greeted with a phone call from a friend who said how much he loved the first episode of *Ghar Jamai*. Even as I wondered where the preview happened, he spilled the beans. The episode was telecast at half past seven in the evening on Zee TV. I failed to understand how another channel could have telecast an episode pre-sold to Sony, that too on non prime time. I enquired further. Maybe he had seen a repeat telecast of the first season. "With R Madhavan in it and your name as Director?" he shot back. I froze. This was like a nuclear leak from an espionage film. It couldn't be happening! Only Bansal would have the answers. Pleading helplessness, he gave me a version that I couldn't chew on. Apparently, Zee was upset when they learnt that Bansal had sold a premier, star-studded brand like *Ghar Jamai* to another channel. So, the latter was emotionally arm-twisted to sell it to Zee. The subsequent breach of contract with Sony would be handled by Zee's legal team and Bansal indemnified. He would return the monies Sony had paid him. The first episode had to be immediately put on air so that Zee could lay claims to ownership. I asked him whether he had stopped to ponder about the embarrassment and flak I would face at Sony. But he dismissed any cause for worry. Zee would flaunt *Ghar Jamai* on prime time with a promotion campaign that would be the envy of Sony. Besides offering me more shows in future in return for my co-operation. The Thailand unwinding came undone. I sunk into my sofa, trying to make sense of the unimaginable turnaround.

The folks at Sony, justifiably, looked bamboozled. I couldn't blame them for coming down on me like a ton of bricks. Dasgupta and Kohli sounded like an off-key choir condemning the breach of trust. But that was only the beginning of my troubles. A clause was laid in front of me like a cyanide pill for a convict. I was to have nothing to do with *Ghar Jamai*. That would tantamount to me being an accomplice in crime. I was too stunned to react. *Ghar Jamai* was my baby. The idea of its rebirth on television was mine. Yet here I was, being asked to abandon my creation. I tried to reason with Dasgupta. It wasn't my fault. I wasn't even around when it was all engineered. But they wouldn't care less. If I chose to go away with a man who had defrauded them, I would have to relinquish *Chamatkar* too. Additionally risk being blacklisted by the channel.

Billie Burke's words came back at me like a bolt of lightning. This was not just bad, it was the toughest I had encountered so far.

The solution to the conundrum was made on a vague mathematical hypothesis. This was Topol's *Fiddler on the Roof* moment for me. On one hand, there was the option to continue with Sony, on the other hand, *Ghar Jamai*, a show about to take off with high profile actors, would be given on a platter to some lucky, though less deserving, candidate. On one hand, I could decide not to give in to Sony's pressure tactics, on the other hand I would kiss goodbye to a hugely successful series and a prominent channel. On one hand, I could accept Zee's offer to put me on a pedestal, on the other hand...enough!! *There was no other hand!* I had no choice but to go with *Ghar Jamai*. *Chamatkar* had reached its 150th episode, *Ghar Jamai* was just beginning. I couldn't overlook the new for the old. I was aware that I was only trying to convince myself. Bansal and Zee's glee was unabashedly on display. I had played into their hands. Kohli and Dasgupta reviled me for unethical behaviour. I was the fall guy, the scapegoat flavour of the season. Partho Ghosh had it tailor-made for him. Just when he was hoping I would step down so that he could bring on a director who charged less, the elements obliged. Tormented, I tried reasoning with Kohli one last time. But she would hear nothing of it. And it only agitated her further when a prominent newspaper quoted me on the fallout. I realised that it would take me forever to mend these burnt bridges.

Ghar Jamai opened on Zee to a whopping 14 points on the rating charts and stayed there for several weeks. I gradually got over the trauma of being indicted for a crime I didn't commit and soaked in the success of the show. It was the first instance of the lead actor of a serial's first season returning to direct its second outing. Zee's overseas footprints, particularly in the United States of America, widened the viewership for the series. The Indian American audience, in a feedback study, found it "the wittiest and finest comedy from India so far". Those words were balm for my troubled soul. It was sweet justice for resisting the temptation to go over-the-top like those awkward farces disguised as comedy. Shah and Madhavan resembled Tom and Jerry as they indulged in a game of being one-up. Though Satish Shah preferred to look at his Mr Mehra as Hagar the Horrible. The scripts adhered to the intended comedy of manners, even as the Zee executives were baying for some less subtle stuff. Sony, not to be upstaged, struck back with a comedy, *Hum Sab Ek Hain*, that had multiple Indian regions locked in a culture conflict in one huge residential complex. It was their way of saying that what *Ghar Jamai* could do, we could do with a bigger roster of actors.

As we neared the 70th episode, I had a visitor one night. It was Madhavan, Maddy, as we had now begun addressing him. He sat me down and, like a scriptwriter, narrated a story. A true story. Mani Ratnam, the celebrated director of Tamil films like *Nayakan, Roja* and *Iruvar* was impressed by his showing in the series. He was looking to cast him in the lead in a new film he was planning *Alaipayuthey*. It would be a life-changing moment for him. But then, he couldn't be part of *Ghar Jamai* any more. Would I accede to his request and free him of the obligation?

I did not think twice. There was no way I would tie an actor down to a television series, when a career in cinema beckoned. We shot an additional five episodes and bid goodbye. Maddy went on to star in Ratnam's film and became a major star in Tamil Nadu. He returned to the Hindi fold just when I was to debut as a film director with *Dil Vil Pyar Vyar*, India's first retro-musical, based on the published compositions of R D Burman. Years later, around 2016, Maddy felt that *Ghar Jamai* should be for perpetuity. *Ghar Jamai - The Movie*, sounded like a great idea. I went back to Bansal and Subhash Goel, the chairman of Zee. They politely desisted from parting with the rights. "We don't give away our intellectual property," were Goel's parting words. I smiled. 'Property' that was given to them by the man who had created it. Creativity had become a real-estate deal. Whoever bought it, became its owner.

The taking of *Ghar Jamai* from Sony marked a watershed moment in the annals of Indian television. It sparked off the first-ever channel war. A face-off that bares its fangs to this day. Software producers, actors and directors were now made to sign contracts on the lines of the age-old studio system and had to swear allegiance to the channel they appeared on. No more cradle-snatching. Any alliance with a rival was akin to selling out to the enemy. A breach of trust, like the *Ghar Jamai* trade-off.

THE BUSINESS OF ENTERTAINMENT

Their incessant cawing was playing on my nerves. The cacophony of the congregation on the tree opposite my apartment sounded like a choir gone awry. Then suddenly, as though on cue, the crows took to flight, only to re-assemble in a minute. They had devised this game to keep themselves busy and entertained. I desperately needed to emulate their feat, if only to rid myself of the aftermath of the fire on the sets of *The Sword of Tipu Sultan*. This was no time to play a sympathy card with friends and producers. In fact it was time to take the plunge. As producer. Not that the grass looked greener on the other side, but simply because I couldn't stay unemployed any more. My software engineer friend, Shivashambhu, was very clear that entertainment needed to be a business and I should have my strategies worked out. He even suggested a name to that effect. He aptly christened my company, Entertainment Business Corporation [EBC]. At that moment, I had no inkling that tackling the 'business' aspect wasn't the same as producing entertainment.

"Let's take a walk and talk", he said as we left his office and headed towards his Beach House apartment in Juhu. It was one of those sultry afternoons of 1996. I was connecting with Shekhar Kapur after quite a while. The walk was *déjà vu* - of when we had walked on the streets of Pune delivering dialogues for that long take in *Mahanagar*. He was the creative head of the newly instituted Business India Television channel [Bi TV]. I figured that it was a good way to launch my production house. Under his auspices. "Go the full hog", he suggested, as we discussed the style of comedy to be deployed in *Memsaab* [Woman of the House], the sitcom that Bi TV had approved for one of its opening slots. The central character was loosely inspired by Lucille Ball [*Here's Lucy*!] and possessed all her fumbling, feather-brained traits. The script is the thing on television and I was fortunate to convince three veteran writers of the time to pen the episodes. Bhushan Banmali [filmmaker Gulzar's erstwhile co-writer], Satish Bhatnagar [a key member of B R Chopra's script department] and Ranjan Bose [who had a long association with Basu Chatterji and his films]. Tanaaz Currim had an effervescence few theatre actors matched. Her only stumbling block was the language. Being a Parsi, Hindi wasn't one of her comfort zones. But there was the enthusiasm to work hard and learn. She wouldn't want to chuck a title role because of a linguistic handicap. She took on the role of the madcap housewife with a fervour that made me forget that I had originally approached Radha Seth and, later, Sharon Prabhakar to take on the part. As her harried husband, Harsh Chhaya was the foil who revealed a comic talent strangely not explored after *Memsaab*. But Prabhakar remembers the offer to this day and occasionally appears to rue her decision not to do it.

The pilot was shot by veteran Alok Das Gupta, the cinematographer of the cult comedy *Chalti Ka Naam Gadi* and filmmaker Shakti Samanta's *Aradhana, Amar Prem* and *Amanush*. But the ailing Gupta, expressed doubts about handling the pressure of a long-running series I looked around and recruited a bright young lad Manoj Bellare who had cut his teeth with Baba Azmi. Bellare warmed up to television demands and went on to film most of my projects and the partnership lasted for more than a decade. The shoestring budget did not deter me from a luxurious three days shoot for each episode. Attention was paid to minute details of scripting, casting, set décor, camera work and performances. *Memsaab* discovered relatively new faces who went on to become household names on the tube. Amongst them Sanjay Mishra, Sandhya Mridul, Amit Behl and Navni Parihar.

Being your own boss did have its advantages. Or so I thought. The transition from terrestrial to satellite was bound to court problems. The folks at the newly constituted satellite offices had this air of superiority, tending to look down on Doordarshan (DD) and dismissing pilots as DD-influenced products. I had shot the pilot of *Memsaab* on the prevailing high band recorders and tape and upgraded it to Beta resolution. The Bi Tv technical check team smelt a rat. I had to summon all my wit and technical upgrading facilities to stop them from issuing reshoot orders. To become a producer with a hundred thousand rupees in the kitty wasn't easy at all.

Memsaab went on air and was the first Bi TV show to attract a sponsor, even if only a city-based fashion store. Fourteen episodes down the line, the payments that were trickling in so far, dried up altogether. The production ground to a halt. I had exhausted my investment and the debts to technicians and suppliers had reached an embarrassing figure. The folks at Bi TV finally let the cat out of the bag. The channel was neck deep in financial trouble. They offered to return the rights of the series in lieu of me waiving payment. Better the crumbs than nothing at all! Armed with a payback of fourteen episodes, I sold the show for a two-time telecast to Star Plus. The weekend telecasts elicited quite some acclaim, but fourteen weeks weren't enough to build a new audience. The paltry sums were handy though. I paid off the actors and technicians, but couldn't foot the bill of Manu Dadlani, the owner of a post-production studio Video World, whose edit suite I had hired. Dadlani, would have his pound of flesh. Years later, on the sets of *Hera Pheri* for Star Plus, I had a visitor. Dadlani it was. He demanded that I pay off his dues, now that I was engaged as a director. The abrupt closure of the channel that bogged me down in a five hundred thousand rupees loss wasn't his concern. Rightly so, I thought. Sattee Shourie bailed me out by advancing me a cheque to see Dadlani off.

This move left me pondering about the unforgiving nature of show business. Here was Dadlani, a man who had even launched a series with me called *Butlerjee*, based on Wodehouse's improbably wise, comedic creation Jeeves. I was still to receive my remuneration for the pilot I shot. Regardless of that, he chose not to spare what I owed him. Well, you live and learn, as they say. Expect no favours and do not be shocked by the business-like ruthlessness of the world. His monies recovered, he went back to being a friend. His customary birthday greeting would beep for years, until he suddenly stopped.

I was keen to dismiss the Bi TV experience as a one-off aberration. In an attempt to keep the company afloat, I found the newly-opened television wing of NEPC Airlines an invitation to continue as producer. This time it was a comedy of three generations that lived under one roof. Even the location was chosen to represent the hierarchy. The patriarch stayed on the top floor, the middle generation on the mezzanine and the young blood on the ground floor. The affinity of the grandfather for his grandchildren drove the parents up the wall. *Parivaar*, warm, funny, with an occasional tear was designed for all ages. This time I faced a bigger challenge. I was given a ridiculous figure of a hundred thousand rupees to film each episode. The actors and technicians were hired on heavily discounted fees. As producer, I would be happy to break even and maintain a turnover. Like in *Memsaab, Parivaar* discovered another set of bright actors. Anoop Soni, Riju Bajaj, Anita Kulkarni, Joan David, Hemant Pandey and Amit Behl amongst others. They rubbed shoulders with veterans like Rakesh Pandey and Meenakshi Thakur. Ranjan Bose continued to weave his glorious middle-class humour, an attribute that had rubbed off on me after working with the champions of the genre - Sai Paranjpye, Basu Chatterjee and Hrishikesh Mukherjee.

Parivaar didn't even get as far as *Memsaab*. The cheque taps were parched after the eleventh episode. This time I could see it coming, but not early enough. I froze production and boarded a flight to Chennai to sound the alarm bells with the Khemkas, the owners. The usual syrupy talk ensued. I was like a brother to the corporate family, so non-payment of dues was unthinkable, blah, blah, blah. My second name should have been Lord Gullible. I waited for six months for the cheques to show up in the mail as promised. Before that could happen, the owners came up with another bright idea of compensation. They would issue coupons that could be redeemed as flight tickets on NEPC airlines. But even as that carrot was kept dangling for a long while, both—the television channel and the airlines wing of the company—downed their shutters. I learnt that six hundred crew members of the airlines had been issued the pink slip. In Mumbai, a furore amongst aggrieved producers like me, evoked no response. The Khemkas had disappeared from the radar.

By a strange coincidence, I had yet again ended up with a five hundred thousand backlog. A cumulative deficit of ten lakh rupees. It was a case of right content, wrong channels. I was left with no choice but to emulate the corporates who had commissioned me to produce for television. Like their channels, EBC closed shop. I have to admit though, the new experience was a valuable lesson learnt, for a heavy tuition fee.

THE TWILIGHT ZONE

It wasn't *just* the star factor that was at work here. I had shared screen space with the intense actor in *Bedardi, Dil Kya Kare, Ishq* and *Pyar To Hona Hi Tha*, but there were other incentives that were the clinchers. Ajay Devgan's (now, Devgn) maiden television production *Devi* [2001], was an attraction, simply because it came at a time when channels were kissing weekly slots goodbye. At a press meet to announce the weekly in the time of dailies, I whacked Gabriel Garcia Marquez's title and made it my own. I likened *Devi* to 'Love in the Time of Cholera'. The time, energy and thought that could be devoted to an episode a week, was virtually non-existent in the daily format. Ensconced within four walls or multiple staircases of a sprawling house, the pressing need to deliver an episode a day probably could ill- afford the luxury of outdoor spaces and elaborate camera movements that would entail time and expense.

The writers press the panic button if any episode drops its rating resulting in decibel levels being raised all round. Devgan was clear that *Devi* wouldn't opt for such tactics to keep it going interminably. His ground floor Juhu office was the operation centre for the series. It was from this place that Ajay's father, Veeru Devgan, had designed all those exciting stunts for several popular Hindi films of the 70s and 80s. Quite naturally, the place imparted the feel of an era, when cinema was stand-alone and was available only in theatres. Television had infiltrated like a super spy that blew the cover off the movies and its stars. Along with it, their secrets, non-proximity and enigma.

The plot of *Devi* defied the label of a genre. I coined the term 'socio-mytho' for want of anything better. The presence of an undercover goddess in a contemporary setting made it both surreal and eerie. It was Indian television's first full-fledged foray into the twilight zone, albeit devoid of vampires and ghouls. Back in the late 1980s, Ravindra Peepat [an erstwhile assistant of filmmaker Raj Kapoor] had strung together short stories in the genre. *Honee Anhonee* was a slick production and had me playing one of my early grey characters, a brother out to usurp the family property. Doordarshan, true to its 'disbeliefs', had raised a finger objecting to "propagation of irrational thoughts". Ghosts and other assorted spirits had to bide their time till the Ramsay brothers, known for their horror features like *Do Gaz Zameen Ke Neeche*, opened shop on television with the *Zee Horror Show*.

The Ramsay brothers - Shyam, Tulsi and Keshu - had made a living out of spinning horror yarns on cinema screens. With satellite television lifting Doordarshan's embargo, the scope for their stock of horror situations was limitless. Their first episode of the Zee Horror Show with Archana Puran Singh's severed head served on a dinner plate was telecast in 1993 and the series lasted a healthy 364 weeks. Each of the brothers took turns directing episodes while Gangu Ramsay operated the camera. Popular television names like Pankaj Dheer, Deepak Parashar, Vijay Arora, Gajendra Chauhan, Javed Khan, Risabh Shukla and their ilk starred in one-off episodes. Though it didn't merit comparison with America's *Late Night Horror Show* stories, the Ramsay brothers did succeed in weaning viewer interest towards the fright factor on television. The success of the show led to quite a few spin-offs like B P Singh's *Aahat* later in the decade.

With the *Zee Horror Show* focusing on the scream-in-fear quotient, the window for paranormal activity was wide open and *Devi* stepped in. Around the same time, Hollywood-based, Indian origin filmmaker Manoj "Night" Shyamalan had done more than a bit with *The Sixth Sense* and *Unbreakable*, both of which had aroused considerable interest in India. Misha Gautam [film director Desh Gautam's son], who had assisted Devgan in the special effects department of the latter's film *Raju Chacha*, had a penchant for off-beat thrillers. He concocted the plot for *Devi* after revisiting Raj Khosla's hugely popular *Mera Saaya*, the film around a mystery woman [Sadhana]. Not wanting to replicate *Chase a Crooked Shadow*, he wrapped the lady in a divine garb and bounced it off to Devgan. The latter's actress wife, Kajol Devgan flagged off the series at the sprawling Poonawala Bungalow in Mumbai's Madh Island. Madhoo, Devgan's leading lady in his debut film *Phool aur Kante* was recalled to play the girl whom Mohnish Bahl [veteran actress Nutan's actor-son] reluctantly weds to please his parents. He then conspires to kill her, on a visit to the holy shrine of Vaishno Devi, to accommodate his philandering ways. The return of the 'dead' wife into the household, throws his life out of gear and what ensues is a cat-and-mouse mind game. Despite the supernatural element, the episodes refrained from any outlandish treatment, making the mystery seem credible.

After all the initial enthusiasm, and the subsequent filming of an hour-long pilot presentation, it was a pity that Madhoo could not make the final cut. In the family way, her plans of resuming her acting career went on the back burner. To this day she rues how she missed a character that would have made her push her limits. Exit Madhoo, enter Sakshi Tanwar, who was a popular face after playing the virtuous Parvati in Ekta Kapoor's daily soap *Kahani Ghar Ghar Ki* [Star Plus]. Amongst the younger breed of new faces on television, Tanwar was perhaps the most promising. Devoid of conventional good looks, she broke her typical daughter-in-law image with a studied performance. On location too, she and Behl maintained a respectful distance that strangely seemed to add to the friction between their characters. For me, it provided an opportunity to go full throttle on drama, a genre I had left behind after four back-to-back comedies. The series consequently took on the likes of a film on television. I didn't know whether to believe it or not, but the grapevine was abuzz with news about Ekta Kapoor religiously watching each episode and her daily soap directors borrowing a page or two from the camera angles and treatment. The crash zooms and swish pans I had invented were solely meant to recreate an aura of the place. To my amusement, they found their way into every other situation and close-up in soaps. Television became a breeding ground for the camera being used like a broom.

I remember reading that Italian master Bertolucci had once condemned this indiscriminate style. I had not intended this, but I silently plead guilty.

The biggest incentive for me to pick up *Devi* was, of course, the channel that aired it. It marked my return to Sony, with all errors and omissions overlooked. Though the old guard wasn't at the helm of affairs now, it was time that once again mended broken bridges. Besides corroborating the cliché that there are no permanent friends or enemies in show business.

It was perhaps a journey I would not have undertaken on my own. A pilgrimage to the shrine of Vaishno Devi in Jammu's Katra. *Devi* was the first series to film there although Gulshan Kumar, the man who founded T Series, a music company, had obtained permission to do a few devotional videos hitherto. So the invitation appeared godsend. The plot to kill Tanwar's character by luring her to the shrine and then pushing her off a cliff was kept under wraps from the authorities. We were only required to film the arduous walk up the steps and the *darshan*. The actual 'push' would be executed at Tiger Point, a steep mountainous area that matched the terrain of Vaishno Devi, closer to Mumbai near the Western Ghats at Khandala.

The trek upwards from Katra began after sundown. It served the purpose of keeping the sun off your back, but did not provide for the fatigue that had set in after an eight-hour shoot promptly after landing in Jammu. So Tanwar, Behl and I - as a unit - commenced the climb. Paved with devotees and music cassette stalls, the route was a mélange of images. Battling sleep we kept walking, as though an unseen force was prodding us on. In a career that now spanned close to two decades, I had mingled business and pleasure. But this amalgam of business and pilgrimage was a first. And not without its ironic moments. A group of devotees who crossed us chanting *Jai Mata Di*, the refrain of the Goddess, stopped in their tracks on recognizing Tanwar, the daughter-in-law from *Kahaani Ghar Ghar Ki*. Devotion took a back seat as they stopped chanting and instead chose to discuss the soap and its seemingly unending course. Discussion over, they picked up the chant and were on their way. This was God taking a back seat while obeisance was being paid to television.

The fourteen kilometer climb was covered at the break of dawn. Forty winks and a quick shower later, we were led into the sanctum sanctorum by crawling through a tunnel. Legend has it that even the most obese yet 'pure' devotee manages to wriggle himself through the narrow space while the leanest yet impure of heart could not. But the less adventurous among us preferred to walk through a normal tunnel constructed on the side. Worship done, work took over. We began filming while climbing down and wrapped by sunset when we had reached base at Katra. Surprisingly there were no signs of fatigue on what was otherwise a strenuous day of work after a sleepless night. It was either passion or the divinity of the place. I would like to think it was the latter. We could all do with a little miracle in our lives.

Devi debuted with television rating points of 3.8 and peaked during its run at 6.9. It was amongst the last of the successful weekly soaps. Even here the rapacious virus of cutting corners struck. After about

70 episodes, the channel began eyeing a one hour slot for the show with enhanced budgets. But Misha Gautam, also co-producer, had reason to not rethink the director's fee. It had a Partho Ghosh ring to it. The familiar sob story of a loss ridden balance sheet. I couldn't figure out how a show that was completed on schedule and fetched bonus marks for the producer on the ratings chart could register losses. After the prescribed first season of 52 episodes, Gautam appeared to have differences with Devgan. There was this creepy feeling of *déjà vu* and I opted out rather than being hung out to dry. Expectedly, another director came on board at one-third the price. I watched the 'new' *Devi* every Friday night. Every cliché that I had judiciously avoided during my tenure, marred the episodes, turning it into an hour of mumbo jumbo. A sorcerer, and even the goddess herself, started manifesting themselves, subtlety be damned. But like someone said, God's second name cannot be 'damnit'. Tanwar, too, found herself being replaced by another actor, Juhi Parmar. The show managed to cling on for another fifty episodes. From the fables to this day, the golden goose has always been up for the kill.

Whether it was the popularity of *Devi* that made producer Amar Bhutala and Sony reach out for Harkisan Mehta's Gujarati bestseller *Sambhav Asambhav*, they wouldn't tell. Bhutala, with whom I had completed the very satisfying *Main*, had been clinging on to the rights of Mehta's reincarnation saga for three years. But in the summer of 2003, I got together with veteran Vikram Gokhale,, Sangeeta Ghosh, Shakti Anand and Pooja Ghai to enact another twilight zone experience. On the death anniversary of Gokhale's wife, his son Anand gets his fiancée, played by Ghosh, to meet his father. Ghosh is enveloped by visions of a previous birth and her proximity to the would-be father-in-law. The reincarnation theory of three lives in disarray was clearly treading on thin ice. It could implicate incest. A delicate balance was what I set out to achieve, playing up the mystery and its unfolding rather than delve into a moral discourse. The maturity of viewers would be tested. I realised that they preferred to see a goddess-in-a-wife, in *Devi,* rather than reconcile to the idea of a wife returning as a daughter-in-law. *Sambhav Asambhav* did not match the ratings of *Devi,* but challenged the director in me. Constraint and sensibilities were the passwords to unravel this drastically unconventional conundrum.

Trends revealed that episodic stories of the supernatural were preferred to long-running soaps. *Aahat,* by B P Singh, provided the right doses and entrenched itself as the new long-running 'horror' show after the *Zee Horror Show.* Characters that returned from the dead piqued audience interest. Even if conveniently resurrected like in the daily soaps that lined the end of the decade. They also revived dead ratings. Reincarnation, incidentally, had become a perfect antidote to a writer's block.

BACHCHAN'S BILLIONS

Circa 2000. It was brewing for a while. Talks about film star Amitabh Bachchan's foray into television. The rumour mills were reveling in the attributes. If it wasn't a career on the cusp of reinvention, it was supposedly the debts that weighed him down. Star Plus' Sameer Nair, however, went about it with Winston Churchill like efficiency. During one of my ideating sessions with him [when directing those three shows for Star], I reacted with child-like excitement to the Steven Spielberg portrait strategically placed on his television set. "I have him observing me all the time", chuckled Nair. Obviously the inspiration to pull off ambitious projects came from the right quarter. "*Who Wants To Be A Millionaire*", the hugely successful and popular international show was being discreetly sourced for the Indian market. The show played all over the world, except Japan, that did not advocate the concept of "gambling". A master move by Nair, to combat the rival Zee network and resuscitate their rating points. But not even Bachchan, by his own admission, had foreseen the catapult for Star. From a lowly number three, to the top of the charts.

Bachchan's participation evoked the expected scepticism. I was privy to groups turning into all-knowing prophets of doom. "*What works in formula films will not work on TV*", "*Imagine diminishing his status to that of a television host*", "*Did he need this at this stage of his career?*" "*I give it three weeks before it bows out*" - the self-styled critics were having a field day. Strangely, Bachchan himself echoed some of the sentiments. "Yes, I was most apprehensive about the idea of going on to the 'small screen', as were most of my family members. I felt that the uncertainty of my ability to pull off something like this was weighing more than the actual danger of reducing my size from 70mm to 21 inches. But as is with most pioneering efforts, since there were no yardsticks or examples to use for reference, I merely took the decision, and the plunge. I have never thought of myself as being in possession of any stature or for that matter being some kind of a star. I looked upon this as another job to be done and that is how I approached *Kaun Banega Crorepati*."

But yardsticks did exist. The fact that most hosts of '*Who Wants To Be A Millionaire*' around the world had been news anchors, moderators or television presenters must have been playing on his mind, but Bachchan, the thespian that he is, betrayed no nervousness. "I would assume that by bringing mention of news anchors, moderators and television presenters, you somewhere proclaim them to be of lesser quality and status, in comparison to movie actors. Nothing could be more incorrect. Having played both roles, I can state with certainty that they are both equal in their quality, intensity and effort. In many ways television is more strenuous and exacting because one has to be constantly thinking out of your mind in *ad-lib* fashion, unlike cinema where there is a written, predetermined format. I am no thespian, but even if I were one for arguments sake, my response would have been the same."

Of course, it wasn't a cakewalk. The pressure to live up to the images of earlier hosts like Regis Philbin loomed large. Star TV carted Bachchan to London's Elstree Studio for a ringside view of the game hosted by Chris Tyrant. The management and the presentation of the show impressed him greatly and he told Star that if they could provide similar production values, he was on. "They did, and I came on. The reference points on how the show was to run were given to me, but most of the language and the atmosphere for the show, including the idea of a 'prelude' before each episode was mine. I saw Regis much after I had finished with the first season of *KBC*. Regis was a better talk show host, with *'Regis and Cathy Lee'*, a very popular show, rated among the top three breakfast shows in America. Incidentally, I was once a guest on it, way back in 1990." But while Philbin still has difficulty in getting names right, Bachchan demonstrates his fine skills in perfect Hindi and English.

It was intriguing to see the actor in him grappling with the host who was taking over. Although I felt he was warming up to don the mantle fully, Bachchan didn't express much concern. He admits to dutifully following the black book on production to the tee. "And yes, add a few from my own personal vocabulary. The expressions that became associated with the show were in fact off the cuff remarks that I would teasingly indulge in during the rehearsals. I kept up with them in the final version too, without ever being conscious that they would become popular".

The quiz show, as it eventually unfolded on prime time at 9, turned out to be just the perfect escapist entertainer that the small screen was wanting. Most viewers used to pride themselves by knowing the first ten answers. Some even imagined themselves scoring over the lucky ones on the hot seat. The 'soft' beginning was what Bachchan warmed up to. "Yes, most of the first few questions were relatively easy, but as we went up the money tree they became a lot tougher and there were many revelations. A sort of a learning experience for me too".

Kaun Banega Crorepati was the forerunner of revenue earning for mobile network companies. I once called in to "enter" the contest only to find the lines congested. In fact, the waiting period itself would have upped their profits. It was often argued that people contested the show more for the awe of being at handshaking distance with Bachchan, rather than demonstrate any general knowledge skills. A point that Bachchan vehemently denies. He insists that I drop the "awe" bit. 'They all came to play a game, to win. Of course, I empathized with contestants and felt awful when they lost out. That was by far the most difficult part of the show". Quite often the "come on" look on his face seemed to collaborate with the feelings of participants and will them to win. But Bachchan denies ever developing a bond with those on the hot seat. "That would be against the rules if I collaborated or even gave a hint of it in my behaviour."

I am not sure where the rumour originated, but I suspect it had its roots in versions of the game in the United Kingdom. Audiences seeking the ultimate escapism would run out of patience when participants would fall short of the big prize money. Hence, the pressure was on the channel to ensure that someone wins at regular intervals to keep the excitement of the viewer going. They did, with an episode that spilled over to the next evening, keeping the audience on tenterhooks. When the one crore bubble finally burst and the confetti exploded on Mr Bachchan as he declared "you have created history!", to a beaming Harshvardhan Nawathe, the first winner in India, doubting Thomases reared their head. *"Was this one rigged?" "Did they stage-manage it for TRP?" "Ah, so cleverly done to put the punch back in the show"*. I guess that's the risk factor most reality shows have to live with...the authenticity of a win. Mr Bachchan sidesteps the issue with the class of a batsman refraining from fishing outside the off stump. "I am unaware of this philosophy. You would need to address this to the management that ran the channel".

Kaun Banega Crorepati held on doggedly for 300 episodes on the trot without a first-season break. That could well be a record of sorts for its genre. Bachchan's charisma was largely responsible for the dedicated audience. But then, there was always the fear of tiring out. Of audience fatigue setting in. And this show was no exception. It bowed out to return in different avatars. A second season, and a kids' special that ran on Sunday mornings. Besides spawning several other look-alikes chaired by other film stars like Anupam Kher, Manisha Koirala [*Sawaal Dus Crore Ka*, Zee] and Govinda [*Jeeto Chappar Phad Ke*, Sony], it also opened up a Pandora's box of reality shows. Suddenly "reality" was the new mantra... quiz shows and song-and-dance contests were more attractive than the soap. If Mr. Bachchan was amused, he wouldn't tell. "Yes, several attempts were made towards similar programming, but the uniqueness of *KBC* could not be replicated". He doesn't want to risk a wager on the trend either. "Television aficionados would be better placed to assess whether the reality show boom was inspired by the popularity of *KBC.*"

Neither does he seem to regret having missed out on the third edition of the show. It is still ambiguous why the channel chose to field another anchor. Was the youth appeal of Shah Rukh Khan a better bet? Or was it merely to effect a change of scene? The move was reflective of the mounting pressure on channel heads to perform. It marked Khan's return to home turf after *Fauji* and *Circus*. Though he exuded his trademark effervescence, KBC faithfuls were yet to get over the Bachchan persona. He was to the show what Sean Connery was to Bond. Roger Moore, Pierce Brosnan and even Daniel Craig all came a close second. The result was the curate's egg. The third instalment's charm gradually wore out and left the game show's return with a big question mark. Mr. Bachchan's dignity and diplomacy held forth. "Star TV chose other, more popular, stalwarts to conduct the show. That was their call. I am happy that I was able to be a part of it initially".

Bachchan remembers Siddarth Basu, the producer of KBC, mentioning Vikas Swarup's book, *Q&A* which was published while he was hosting the show. Danny Boyle's 2008 film, based on the book *Slumdog Millionaire,* cast Anil Kapoor in Bachchan's role with the latter 'appearing' in an autograph sequence. It swept every major global citation including the Oscars, but left an oddball feel in many an Indian viewer's mind. Not Bachchan's though. He doesn't subscribe to the view that *Slumdog Millionaire* rode off the success of the show. In fact I was quite surprised that the climax of the film, where the show was telecast live for sheer convenience of the script to bring together the estranged lead pair, didn't bother him. Bachchan maintains that it was a beautifully scripted film and the idea to incorporate the game show, quite creative and unique. For me, it was Danny Boyle's reputation that preceded him.

At the end of the day, *Kaun Banega Crorepati* led people to participate with childlike excitement. Was it just the lure of money or something else, is a query that foxes Bachchan too. "I have no idea what it was, but I would imagine the very format, the production values and the spirit of the winning and losing contestants, all contributed. The audience adopted this baby as their own and personalized it in their everyday life. They watched it and played along with it too. It became a family affair, both entertaining and educational, an almost unbeatable combination". One would guess that with the economic slowdown at the turn of the decade, the show would be just what the doctor ordered. The perfect prescription for quick money and escapism. To borrow a phrase from Bachchan, "another unbeatable combination"!

After three editions, *Kaun Banega Crorepati* shifted base from Star to Sony for its subsequent seasons. With Amitabh Bachchan returning as host. And the show returning admirable ratings. The fifth season saw contestants who were selected from the hinterland. Small-town hopefuls who chased an improbable dream. The media labeled it as "peddling misery porn" to inflate ratings. But when a bashful computer teacher from Bihar, Sushil Kumar, won the first ever five crore booty in 2011, it was an epiphanic moment. It exuded more drama, euphoria and suspense than the very-fabricated soap operas. An elated Bachchan exulted "*adbhut*" [amazing!] and later blogged "What a sensational day in the studios of KBC! A young man from the interiors of Bihar, earning a meagre salary of just Rs. 6,500 per month, coming from the most humblest of backgrounds, reaches the hot seat and cracks the ultimate prize -an incredible feat!" It was very strangely, a mirror of *Slumdog Millionaire*.

2012: I am on location filming my latest biopic *Gour Hari Dastaan—The Freedom File*. Theatre and advertising expert Bharat Dabholkar, who plays a cameo, lets me in on the goings-on behind the scene on KBC. Dabholkar has been recruited to shortlist contestants on the show. Most of them preferred the 'dignity' of Bachchan to the 'feverish presence' of Shah Rukh Khan. Their stories of aspiration and heartbreak too could fill the pages of a fairy tale. There was this girl who made it to the final studio round. Her boyfriend from the village found this the perfect opportunity to get a Bachchan handshake and was all geared up to accompany her to Mumbai, when he met with an accident and was paralysed below the neck. Not to be undone, he asked her to dial his number when she reached the hot seat. That would make him talk to Bachchan. Fate did not take her beyond the preliminary fastest-finger-first round and the boy's dreams crashed.

With different themes for each season the *Crorepati* race crossed its 11th season in 2019. The occasional film being plugged into the game by inviting the stars to play is an entertaining turn. Many a time, a screen hero looks flummoxed by the questions which are quite elementary. But since the prize money goes to their favourite charity, the noose isn't tightened. It's when the real people sit down to play that the adrenaline shoots up. In 2019, Sindhutai Sapkal, the "mother to a thousand orphans" on whose incredible life my first Marathi film *Mee Sindhutai Sapkal* was based, was the guest of honour. Bachchan graciously acknowledged her by touching her feet and mentioning the film that won 4 National awards and made her a celebrity. It was a defining moment for me too as Bachchan had launched the music of the film in 2010. Life was a game show that had come full circle!

Bachchan shied away from the fiction route as he was wary about the demands on his time. Further, the last minute schedules and hurry to upload an episode the very next day, wasn't his discipline of work. But eventually the moment arrived, and *Yudh* with him as the all-pervading patriarch dropped on the Sony network. I had always been euphoric about watching him either live on stage or in a television show. Maybe if *Yudh* had been better designed to suit his long-awaited debut, the Bachchan persona would have commanded more time on the soap operas.

Kismat – Directed by Ramesh Sippy with Kanwaljeet Singh

With the cast of *Ghar Jamai*

In *Kohraa*

Ravi Chopra's *Kanoon*
with Deepak Parashar

Chamatkar – Nandita Puri and Farouque Shaikh

Live on *Star Yaar Kalakaar* with Farida Jalal

On Location in Kolkatta, for *Chamatkaar* with Farouque Shaikh

Shekhar Suman, Sonal Seghal in *X Y & Zee*

In *Amar Prem* with
Farha Naaz

In *Kabhi To Milenge* with
Rati Agnihotri

With Cricketer Vinod Kambli on the sets of *Chamatkaar*

Directing R Madhavan and Satish Shah in *Ghar Jamai*

In *Kabhi To Milenge* with Tanaaz Currim

With Rajesh Khanna at the launch of his Television debut

With Sakshi Tanvar on the location of *Devi*

With my set of actors on location for *Parivaar*

With Neena Gupta in *Amar Prem*

Raj Kiran and Dimple Hirjee in the Ransom episode of *Kohraa*

Joy Sengupta in *Sir,* an episode of the *Rishte* series

In the film *Badshah* with Shah Rukh Khan

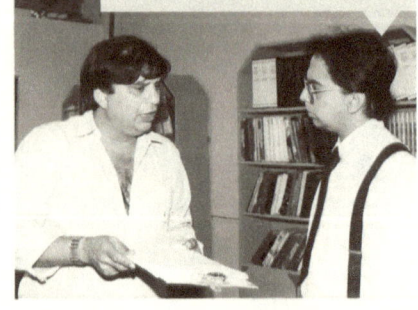

On the sets of *Kanoon* with director Ravi Chopra

K K Menon in an episode of *Saturday Suspense*

Farouque Shaikh and Varsha
Usgaonkar in *Chamatkar*

Rohit Roy, Shekar Suman
in *Hera Pheri*

The first cover to feature me...
with Naseeruddin Shah,
Pankaj Kapur, Sadiya Siddique
and Kiran Juneja

The late Farouque
Shaikh's letter

Farouque Shaikh

Dear Big Boss,
        Wish you the very best
for this evening — and always!
You are becoming like a
TALENT KA MALL!
Everything, high quality,
under one roof!

Tons of luck
Farouque Shaikh

1102, Highland Park A-New Link Road, Oshiwara, Andheri West, Mumbai 400 053
Telephone: Tele/Fax 2636 9893 E-Mail:

EPISODE

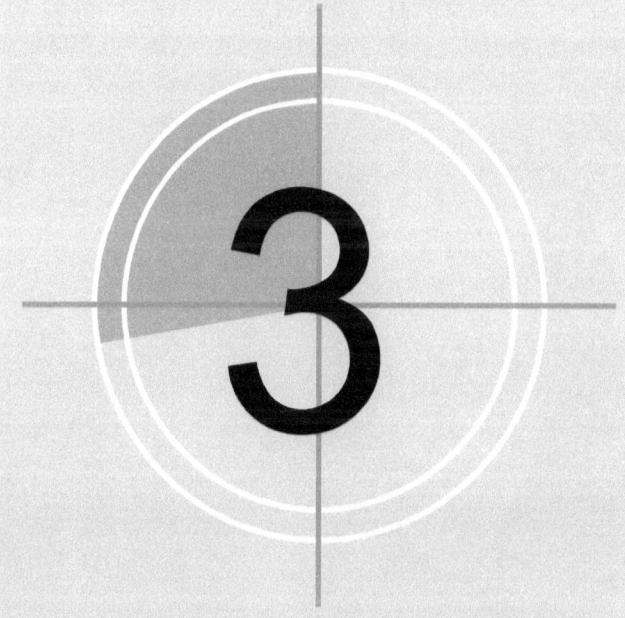

THE NEW BEGINNING

It is said that in California, they don't dispose of trash. They merely turn it into television. I could thank my stars then, that I could not have arrived at a better time in the annals of Indian television. The new millennium has few candidates to genuflect on a Tamas or Mirza Ghalib. This in an age where our television prides itself of a 150 million viewership and close to sixteen thousand crore rupees running in its veins, third on the list after China and the United States. Yet, it appears to be spiraling out of concepts and control, evoking Apollo 13's "Houston, we have a problem". Are we then regarding what is but a diagrammatic representation of the days of glory? Graham Greene may have a hidden hint in his statement- "to achieve the impossible, we must attempt the absurd".

THE TV SUPERMALL

"I find television to be very educational. Every time somebody turns on the set, I go into the other room and read a book". Of course, Groucho Marx had the liberty to say anything and get away with it. I was hoping that Marx's dig and the California trash theory, which I had read with much amusement in an American periodical, would have had their sell-by date. But the cumulus clouds of television programming began hovering around the beginning of the millennium. Billowing into more than two hundred channels, India's television resembled a super *bazaar* that flaunted more take-away counters than fast food outlets.

I scrolled down the channel menu to soak in the variety. On most of them, the revamped Indian family order reigned. Whoever ordained that it was the day of the nuclear family stood corrected by shows that reveled in joint family proliferations. The phenomenon that assumed the label of the "*Tulsi-Parvati* brigade", a synonym for daughter-in-law versus mother-in-law conflicts, had its origins in two shows judiciously cooked up by popular star Jeetendra's enterprising daughter Ekta Kapoor, who along with her mother Shobha Kapoor, set up Balaji Telefilms, their television software company. Ekta whose initial efforts to woo Doordarshan were met with indifference by the higher-ups at Mandi House, returned to her Juhu Bungalow with a vengeance to make *Hum Paanch* a success on the satellite network. The lady who would be nicknamed 'television queen', had visualized the daily episode format as a wishing well for whipping up sentiments in housewives who deserved a break from kitchen chores. She threw in coins of ruminative images and reaped a bountiful harvest. Both *Saas Bhi Kabhi Bahu Thi* and *Kahani Ghar Ghar Ki* altered the way we were on the tube. Smriti Irani emerged as the new face of soaps, embarking on a career in the performing arts almost like taking up a challenge to prove her worth on merit. Quite unsurprisingly she didn't relate to all the melodrama in the soaps she performed in, her life, as she once admitted, being quite the opposite... boring and devoid of the syrupy moments of television despite being a Miss India finalist. Destiny shepherded her into Parliament cutting the umbilical cord with her hard-won showbiz laurels, overnight. Her journey itself, has the arc of a classic female empowerment series... from activist and actress to a governmental order. Star Plus, in the bargain, had finally cracked the TRP *Da Vinci* code.

Kapoor had unwittingly ignited a fuse that sparked off a new hobby amongst software companies - trendspotting. The mother-in-law became the new, all-pervading entity on television. Replicated in every series, she was a picture of contradiction. Bellowing about tradition and family values on one hand and elbowing the daughter-in-law on the other. The rating scales tipped up to 25 points when disappearances, deaths and resurrections occurred. The characters, created by Kapoor and generously preyed on by others, held fort for more than half a decade before the doppelganger effect threatened a lock-out in the soap factory. There was a nine-out-of-ten chance that on any given evening, every channel had a marriage happening in their prime time shows. Women, as either victims or vamps, all decked up in finery with the mascara intact even as they woke up each day. When I broached this, the creative executive of a channel was unapologetic. "Our audiences have multiplied in the heartlands of the country where they revel at the sight of the perfectly made up housewife at all times of the day. Even in bed, she'll have her mascara on", she added without batting an eyelid. The marketing section too, I learnt, had a major say in the brainwashing.

The recurring joke in South India was that in the days of yore disturbed spirits would come out after seven in the evening, now the vamps emerged. As I drive past Balaji Telefilms' imposing building in Andheri, I see a queue of wannabes aspiring to be the next Tulsi or Parvati. They have their pictures and *curriculum vitae* on hand and meticulously hand it over to the security at the window, the look of aspiration on their faces, perhaps their only "natural" moment.

The early breather came in 2003, when Sony picked up the rights of the popular Spanish series, *Ugly Betty,* and turned it into *Jassi Jaisi Koi Nahin.* No one grudged the makers Diya and Tony Singh the element of inspiration. After all, it provided a welcome break from the 'in-laws are outlaws' wave. It also introduced a new talent, Mona Singh, to viewers who willingly gave her a fan base. But even as the *saas-bahu* formula was on the wane, another fad waxed. Around 2008. A Total Available Market (TAM) database revealed that the number of television sets entering lower income group homes was on the increase. That was what prompted writers and channels to land up in the unexplored hinterland of Rajasthan, Bihar and Maharashtra, ushering in the age of the girl-child. *Balika Vadhu* [the child bride] on the, then, newly-launched Colors channel initially struck as a whiff of fresh air addressing an age-old social issue. The writer, Purnendu Shekhar, an ex-Zee television executive, had written the script in 1992 and intended it for a movie. The show professed to trigger off a change of heart in families craving for a male heir, until it landed itself in Parliament in 2009, when a member damned it as a "regressive, anti-law show that glorified child marriage, while offering platitudes at the end of each episode". A show that intended to act as a reflection of the practice of child marriage and lack of women empowerment, had begun working against itself.

Then the fall-out began. A band of self-appointed pundits on an 'eradicate social ills' drive, invaded channels like Zee, Star, Sony and Colors with titles like *Agle Janam Mohe Bitiya Hi Keejo, Uttaran, Na Aana Is Des Lado, Bairi Piya* and *Geet Hui Parayi*. Rural India, hitherto considered unworthy of television upgrade, found unexpected patronage by television honchos. Local terms like "*maasa*", "*gauna*" and "*hamaar*" became the new lingo.

The out-of-the box thinking was, on the face of it, a good measure to adopt. A badminton star finds her dreams shattered after a man, her father's age, molests her. The series *Kaali Ek Agnipariksha*, appeared to have been inspired by real life—the Ruchika Girhotra case in 1990 that involved the molestation of a 14 year old girl, Ruchika by the Inspector General of Police S P S Rathore in Haryana. A spate of honour killings found their way to the tube with *Rishton Se Badi–Pratha*. Even the reservation policy found a voice with another stretched title, *Armanon Ka Balidan Aarkashan*. Bridegroom kidnapping, a matter of concern to young brides in Bihar and Uttar Pradesh, found an outlet in *Bhagyavidhata*. Perhaps the one that outdid them all was the story of a dwarfed girl, *Baba Aiso Var Dhoondo,* that featured a real-life dwarf, Juhi Aslam who was subjected to ridicule and isolation. But the 'causes', pitched as hyperintense drama found it trendy to glamorize and revel in exotica, rather than project stark reality. This 'purported' face of truth included dominant characters like Ammaji in... *Laado* having no qualms about her son remarrying when his wife couldn't bear him a child. Besides, several other instances like abuse, rape, female infanticide and domestic violence perpetrated on girls in their late teens added to disconcerting queries.

With farmer suicides, widow remarriage and honour killings, the spectrum of social evil was complete. The relevance factor in *Mann Ki Awaaz Pratiggya* went as far as having the educated small-town protagonist opting to marry an eve-teaser. And later, her in-laws plotting to burn her alive. Obviously, the signals sent out weren't too healthy. I caught a viewers' poll on television with a boy rooting for a wife like Anandi from *Balika Vadhu*. One who would do everything for her husband, including school homework. For millions of viewers, these soaps had become a daily fix, an insidious entrapment. Romanticising social issues as a representation of Indian culture, is not an act that modern day television pleads guilty of. It didn't take us long to deduce that the soap factory had merely come "under new management". *Hum Log, Rajni, Stree* and TV18's *Bhanwar* [an episode of which, cast me as a parent who indulges in child-abuse] and Aruna Raje's expose' of male chauvinism *Shaadi Ya...* had approached the reform cell with far more restraint and conviction.

In an interview to the media, the erstwhile programming chief of Colors, Ashwini Yardi, had justified the excessive social consciousness content as great improvements on the prevalent kitchen politics. But, her defenses were culled by the protests of Kishore Tiwari of the Vidharbha Andolan Samiti who was aghast at the misleading portrait of farmers in *Bairi Piya*. Television executives, dismissed these barbs, claiming that the end result was positive and the woman emerged as a revolutionary icon. Rajesh Kamat, then CEO of Colors, was quoted saying that revenue pressure made it mandatory to be a smart operator rather than a safe operator. Star India's Anupam Vasudev was a willing accomplice. "It's about programming better, staying ahead of the game", he declared. In what seemed an attempt to break the clutter, big-screen director Sanjay Leela Bhansali opted to adapt Govardhanram Madhavram Tripathi's four-volume Gujarati classic *Saraswatichandra* into a long-running series[2013]. The novel had been adapted into a film of the same name in 1968 featuring Nutan. An off-beat romantic drama of a man who seeks to redeem his ties with his betrothed after she suffers a bad marriage, the soap made television stars of its lead pair Gautam Rhode and Jennifer Winget.

As though to underline their theories, the soaps are proving to be popular in the neighbourhood too. In Afghanistan, the gun-toting rebels, it seems, ease their hold on the trigger when they watch Indian television beamed into their lair. A smart aleck observer commented that this was the perfect opportunity for vested forces in Afghanistan and Pakistan to annihilate the enemy. With software outsourced from India's television supermall, of course!

Afghanistan's indulgence may be attributed to its proximity to India, but the surprise was sprung by a report from Brazil where the most popular soap in 2009 was a series about Dalits and Brahmins titled *Caminho Das Indias* [Passage to India]. Brazilian actors play everything from a *pandit* to a *bahu* to a patriarch, dressed in *sarees, kurtas* and other Indian ethnicity. That Brazilians like Indians, are suckers for family-centric sentiments, explains the eager wait for an episode each evening. The *bindi*, the self-imposed laws of untouchability, arranged marriages, the dowry system and other complexities have led the average Brazilian to discover more about the psyche of India through the box. Like on Indian television, the authenticity of such a soap did lend itself to questioning there too. Like us, they, too, have come to live with the shenanigans of glamorized drama.

The 'rural awareness programme' would no doubt hit a saturation point like its predecessor. As each trend hits a trough in TRPs, the search for the next-big-concept begins. So the formulae roll on-television writers bear the brunt of it. They have the unenviable task of producing scripts that do not let audience interest waver. They could do with a bit of affirmation from Michael Preece, script supervisor on films like *Mutiny on the Bounty* and *Ben Hur*. He also directed most of the episodes of *Dallas* and *Streets of San Francisco*. He said, "Don't you worry, every third episode is a good one". Yet, until there is a drastic increase in the number of households used for sampling by the ratings companies, the challenge persists. TAM, a subsidiary of the US based AC Nielsen company, monopolises the ratings measurement barometer. The viewing preferences of about 8000 households determines which programmes make it to the advertisers' budget. The Information and Broadcasting Ministry urged the number to be increased to at least 30000 in the ensuing years. Still paltry by Indian viewing numbers. The proliferation of some dubious agents, who bribe the metered households with plasma screen sets and manipulate ratings of shows, is another grey area that has reduced the credibility of many a popular show. The accusations of manipulating ratings culminated in NDTV taking on AC Nielsen. The court case prompted more broadcasters to raise a timid finger like we did back at school. I see "rigged" becoming the watchword in India. Be it elections, cricket matches or television.

Regardless, general entertainment channels continue their consumer-driven agenda based on "market-research". Their templates include mega episodes, crossover shows, in-show promotions of upcoming films and weekend spillovers. The exposure to long hours of passivity throws up a question, "Why has television come to mean everything but what it was meant to be?" Earlier we were stimulated. Today we are carpet-bombed. There isn't even space for end credits as we watch shows telescope into each other for fear of losing eyeballs! There could be both a psychological and sociological explanation as to how they arrived at this 'model'. It is, common knowledge that no one dresses up like those women, not even the Tata and Ambani daughters-in-law. One could conclude that all that display of clothing and jewellery is subtle salesmanship at work.

Which brings me to the case of a pet rabbit Jia Xiaoyu in China which is hooked on to South Korean soap operas so much that she doesn't desist from tearing open pillows and attacking her owners if they switch channels. It isn't too comforting then, that rabbits multiply the fastest.

THE LAST LAUGH

"The human race I prefer to think of as the underworld of the gods. When the gods go slumming, they visit the earth. And what they saw mostly was uncelestial folly." God of comedy, Charles Chaplin's words might just ring true, if he decides to pay a visit to the genre on Indian television, with its modern-day curmudgeons trying to stick a knife into our funny bone in the hope of eliciting laughs. A 2009 study by a German academic revealed that humour is actually not meant to lighten the atmosphere but an act of aggression. The ability to make others laugh is seen as the control which people exercise to show they are in charge. That aptly defines Chaplin's craft. Television's most popular genre had lost its way in the beginning of the millennium, buried under the daily soap opera wave. Strangely the abandoned soul found a rescuer in cinema but its recycled big screen avatar was a hugely underwhelming effort. In the middle of the last decade, the Sony channel officials thought it an opportune moment to have a dedicated comedy station. They converted SAB TV which they had shopped from the Adhikari brothers into a full-fledged channel for comedy shows.

In their hey days, American humourists Woody Allen and Carl Reiner along with their boss Sid Caesar were popularly known as the triumvirate which had cracked the code to successful comedy. In his writers' room, Caesar formally dressed, would brandish a fake machine gun in front of his writers. If a joke went home, the machine gun would be silent, but one sour punch-line and the gun would go off "shooting the line down". It was indeed the misfortune of creative heads and comic writers in India that this technique wasn't heard of. If they had, my guess is that, most of the writers would have learnt to bite the bullet.

If Kundan Shah was bemused by the new form R K Laxman's Common Man had assumed in *R K Laxman Ki Duniya* on SAB TV, he did not tell. For, he distinctly recollected the author as one with an oblique vision, when he set out to produce *Wagle Ki Duniya* [Doordarshan 1988], a tribute to the cartoonist's creation. "I think Girish Karnad was first approached to direct the series but couldn't be on the same page with Laxman. Then I was recruited. Laxman was one of the geniuses I met in my lifetime, the other being the poet Majrooh Sultanpuri. I was a student in front of Laxman." Shah initially classified the cartoons into compartments. Office, school, home, streets and government cabins. But he soon discovered that the caricature in a cartoon was different from the human shape it would assume in an animated form. Pertinent, when one observed the criticism that Steven Spielberg faced from some quarters for going overboard with the motion control technique while filming *The Adventures of Tin Tin*. But the foot-in-the-mouth moment for Shah was when he inadvertently addressed Laxman as "Mr Wagle". "What did you say?" remarked the writer. Shah realizing his gaffe, quickly rectified it to "Mr Laxman". Upon which the maverick satirist surprised him. "Thanks for calling me Wagle, I feel more at home". Followed a reading of the episodes in Laxman's house. The central character Wagle, indulged in double-takes, which had the unit in splits. But Laxman promptly applied corrective measures. "Don't attempt an obvious comedy" was the funny man's dictum. "We had to become Laxman to see his point of view, the new version on SAB TV did not go beyond using his name". For me, as an actor, *Wagle Ki Duniya* had remained an egregious omission. So I sought to make amends by sending feelers to the creative producer of *R K Laxman Ki Duniya*, about my desire to feature in it. After Shah's observation, I wasn't too unfazed when my friend Balwinder Singh Suri did not get back.

Comedy in the satellite era did have its enjoyable elements. Rajiv Mehra after *Zabaan Sambhal Ke* had moved out of the Metro channel into SAB TV to create *Office Office* [2001] with a new set of actors, while retaining Pankaj Kapur to play the harried Mussadilal, a victim of red tape. The socio-political bite that was missing on television after Om Puri's portrayal in Basu Chatterji's *Kakaji Kahen*, was back. Musaddilal was, in many ways, the antithesis to Chatterji's *Rajni*. He was the hapless common man driven from pillar to post in government offices as he sought to over-ride corruption and plain indifference and find a way out of a knotted situation. It was a cattle-class Indian's adventure through bureaucracy - spiked, stirred and shaken.

Satish Shah was candid enough to admit that *Ghar Jamai* was the precursor to the hilarious concept of *Sarabhai Vs Sarabhai*, a family of fumbling members, who failed to see eye-to-eye with each other, leading to situations of one-upmanship that made the 2004 show on Star One, probably among the last of the truly funny times on television. Satish Shah played in tandem with the infectious energy of Ratna Pathak Shah. Sumeet Raghavan, Rupali Ganguly and Rajesh Kumar were the catalysts to each episode, resulting in a healthy run of 60 weeks. An attempt to revive the camaraderie in 2017, only met with partial success. However, my dream project during those days, was to do an adaptation of the popular American play, *The Odd Couple*, with the biggies of the small screen-Farouque Shaikh and Satish Shah. It remained a dream, thanks to the prohibitive budgets and channel policies being revised to make a production of this scale unfeasible.

The one that had taken the cake, and the bakery, as far as political satires went, was the BBC sitcom *Yes Minister*, back in 1980. The sequel *Yes Prime Minister* came on in 1986 and played for two years. The British producers found the Indian political scene more than conducive for a Hindi adaptation. They collaborated with NDTV to produce *Ji Mantriji*! with the versatile Farouque Shaikh playing the eponymous part. Whilst filming *Chamatkar*, Shaikh had raised my adrenaline levels by recommending me for the crucial part of the department secretary in the show. It was eventually played by Jayant Kripalani. The British and European references were replaced with Pakistan, SAARC and the Commonwealth. Befittingly, R K Laxman caricatured the opening title. Star TV bagged the rights for the season of 38 episodes.

As a major part of the decade passed sans comedies, I was prompted to probe further. A senior programming executive remarked with nonchalance, "Oh, comedies are no longer the flavour on television". It was akin to saying that there should be no more children in society. An axiom like that certainly wasn't sweet music to its exponents like Kundan Shah, Basu Chatterjee and their tribe. I found myself being distanced from the tube, but in the summer of 2007, I gave the nod to a sitcom planned by my friend Dr Anuj Saxena who had earlier flirted with films [*Sar Aankhon Par*] and other shows as a lead actor. Amongst them, Aanand Mahendroo's *Aasman Se Aage*, an ambitious adaptation of Ayn Rand's opus *The Fountainhead*. Vikram Bhatt directed the series that was eventually relegated to the backburner as Mahendroo found the budget beyond his capacity. Saxena's credentials as the owner of Elder, a thriving pharmaceutical company, fetched him bigger glory but show business remained the apple of his Eden. The concept of *Gupshup Coffee Shop* had a premise not attempted in television comedies in India. A café run by four women and the ensuing owner-patron interaction was reminiscent of what the Coffee Day, Starbucks and Barista chains have turned out to be. Navneet Nishan, after Tara, had an opportunity to go stellar with co-actors Sudhir Pandey and Eva Grover. Anuj Kapoor and his team from Sab TV greeted the opening episode with a warm round of applause, giving me reason to feel that television wasn't so painful after all. But, maybe I had spoken too soon. After twenty episodes, the sentinels of creativity bared their fangs and tweaked the scripts. The suggested raise in decibels of the sit-com and rather illogical plot points were not in keeping with the original concept. My protests weren't underplayed either. The channel officials were apparently peeved by my disagreement on their play-safe approach.

Saxena called me one night to plead helplessness. The channel had asked him to opt for a change of director. I chose to not hide my disillusionment with the mindset of creative heads. The series folded up after another six episodes, disproving their theories, but raising a vital query yet again. Do channel heads ever pause to think that the responsibility for a good show lies as much with the director as on their broad Atlas shoulders? That, when they step in with their team of writers, they quite often end up proving the too-many-cooks theory right? Or is the constant pressure to out-perform preventing everyone from playing their natural game?

Burying memories of *Gup Shup Coffee Shop*, I spent the best months of 2008 completing my feature *Red Alert - The War Within*, an incisive look at the Naxalite conundrum in the country. That was when television beckoned again. This time the caller had impeccable credentials. With roots in television. Shah Rukh Khan had just floated Red Chillies Idiot Box ["We think out of it" was the refrain] the television wing of his film company and chose to flag it off with a tribute to the favourite sitcom of the eighties, *Yeh Jo Hai Zindagi*. The thought of reconnecting with this chapter of television history fascinated me. It had the added bonus of veteran Aziz Mirza playing script supervisor. Mirza wasn't oblivious to the state of television at that point. Rather, he appeared intimidated by the dictates. He often 'feared for my life'. "I shudder to think how you are going to cope with the system and its demands. I am glad I am not in your shoes". I didn't know what to make of it. Be flattered or demoralized. The brainstorming over the scripts was an uplifting experience. Experience and wisdom that otherwise came at a premium, in these times were mine for the taking.

Yeh Jo Hai Zindagi proved to be a tricky customer. It couldn't be replicated verbatim and yet the fervor couldn't be overlooked. With Mirza's team of writers, this was turning into a challenge of adaptation. Though rights to the original series were purchased from the Oberois, I preferred a change in name.

Ghar Ki Baat Hai, had a more focused ring to it than a generic... *Zindagi*. The cast had its task cut out too. Sumeet Raghavan, Juhi Babbar and Swapnil Joshi reprised the characters played by Shafi Inamdar, Swaroop Sampat and Rakesh Bedi. Ali Asgar took on the daunting task of doing a multi-faceted Satish Shah. While Jayati Bhatia, with that twinkle in her eyes and newcomer Deven Munjal moved in as the cacaphonic neighbours. I was keen to design the show on the lines of the classic American sitcom. A three-camera unit made a vital difference to the presentation, achieving a crackling edit pace and interesting match-cuts seldom experienced in Indian productions. When Khan watched the first episode, I hung on apprehensively. It took a while, before I could breathe easy. At the media launch, he reminded the gathering of our association in *Baazigar, Baadshah* and Aziz's own *Yes Boss*. "Anant *saab*", he kept referring to me, a rather benevolent gesture, I thought. Better half Gauri Khan's mother turned out to be the show's most avid watcher. There was another surprise in store. The film fraternity, generally cold to television shows, found *Ghar Ki Baat Hai* a refreshing change from the regular television beat and even looked at it as an anti-depressant for the weekends. Many a past associate of *Yeh Jo Hai Zindagi*, gave it a thumbs-up rating, stamping the final seal of approval. Only Shah Rukh didn't keep his promise of an episodic appearance. He sent Juhi Chawla and

Irfan Khan instead.

NDTV Imagine was run by my friends, the old warhorses from Star, Sameer Nair and Shailaja Kejriwal. They considered the two aces in their hand - a revisit to *Yeh Jo Hai Zindagi* and Shah Rukh Khan as producer. They thought of what could have been a perfect gamble. Play *Ghar Ki Baat Hai* on the weekend and garner viewership without competition. I tried to reason with Kejriwal. This was akin to listening to Elton John's soulful *Blue Eyes* on Mumbai's pothole ridden roads. The desired effect could only be had on New York's freeways. The right show on a wrong slot was ill-advised. The records were there to see. No past instance of weekends attracting eyeballs for fiction. The slots were as good as dead. She brushed my thoughts aside with a casual "don't teach us marketing", quip and proceeded to programme it for Saturdays and Sundays. We did not have to wait long to realise that the marketing bubble had burst and doused us with the effluents. The lack of viewer awareness led to the show remaining content with a first season of thirty-two episodes. There were 'plans' afoot to get the second season on to a more orthodox slot. Those plans had to be aborted as NDTV was merged into Turner and the policies revised.

In the meantime, comedy had perceived a new platform for its risibility. The stand-up comedy acts, appropriately titled *Comedy Circus, Laughter Challenge* and other such permutations, redefined the over-the-top farce. Each channel laid their claim to having discovered the new magicians of humour. Lampooning and mimicry became the mainstay of the skits featured. The judges included Archana Puran Singh, Arbaz Khan and cricketer Navjot Singh

Sidhu who couldn't bring themselves to be critical of the channel that hired them. They were often caught laughing louder than the viewers, when grappling with words of praise after each stand-up. Not surprisingly, my memory bank triggers off the starting years again. Black and white images of Adi Marzban and Baban Prabhu, television's first stand up entertainers. The *Hasya Kavi Sammelans* featured poets like Surinder Sharma, Pradeep Chaubey, Ashok Chakradhar, Shail Chaturvedi and Hullad Muradabadi. Jaspal Bhatti, with his inimitable, self–mocking shows like the popular *Flop Show* displayed a Buster Keaton kind of deadpan humour and political satire. Less raucous, more funny and yes, no loss of innocence. The new kid on the block Kapil Sharma, was the only one who got quite close to that.

The new millennium saw SAB TV devote their channel exclusively to comedy. Their big catch, *Tarak Mehta Ka Ulta Chashma,* based on the satirical writings of Tarak Mehta in the Gujerati periodical *Chitralekha* titled *Duniya Ne Oondha Chashma,* was promising to begin with. The myriad situations that a housing society member faced was just what the middle-class subscribed to. The curtains went up in 2008 and despite running out of episodes by the original author, the producers [Neela Tele Films], kept it going. A daily comedy is a tall order and when faced with the task of meeting the benchmarks of the author's episodes, the proxy writers have a task on hand not to let the series run out of steam. With a faithful audience in Gujarat, the elementary treatment in *Tarak Mehta Ka Ulta Chashma* doesn't appear to have been a deterrent to viewership numbers. Though one does miss the take of the author's eye-view in the newer episodes. In one scene, an auto-rikshaw driver exults at the mere mention of the name "Mallika". "Where's Mallika Sherawat", he excitedly enquires. Comedy scripting's golden rule of avoiding names-dropping to extract laughter doesn't appear to hold forth anymore. It is an easy escape route for writers, something I had judiciously avoided in the scripts of *Chamatkar*, despite the frowns of objection from the opposite end.

Trends around the globe in the past two decades offered sharp contrast. While the British appeared to be turning their back to comedy, American television networks were banking on the genre to laugh away difficult times. The targets for pot-shots were ethically suspect lawyers, dysfunctional families, high school singing groups and detectives. *Friends, Seinfield* and *Frasier* had lit up living rooms and moods in the early 1990s when the US was mired in recession. ABC's entertainment president, Steve McPherson, was out to redefine the family comedy. Also, sitcoms were more economical to make. So, while America got to laugh driven by social necessity, I fell back on my collection of *Friends* to remind me how to smile. Or a collection of the *Seinfield* scripts. On our television screens, though, Parliamentarians continue to unintentionally raise the chuckles. Unlike most manufactured comedies, they unwittingly turn out to be topical and socially relevant.

REALITY
BITES

"TV has proved that people will look at anything, rather than each other"- Ann Lander, American columnist, media celebrity

The pachyderm wound its way into Cusrow Baug, an exclusive Parsi colony in South Bombay. A camera team followed as it stopped outside an apartment on the ground floor. An elderly lady answered the doorbell and the look on her face on seeing the elephant was worth a million bucks. "You are the lucky winner of the Maharashtra Mammoth Lottery draw last night", I informed her, ushering the animal towards the door. She tried to scream, but failed. Her voice squeaked, "You keep him, give me the cash instead". I pointed towards the camera and declared, "Smile madam you are on camera". The million-dollar expression was replaced with a billion-dollar look. *Freeze! You are on Camera*, was the Indian version of the popular international show *Candid Camera*. For me, as the anchor on the show, these were the tentative steps of reality television on Doordarshan in the late 1980s. Situations unscripted, to expect the unexpected. Several years later, rip-offs like the MTV *Bakra* followed suit, but *Freeze!*.. pioneered the trend, raking in ratings even on *The Breakfast Show* on Doordarshan. Jhelum Ratna, whose Collage Communications produced the show, was initially skeptical about me playing anchor. A known face would be a dead give-away. But I used the familiarity to advantage, often pretending to be an accidental passerby at the sight of the 'crime'. The victim, recognizing me, would open conversation about picking up an abandoned suitcase or attempting to run a car on pencil batteries, unaware that every move and word were being recorded by a hidden camera.

Reality shows became the new talent malls. Its demands were somewhat alien to people like me, who hail from a time when the nearest ticket to exhibiting whatever talents you possessed, was the school annual day or inter-collegiate contests. Today it's the magic window that sees children herded and goaded by unrelenting parents to accomplish in three months what it took the previous generation more than a decade to achieve.

The term and formats are imports from the West. American television programmers invented the formula of ordinary people playing into the hands of what appeared as unscripted shows. *American Idol* [*Indian Idol*], where contestants sing themselves to fame; *Survivor* [*Survivor India*], about being the fittest when marooned on an island or in a jungle; *Big Brother* [*Big Boss*], with selected social figures under house arrest; *Fear Factor* [*Khatron Ke Khiladi*], that turns celebrity names into daredevil stunt persons; *The Moment of Truth* [*Sach Ka Saamna*], that had participants failing a lie-detector; *I'm a Celebrity, Get me Out Of Here* [*Is Jungle Se Mujhe Bachao*], with more celebrities subjecting themselves to

Mowgli and Tarzan territory; and the *Got Talent series* [*India's Got Talent*], which gives skilful circus artistes the blues and *Temptation Island,* invoking the primitive instinct of Adam and Eve, were some of the popular 'real' attractions that found their way as syndications across the globe. 2005 saw the big spurt of these 'reality' imports in India.

Reality shows are akin to pressure cookers for participants and audience alike. The repulsive thought of gulping down mashed worms [*Get Me Out of Here*] or freeing oneself from shackles in a tub of slithering lizards and cockroaches [*Khatron Ke Khiladi*] is complemented by the gawking nature of the viewer. Channels believe that all this is pushing the innovative limits of show business in keeping with changing world temperament and taste. In fact this is where normal life is manipulated and refunded to the viewer as the real thing. One could trace the acts on *Entertainment Ke Liye Kuch Bhi Karega*, an offshoot of *Got Talent*, to the freak shows that were crowd-pullers in the West of the 18th and 19th centuries. So, while we wince when participants delve into circus acts like setting their body on fire, drinking milk and squirting it from the eyes or swallowing swords as a mark of their special talent, celebrity judges are caught on camera rooting for the weirdo acts, probably because they match the implausibilities of situations in formula films. British broadcaster Robin Day nailed it when he observed that, "Television thrives on unreason and unreason thrives on television, striking more at emotions than intellect". The growing demand for the genre has made the non-fiction segment a tough competitor to the long-winding soap operas, with audiences stopping by to catch the blurred 'soap' in 'reality'. Every general entertainment channel opts for at least two of these non-fiction reality set-ups during any given year.

Although Amitabh Bachchan fights shy of acknowledging any Orwellian influence in *Big Boss*, where he played pop philosopher in its third season, I cannot desist referring to one of the seminal texts of the last century, George Orwell's futuristic purgatory 1984, where the ministry of war was projected as the ministry of peace. A context that can be squarely transported to the Big Boss milieu where they first manipulate a normal lifestyle and then proceed to systematically shred it, while the viewer is made to believe that it is all a real-life occurrence. Bachchan, however refrains from thinking that the show, deliberately coerced individuals to come out with their worst. "But, the way in which viewers became involved with the characters in the 'house' was most revealing for me. They almost started taking a personal interest in their behaviour or the behaviour of others." The expulsions from the house of sin are followed up with specially edited video clippings that resemble "in fond remembrance" videos. Of those, who will no longer be amidst us.

After its thirteenth season, it is now obvious to the viewer that the show provoked contestants to escalate the conflict. As the inmates act themselves out, they tend to get crasser and even more self-centered, while the channel laughs its way to the Television Ratings bank. The participants are carefully handpicked from failed stars, controversial godmen, political figures, lawyers, even an ex-convict, bench-warming cricketers, wrestlers of both the conventional and Sumo variety, models with attitude, porn stars and transgender biggies. For every swear-word, fight, back-stab, flirting and bitching act, the entertainment quotient rises. I watched my *Memsaab* lead, Tanaaz Currim, spar with her husband Bakthtiyar Irani. They fought, conspired, kissed, fought again. So did several other television stars. Rupali Ganguly, the late filmmaker Anil Ganguly's actress daughter and her colleague Kishwar Merchant, however, chose to see some positivity in the being-bad exercise. Ganguly claims it to be life-changing, teaching you-amongst other things tolerance and acceptance. One thing is for certain–never has one been paid so much to be this bad. Seldom has a show been mostly disliked, yet most watched. Joan, Jett and the Blackheart's popular number 'I hate myself for loving you' could well be the recurring refrain here.

Bachchan, a stickler for humility and dignity, may appear to be in the wrong space with *Big Boss*. But he had reconciled to the idea of having to speak to the contestants after every week and read their minds towards incidents that transpired in his absence. "I felt it would be too harsh to grill or counsel them, after they had been through worse through the week. But just talking to them in a pleasant manner and getting them to be comfortable with what they would confide in me, was, to me, more important and in some cases more revealing." He did not sign on for another season. Sanjay Dutt and then, Salman Khan moderated. Their "bad boy" image, was more in keeping with the nature of the show. For me the amusement stemmed from watching fulminating members of Parliament thump their desks in protest against the entry of Sunny Leone, rated amongst the top twelve porn stars of the world. Later, Shekhar Kapur publicly declared that "Indian television has lost it", in protest against the 2.5 crore rupees paid to *Bay Watch* star Pamela Anderson to feature in *Big Boss* for a mere three days.

The *Big Boss* syndrome spread its wings to regional spin-offs too. Marathi, Tamil and Malayalam. I often meant to ask my *Papanasam* and *Vishwaroopam 2* lead actor, Kamal Haasan, what prompted him to play host to the show in Tamil. When I eventually did, he dismissed it with his disarming smile. It was a totally unplanned moment, when I accompanied him to the "Big Boss house" on a promotion run of his film *Vishwaroopam 2*. Actor Mohanlal was the host on the Malayalam version and three 'long-lost' South Indians, ended up talking to an audience about our native roots, habits and our oft-arduous, yet enjoyable, journey in show business.

Back in the day, at Don Bosco's, we could never have foreseen a situation when we would be discussing the goings-on in last night's reality show. In fact, there was nothing to faff about except last night's homework. Today, I am both amused and disturbed to discover that schools have found a new use for their compound walls. Banners that proclaim the names of students who have appeared and won reality competitions on television. The roll of academic honour that used to adorn the portals of our *alma mater* seems only secondary now. These flexes are launching pads for the young and restless who do not mind the excruciating pressure and occasionally humiliating moments on national television for their thirty seconds of fame.

I read with alarm, instances of participants like Susan Boyle who found herself in a rehab centre after being booed out of *Britain's Got Talent*. Closer home in Calcutta, a singing contest elimination confined a young girl to a comatose condition. What is more disconcerting is that talent on display on shows like *American Idol, The Voice, Indian Idol, Sa Re Ga Ma Pa* and others rarely make it big on the professional scene even after winning titles. We haven't seen another Shreya Ghoshal in the past decade. True, there *was* Abhijeet and a few dancers-turned-choreographers but, for most of the time, these names appear more channel-driven and mentored rather than real talent of the future. Singing cover versions beautifully does not purport to be a barometer of true vocal merit.

That, then, is the sea change that has happened to singing contests. The real fun was participating in *Star Yaar Kalakaar* [Sony], amongst the earliest invitee singing contests on the tube hosted by a radiant Farida Jalal. As the celebrity guest, there was no competitive pressure and I was allowed to sing my favourite number. It had to be *"Oh mere dil ke chain"*, Kishore Kumar's lilting ode to love. I dedicated it to my father. It was one of his favourite numbers. He doted on it, along with Lata Mangeshkar's rendition of Ghulam Mohammed's, *"chalte chalte"* [*Pakeezah*]. My team won all rounds hands down and I bagged an all expense paid trip to the Far East. That the flight tickets never came didn't rob me of the experience of belting out live numbers to a television audience.

As I speed down the Juhu roads, a UTV Bindaas channel hoarding flashes by. I slow down to read, *"Just because I am bindaas, does not mean I do drugs, just because I am bindaas, does not mean I sleep around"*. It was sounding falsely apologetic, almost like applying for anticipatory bail. I'm a little unsure if MTV is being sarcastic when it calls itself, "The channel that your mother used to warn you about"? Along with other channels like V and Bindaas they have hatched a catch-them-young-and-throw-them-to-the-wolves strategy. *Emotional Atyachar*, inspired by Fox Reality Channel's *Cheaters*, is one that capitalizes on infidelity as a, supposedly, human characteristic. While detectives followed the suspects on the American show, here 'hidden' cameras spy on couples cheating on their partners and set the stage for a confrontation between the cheater and the cheated. There have also been bizarre instances of girls and boys approaching the channel to test their spouses' loyalty. Quite often, the show has been accused of being fixed, of participants being saddled with fake boyfriends and instructed how to kick, wail and slap each other. Youngsters are lured with the ticket to television fame and those who aren't willing customers are paid a packet to simulate the situation.

Identical juices flowed on *Spitsvilla*, a free-for-all crash course in bitching about other contestants. The MTV tag called it as 'a one-of-its-kind-hunt-for-love show'. Borrowed from the American dating reality show *Flavor of Love*, it prods young boys to find the girl of their dreams from twenty probables, who battle politics, stress, exhaustion, a hate club, fear and bad television [!] to emerge as the eventual choice. Do spare a thought for the ones evicted. They are humiliated and dumped, but then, they do bring it upon themselves. In comparison, the tedious fights and controversies in music and dancing talent hunts are innocent banter. Some of the voices are a revelation but, like I noted earlier, fall short of being discovered in the world of film score recordings. That, then, is the innocence that television has discarded by the wayside. Bullying and bitching have replaced traditional rivalry. The Bindaas channel aired a boys versus girls reality show called *Dadagiri - Revenge of the Sexes*, where the contestants are subject to revulsive tasks and brainwashed to say, "I have to slay the competition by hook or by crook". I knew Shifa Maitra, the creative director of these shows as a gentle, sensible and rational programmer. Maybe loyalties to the channel tempted her to start believing that the taboo on sex and love has been lifted. "There is nothing private or sacred anymore. People are talking about *Emotional Atyachar, Love Lockup* and *Dadagiri*, even if they aren't liked. So, we can't be ignored", she concluded. Bold, brash, public display of affection are the entertainment demands of a 'right here, right now' generation in the 15 to 24 age bracket. For them, love hangs by a thread. Compatibility is questioned at every turn. Tolerance levels have plummetted. Television, I guess, has become the no-holds-barred escape adventure.

Unearthing primitive emotions was one thing, but unwinding to the mythological age was what took many by surprise. Conducting a *Swayamvar* [a ritual where the bride chooses her man amidst several suitors and garlands him, like Sita in the *Ramayana*] in these times may appear preposterous but NDTVImagine subscribed to the game of marriage and declared, "The more unbelievable it appears, the more real it is". The first candidate was actress Rakhi Sawant. There were 16 men waiting to woo her on television and perform tasks to stress their eligibility. Perhaps the idea was to make us smile through it as sweet revenge on the men brigade which was notorious for asking a prospective bride to go through several chores before approving of her.

A week before the finale, I received what looked like an ancient red cloth scroll. It requested my presence at "the final night of the country's biggest *Swayamvar* as Rakhi Sawant chooses the man of her dreams. "We would love to have you to bless Rakhi and join in the celebrations". I didn't consider myself qualified enough to be a dispenser of blessings, so I stayed away. But the voyeur in me switched the television set on to a deferred 'live' telecast. As the guests cooed, pretending to actually see off a bride, the lady voted Elesh Parujanwala from Toronto to the marriage throne. Just as we waited with bated breath to know whether the next marriage would actually be made on television, she got away with the formality of an engagement. Sure enough, even that did not last long. But the die had been cast for the concept. Ashish Patil who was heading MTV India in 2009, had his say, "Rakhi Sawant is like a train wreck". You can't take your eyes off her. They were fair to the opposite sex, the next time around. The late politician Pramod Mahajan's son, Rahul actually took the marriage vows with a girl called Dimpy. And in the third season, a television actor Ratan Rajput was surrounded by suitors from as far as Ireland and Poland. What next on the anvil? Not a ritual like Sati [where wives accompanied their dead husbands on the funeral pyre] I hope.

Siddharth Basu, the quintessential quiz master of yore, found himself caught in a decade where he had to take a quantum leap from his origins with *Quiz Time* in the eighties. He has masterminded many a show in this genre, the most popular being *Kaun Banega Crorepati*. Now as head of Synergy Communications his production company, he toyed with the Indian version of BBC's *Dancing with the Stars*, a celebrity dance show. I was flattered when he called it *Jhalak Dikhla Ja,* which was the chartbuster number from a film I had made, titled *Aksar.* Then in 2009, he set out to probe the darkest corners of a person's conscience. *Moment of Truth* turned into *Sach Ka Saamna* on Star Plus. This was a hot seat where participants squirmed answering discomforting questions like, "did you have an affair with your best friend's wife?" If they confessed, they won a point, if they were caught lying, they were expelled. It was a lose-lose situation either way. Actors Urvashi Dholakia, Yusuf Husain and cricketer Vinod Kambli were amongst those who took on the lie detector. The shock of facing one's personal demons in full public view added to the sensation of the exercise. Contestants were aware of what they were getting into, while viewers feasted on the skeletons tumbling out of every closet. Although Basu felt that many contestants felt cleansed after the confession, the show made the church confession box look a more secure option.

Sach Ka Saamna and *Swayamvar,* however found their nemesis in the regression show *Raaz Pichle Janam Ke.* This believe-it-or-not experimentation had participants volunteering to revisit their previous lives. A psychologist performed the act of hypnotism or alpha-theta medication as she described it, that sent the subject hurtling back in time. The images, created as visual representations of their past raised more of a chuckle than awe. Shekhar Suman, Monica Bedi, Celina Jaitley and Chunkey Pandey were among the ones who visited their previous forms. The medical fraternity, however maintained that such 'memories' of a past life may only be the projected imagination of an individual. Many were of the opinion that the concept called for elaborate research. Not surprisingly, several fingers were raised and the reality quotient questioned. The channel maintained a hypnotised silence. After two instalments, the show was spoken of in the past tense. No more seasonal activity was reported.

The genial British actor Sir Alec Guinness, unwittingly, adds to my commentary of the times in his diary. A television programme on the Southern Charm Pageant in Atlanta, Georgia, had American mothers imparting to their little girls, the art of seduction. Guinness says he was aghast as he took in the sight of these aspiring mums. When a five-year-old was accorded the Queen of Queens crown, he shuddered to think of the future she was walking into. The Warholian hunt by youth for those 15 minutes of fame, reminds me of the dramatic lines of *The Fight Club*. "We've all been raised on television to believe that one day we'd all be millionaires and movie gods and rock stars. But we won't. And we are slowly learning that fact. And we are very, very pissed off."

SILENCE OF THE LAMBS

The place was decrepit in comparison to Sridhar Kshirsagar's aesthetically done up Astra Telecast. To think that this was the 2010s! The board proclaimed the name of a software company named after its lady boss. The door was opened by a girl pushing her late twenties. The sinews of her face stood out trying to place me. Eventually, the villain of the whodunit *Khiladi* registered and she leaked the news of my arrival to people inside other cabins. "They are auditioning another actor inside". she revealed, giving me the feeling that of cops waiting to investigate me. "I am the creative head of this show called *Palkon Ki Chaon Mein*, she continued, "I occasionally write too, but I cast, make shooting schedules and I have a documentary script that I am longing to make". It was a 30 second education in introductions.

During the best of times I had not gotten myself into a situation like this. For long, I had refrained from audition sessions and preferred to stay away. These auditions were mostly meant for "those who came in late"- the programmers and executives of channels who had scant knowledge about names like Gulzar and Ramesh Sippy.

However, this time my exploring instincts got the better of me and I found myself sipping coffee in a bath of sugar and staring at a wall that was plastered with a lady trying to exude some sunshine on her face. This, I assumed, must be the lady of the nameplate. As I sat there - bewildered and impatient in turns - the image of actor Kanwaljeet Singh floated in front of my face. Not without reason. The time was the mid-nineties. I was going about my duties as honorary casting consultant for Jijo's *The Bible.* Maybe my being a Malayalee who could communicate with him, prompted him to believe in me. The '*mundu*' [a sarong for men] clad Jijo hadn't heard of any Bombay talent. Every popular face was a non-entity for him. I introduced Kanwaljeet Singh for a prominent part and left him to Jijo in his cabin. He emerged half an hour later with a look on his face I'll never forget. "After all these years they subjected me to an audition", he sputtered, his plight that of a patient who had been forced to undergo an HIV test. "They don't know who we are, we might as well be aliens for Jijo", I tried to reason with 'Kuku' and calm him down. It was a "physician heal thyself" situation I faced as I waited for my trial. Jijo, after *The Bible,* started an amusement park in Chennai. He found the roller-coaster rides more worth his while.

There was the sound of a door opening, some voices overlapping and the actor being "interrogated" stepped into the reception area. It was the tall and lanky Deepak Parashar. No trace of the hero who had hit it off with B R Chopra's films like *Insaf Ka Tarazu* and *Nikaah.* A quick hello and handshake later, he quickly stepped out for a life-inhaling smoke. The person accompanying him was a thirty-something assistant, who appeared apologetic for delaying the inevitable. He then thoughtfully handed me some reading material, "while you wait". It was a scene from the 200-episode old daily, the lines of which I was supposed to speak for the camera. He then patiently went on to describe the character, that of a missing husband, which the series had, innovatively, kept under wraps so far. He was the repentant man filled with remorse and was begging forgiveness of the wife. It took me but a few minutes to grasp it, but had enough time to think up myriad interpretations as Parashar groped with it for another session. Eventually, he emerged battle-scarred and bid a relieved goodbye.

I was on! I entered the 'room' that displayed more pin-ups of the lady on a vacation, in what seemed like, some foreign shores. Her confident countenance could have been unnerving for under-trials like me. I could 'see' how Parashar would have portrayed the "come-back" husband. I deliberately did not want to pitch him like a wimp. I lent him a semblance of sensitivity and maturity. The man with the camera shrugged an 'okay' and left me with the second most infamous line after "your cheque is in the mail" - "We now wait for the channel to get back".

Something told me the wait would be futile. Sure enough, neither did the channel nor the production crew "get back." The mind did a quick, comparative flashback to the late eighties when I had auditioned for Bernado Bertolucci's film called *Little Buddha*. The rejection came with a politely worded letter from his international casting director, "Though Bertolucci liked you very much, we could not accommodate you in the cast". A letter I have treasured to this day. I wouldn't blame the times. People just don't bother anymore. I had a hunch Deepak Parashar must have landed the part. I took a deep breath telling myself that there were many lessons to be learnt from this exercise, among them shock-absorption, patience, humility and a sense of self-mockery. Anyway, at the rate at which actors keep cropping up in every series, it makes you feel like the whole world is going to a party and your invitation got lost in the mail.

It is well beyond half-past eight. Facebook time. We have all been lured into what is nothing but the pen pal clubs of our childhood in cyberspace garb. But, something inside me shut down. I did the same with the living room lights and sprawled myself on the floor attempting a premature forty winks. The cell phone played my favourite ring tone, the signature opening of the Akashwani radio station. My brother Ravi had downloaded it with great care, "exclusively" for me. It was a journalist friend who was trying hard to be heard, above the loud rumble of a crowd. "Where are you", his voice barked an urgency. Not to be caught napping at an early hour, I lied. "In an edit" I whispered. "Well, I am here, at the Indian Telly Awards for New Talent". I had deliberately given it the skip, despite repeated invitations. What would I do at a new talent parade? The voice continued, "they just announced your name in the Director's category for Sitcoms. You won it for Shah Rukh's serial *Ghar Ki Baat Hai* and you are not here!" "Do me a favour, why don't you go up and collect it for me?" I rambled." "Well, too late, they have already taken it backstage!" "Too bad" I concluded and hung up. I sat up to take stock of the situation. I was new, emerging talent! I was starting all over again. I was back to square one. A few weeks later, a delivery boy was at my doorstep. He held up a black cardboard box for me. It said *The Indian Telly Awards*. I fished out the heavy, golden statuette and smiled to myself. The Red Chillies Idiot Box office called to say that Shah Rukh would like to take a look at it. I smiled again. This was something I couldn't even share on Facebook!

The tragi-comedy has engulfed an entire tribe of actors, producers and television directors who are frazzled by the demand and supply syndrome. From the original lesson of giving a picture to a good story, television has far detached itself and, in the late Ravi Chopra's opinion, entered the *kalyug* phase. Directors on television resemble the hordes of labourers awaiting assignments outside Mumbai's Borivali railway station each morning, not knowing what job lay in store for them. When they land up on a set, there is no saying how long he or she or even the show would last. A few years ago, a software company formulated a new system of remuneration. Directors would be paid by the scene and not an episode. I did not mean to pry, but this episode director was loud and clear as he spoke to his writer on the studio phone. "Write a few more scenes will you, it would mean a few extra hundreds today". Basu Chatterjee had seen packaging and showmanship lording over substance, a decade back. When he filmed two commercials with Priya Tendulkar, over a period of three days, the agencies were of the opinion that he wasn't doing justice to it. "Advertisement shoots are meant to be spread over ten days. So, they stopped giving me work after that". Understandably, today he refuses to look back. "I've seen times which people today haven't. And that is a satisfying thought". His statement was what they would comment in cricket to a delivery outside the off-stump, "well left!" But I didn't miss the sense of resignation to a mutated scenario.

Aziz Mirza's eyes wander beyond the windows of his Khar office as he conjures up an apocalyptic picture. "Is no one concerned that there may not be another Ramesh Sippy, Gulzar or Basu Chatterjee on television?" If so, will television become audacious and original and recall its top-notch creators again? My evenings are often indulged in pondering over the answer. Will there be a patient ear for the studious twerp? Will they clear the air about why the chair is allotted to mass communication school products who are blissfully unaware about who built the ground beneath their seats? One theory that has gained credence is that channels prefer to rein in novices whom they can dictate to, rather than be exposed to experienced directors who will not let them litter in their own backyard. It evoked a regime where they discouraged education for farmers for fear of their own ignorance being discovered. So while many a television star and maker have managed to live in the apogee of their long career, most of today's actors and executives seem to have a use-by date stamped on their career graph.

Amitabh Bachchan, after testing waters with a soap in *Yudh* (July 2014), however, admits that it is difficult not to acknowledge television as a massive entertainment entity growing at an avaricious speed, though he advises caution. "Its returns and turnovers are going to be bigger than film, if they are not already. I have been exposed to the working and the manpower that television in India recruits and the talent that runs it. It is massive and impressive. The rate at which they function and the alacrity with which their creativity just tumbles out is beyond remarkable. What surprises me even more, is the age group of those that manage television outfits. They are all young and within 25–30 years of age. To have such a powerful medium in the hands of those that will guide the future of a nation is admirable." Having said that, he rings the warning bell. "It is also desired and expected that they are able to exercise sufficient maturity to be responsible in what direction this medium must travel. Television has the power to bring in change. Will this generation realise this and act accordingly is what remains to be seen."

The long absence of stalwarts who guided programming during the 1980s and 90s, was becoming very palpable. Sai Paranjpye tried hard to reason how it all faded away. "When I realised that it is no longer the cup of tea I used to relish, I just turned my back, since I know that there was nothing I could now do or contribute. I do not wish to see myself struggling to do what I once enjoyed doing. Television today wouldn't hear of anything less than two hundred episodes. If I were to attempt that, I would be stuck with the damn thing forever. But today's average viewer who leads a mundane life, devoid of any excitement, prefers the glitz and glamour on the small screen. The good women are paragons of virtue and the bad ones are bad beyond belief. So I have switched off. Even the television I watch is of the British and American variety, episodes of Inspector Morse. My only regret is not keeping a record of all that I did. Not a single backup, I was so careless, but that's me!"

Paranjpye's censure of the system found another voice in Kundan Shah. But Shah saw television as a small subset of a bigger world pattern emerging. "It is directed at diverting us from the main issue.

The media all over the world is being controlled by corporate houses. From providing ammunition to both sides in Iran, to controlling consumer choices, the conspiracy is on. Television is only a small lie. There is a bigger one afoot. With everything dependent on the monetary system, corruption is inbred. Corruption of society, mind, body and soul. Television is one of their channels. We have walked into a big trap. The sooner we realise it, the better. "

The despair is deflating to people like me whom television gave a career. It makes one fervently hope for a Kundan Shah or Sai Paranjpye out there, even someone like me, quietly waiting to board that evening local to a studio.

2018 I had turned down more than a dozen audition calls over the years [some under the guise of "look-tests"] and virtually given up hope of bagging an acting assignment on prime time [that I wasn't inclined to direct a routine daily soap, was a foregone conclusion]. That was when an old friend Dharampal Thakur called. I had been cast in a comedy for SAB TV, titled *Aadat Se Majboor*. "No audition, no look-test, just come!" One factor that weighed heavily in his favour was that the series was being shot at Future Studios, which was home territory for me. I had sworn off the far-flung Dahisar, Mira Road sets. The unit of the company headed by Bharat Kukreti and Pankaj Sudheer Mishra turned out to be extremely well organised and allayed any fears of television working recklessly without time restraints. The youthful cast of Anuj Pandit, Risabh Chadha, Vanshika Sharma and Sana Maqbool Khan were a riot. So was the show set in a publishing house where I was boss. TV made me smile again!

EPILOGUE
AN EPISODIC STORY

This church at Four Bungalows, a jostling Andheri locality in Mumbai has a display that I look up to every time I drive past. Jesus Christ stands in what looks like a capsule lift. I wait for him to come down one day and surprise us, but the vestibule seems to be stuck in limbo. Deliverance was what I started this book with and hopes keep waxing, then waning. The television that went missing when I began this book finds itself pushed further into oblivion even as I put the finishing touches to it.

This has been, and continues to be, a career where I have eschewed the fringe benefits. Going against the unwritten norm, if you "are to be part of the fraternity", I was never spotted at the racecourse, shied away from the traditional Diwali card games, shunned alcohol at the five star hotel press meets and have never ever been tempted with a cash loaded packet to tweak a film review. Actions which have often greeted me with a puzzled, "you really don't do all this?" gaze. After all these years, I am still made to feel the odd-man out. Looking back at the hair-pin bends in my career and what fate bestowed, I wonder how differently I could have done it all. When I didn't conform to the in-thing of advertising myself in the advertorial columns of newspapers, I realise that I may have turned into the Indian film industry and media's best-kept secret. Like my actor friend Gary Richardson [who had a migratory season in India after essaying a minor part in Costa Gavras' political thriller *Missing*], says, "We are survivors", making it sound like we were marooned on an island and just about escaping the cannibals'tatum pole.

The intoxication of television slowly, but surely, withered in the face of the hugely successful digital market with audiences weaned into different solid states. The tectonic shift has television viewers cutting the umbilical cord to settle down with their cell phones and tablets that are the new lair for entertainment on demand. The transition was coming with cable operators unable to restrict subscription fees after the new tariff order by the Telecom Regulatory Authority of India that let subscribers choose the channels they wished to watch. The so-called "best-fit" packages did not turn out to customer satisfaction. The channels acted swiftly, too, and readied for the impending revolution. Star developed Hotstar, a web based platform, with Zee following suit [Zee5] and Sony [Sony Liv] registering themselves for the next upgrade. All of which were shaped on the lines of America's hugely successful Netflix and Amazon's Amazon Prime. Netflix, which was launched in 1997 as a media services provider, certainly dragged its feet for an India launch but soon found a subscriber group of a hungry mass of cinephiles. The infinitely long television shows had found an alternative. The season effect of web series. Almost on cue, several software companies took the plunge with the production of web shows almost matching the number of television dailies. Relying heavily on subscriptions, the Indian platforms took their time to find their feet. The more "elite" vendors were of course Netflix and Amazon that upped the ante for budgets and quality control.

By 2017, OTT platforms had turned into a haven for content deemed unsuitable for the general entertainment channels with the additional attraction of an escape from the net of censorship. Subterranean channels with pulp erotica content and titles like *Gandi Baat*, *Dance Bar* and *Bekaboo* among others, slipped in the risqué elements unapologetically, catering to subscribers mostly from the hinterlands, that included the working strata of drivers, staff and security personnel. This target audience revelled in their darkest fantasies coming alive with hitherto dignified relationships of husband, wife, *devar*, *bhabhi* and fiancée brazenly twisted. These platforms, as many as 30 of them, claim to woo a cumulative viewership base of more than 30 million.

It is only the discerning circle that has judiciously avoided the temptation of seeking employment in these shows. I am not sure who recommended my name, but one of the prime web-production companies, Alt Balaji, once sought me out to direct a series for them. When I politely enquired if the show was predominantly adult content, the caller got the hint. He sought time to revert. Thankfully, that time is taking forever. But it must be added to Alt Balaji's credit, that eventually, their content showed a conscious leaning away from pulp origins and drew plaudits for originals like *Bose..Dead/Alive*, *Apharan* and *Verdict: The State vs Nanavati*.

Satellite television premieres have now shifted to the new OTT platforms. Films are aired a few weeks after their theatrical release. Netflix, with productions like Alphonso Cuaron's *Roma* and

Martin Scorcese's *The Irishman* has transformed into the new Hollywood studio superpower, blurring the gap between theatre and the digital platform. Not to be left behind, Disney and Apple are truly on their way too. Television and cinemas are encountering a new learning curve. There is a battle for survival amidst the new technology tidal wave, an occurrence that is a given trend as viewers multiply and gadgets get newer editions.

While the jury is still out on this, I fumble with the keyboard of my time machine that intermittently shuffles episodes that made this journey remarkable, worthwhile and, on the odd occasion, absurd. After all, isn't it all about episodes?

* * * * * * * * *

Your first signs of 'arrival' are when a newspaper columnist asks you about your love life. When *Ados Pados* had completed its run, *The Evening News of India* [now defunct], published an interview that had my single status tucked away in one of its paragraphs. It strangely, provoked an amusing backlash from other journalists like Shireesh Kanekar, a rebellious, colourful character who wrote in his column, "Who is interested if Mahadevan has a girlfriend or not?" Maybe he hated the interviewer for straying away from the main subject! Another friend from the media, the bearded Mohan Deep had other things to pine about. In his column in TV & Video World, the only magazine to feature me on its cover, Deep wondered aloud. "How does Ananth Mahadevan find his way into prominent directors' camps and bag work? After all wasn't he this middle-class guy who hung out from second class compartments travelling to work!"

* * * * * * * * * *

The media had labeled me "ubiquitous". It was probably because I hadn't spared even one-off episodes like *Janki Jasoos* [Hari Atma], *Faster Fenay* [Madhura Jasraj], Kamini Kaushal's children's series *Chand Sitare*, Jhelum Ratna's *Een Meen Sade Teen*, Dheeraj Kumar's thriller series *Apradh*, Mazahir Rahim's *Tane Bane* Ambrish Sangal's *Aadha Sach Aadha Jhoot* [produced by Rajesh Khanna] and Chander Behl's *Prerna*. The hectic routine took its toll. Returning from Mumbai's satellite city of Poona after filming for a series there, I had to walk into the sets of actress Rameshwari's debut show *Maqsad*, being directed by her friend Chitraarth. The scene required me to be lost in thought, crossing a street, when a bus 'hits' me. It very nearly did happen when, in a state of slumber, I walked across oblivious to the heavy vehicles whizzing past. If Rameshwari thought it looked real, it was! Later, laid out on a stretcher after the 'accident', I was supposed to play unconscious. I closed my eyes and lay there. I had no idea when I dozed off, but after what appeared to be an hour, an assistant shook me out of the stretcher saying they had canned the shot. I felt sheepish exploiting a working space to catch up on lost sleep.

* * * * * * * * * *

My foot-in-the-mouth moment happened on the sets of Sridhar Kshirsagar's soap *Manzil*. Kshirsagar's usual suspects were around. Benjamin Gilani, Tinnu Anand, Navin Nischol, Malvika Tiwari and I. As I watched Gilani and Anand perform I had this nagging urge to tell Kshirsagar that the shot could look better if framed differently. He listened to me and then unfurled the director's pride. "When you become a director one day, *then* do it your way". Curt and belittling it may have been at that stage, but it made sense now that the shoe is on the other foot. Even so, I make it a point not to react brashly when an actor walks up with a suggestion.

* * * * * * * * * *

When *Khiladi* co-star Deepak Tijori decided to explore more lucrative pastures, like producing software, he called on me to launch his company *Tijori Inc.* In 1997, we launched a weekend thriller series on Zee, *Saturday Suspense*. The eight scripts we filmed had a contemporary ring to them, particularly one which had a doctor using patients as guinea pigs for an anti-AIDS vaccine he had formulated. The series introduced then theatre actor Kay Kay Menon to mainstream television. An episode titled *Breaking News* had a channel head 'manufacture' news and then flash an exclusive report on his channel. Sounded like imaginative fiction, until recently when I chanced upon a report about the Brazilian police investigating state legislator Wallace Souza, a television crime show host. The crew of the programme *Canal Livre* had been, rather conveniently, arriving just on time at the scene of every new murder in town. Turned out that it was no coincidence. The murders were executed by Souza's men to boost the ratings of his reality show.

The flip side of the coin is the social media network that has been a vehicle for the promulgation of fake news. Surreptitiously posted mostly by political interests, this could endanger society and create disruption in a world already teetering on the edge of religious and traditional differences. Fake news is so widespread and disguised, that it finds a dedicated column in daily newspapers that issue warnings to the gullible.

* * * * * * * * * *

1983. Madhuri Dixit was an unknown name. The fresh-out-
of-a-microbiology-course student was originally headed for a
television debut as the protagonist for a new series to be aired on
Doordarshan, *Bambai Meri Jaan*. A few months after the pilot
was shot, Dixit was auditioned by the Barjatyas for the naïve and
precocious Gauri in *Abodh*, a rural romance in the Rajshri tradition.
Television was yet to realise what they had narrowly missed. On
location for Sridhar Kshirsagar's *Manzil* at the Juhu Hotel, we
looked round to see Madhuri Dixit and Aamir Khan filming for
Dil a furlong away. Kshirsagar couldn't resist the temptation. He
walked up to Dixit, told her what a huge fan he was and then put
forth a request, "Can I touch you?". When I asked him the reason
for this rather audacious act, he replied, "I wanted to see if she was
for real". Two decades later, the star returned to the studios judging
the dance contest *Jhalak Dikhlaja Jaa*. That is, if you discount the
matrimonial show on Sony *Shubh Vivah* [2002], Now married and
back for good from the US of A, she renewed her television ties
playing *sutradhar* on the Life OK channel which was but a new
garb for Star One. "I am only an anchor, linking the shows together
and not endorsing the channel, let alone being a business partner",
she clarified. She's retraced her roots, after all.

* * * * * * * * * *

1995. Himesh Reshammiya's craving to create music found its
outlet in the television shows he produced. *Andaz*, his debut on

Zee, was a product of ambitious casting. I found myself elbowing for screen space amidst big screen entities like Rajendra Kumar, Prem Chopra and Kanwaljeet. Then Shekhar Suman, Kulbushan Kharbanda and Sujata Mehta joined the party. It was a party sequence at the Horizon hotel in Juhu. Chopra, taken aback by television's unduly long working hours, threatened to quit the sets at nine. Reshammiya along with his father Bipin, rallied to hold the overcrowded fortress and appease frayed egos. The theme of *Andaaz* was also his first score. *Amar Prem* and *Aaha* followed recruiting more star names like Farha Naaz and Farouque Shaikh. Television became a distant memory for Reshammiya ever since he strode into the territory from where he sourced his actors - films. He may not admit it, but his score for my film *Dil Maange More*, was as good as the chartbusting album *Aksar*, a few years later.

* * * * * * * * * *

He took pride in being the 'first superstar'. Not without reason. Not many can boast of fifteen consecutively successful films. A black and white sketch of him in *Anand* smiled at me in his office. Rajesh Khanna was at the window watching life pass by at breakneck speed below. He turned around in characteristic fashion and declared, "I stand here every evening and think. And I have decided. Why not, I'll do television. The reach of TV is much more than cinema today and one episode of my serial is likely to be watched by more people than a super-hit film". Contemporaries like Bachchan had already gained a foothold, but Khanna was insistent that he did not want to do a game show or a talk show like *Movers and Shakers*. Fiction it would be for him. He loved dramatics. Dinesh Bansal, who was instrumental in his eyeing the small screen, celebrated with a media launch at a five star banquet. It was a star studded event with Maharashtra cabinet ministers, wife Dimple Kapadia and a whole lot of guests turning out in their fashion statements. As master of ceremonies, I sang the initial refrain of his popular *Aradhana* number *"kora kagaz tha yeh man mera"* before heralding the comeback of a man who had seen everything from dizzying stardom to sticky politics. Khanna turned on his charm with a lady who was trying to quieten her wailing six-year-old. "Show her *Haathi Mere Saathi*", he prodded, invoking memories of the film that had children hooked in the 1970s. Khanna had promised Bansal exclusivity and the latter spent a good ten lakh rupees for the first four episodes of *Batwara*, a partition drama. But, as was expected, producers made a bee-line for Khanna. Now there were 4 of his projects on sets, one of which found a telecast slot before *Batwara*. A furious Bansal landed up at Khanna's office and dumped the recorded tapes into his dustbin. Khanna pleaded and protested, but to no avail.

The banter shifted to a location at Goregaon's Film City. As I was sharing screen space with him for the pilot of a new show, he walked me down his memory lane. From humble beginnings in the late sixties, when he gave up an offer to play the lead in *Farz* to Jeetendra ["that wasn't the kind of role I wanted to begin with"], to sealing his status with *Aradhana*. A commotion interrupted his thoughts. A wild group of fans had just emerged from the adjoining sets where Bachchan was recording an episode of *Kaun Banega Crorepati*. It was their lucky day. Two superstars on one floor. As he autographed their books he slipped one of them with Bachchan's signature to me and then flipped the page to reveal his. "You notice the difference? he asked me. "He simply signs his name, while I write *Love, Rajesh Khanna*. Love, that's what makes all the difference", he insisted in that romantic tenor of his.

I caught up with him again in the winter of his discontent. He was now a frail man, a pale shadow of his former self. He doggedly put his ailment on the back burner a la *Anand*. In fact I could sense *Anand* playing all over again at *Aashirwad*, his Carter road bungalow. But the crinkled eyes and smile expressed a desire to do one more film. I mooted the idea of a sixty-year-old man who is drawn into a relationship by an advertisement in a matrimonial column. I called it *"Old Wine"*. We could get Sharmila Tagore to play the love interest. It would be *Aradhana* and *Amar Prem* all over again! The thought appealed to him and he couldn't wait to read the script. Literally. He left without a goodbye. As he had mentioned on that Film City set, he would love to be remembered as the last of the romantics.

* * * * * * * * * *

The Raja of Mandi in New Delhi had an unexpected visitor in 1976. The newly appointed director General of Doordarshan, P V Krishnamoorthy. The latter was saddled with a tall order. To evict the Raja from his premises so that Doordarshan could move in. Threatened with the government's acquisition of his property, the Raja sold out. That was the first big sale at Mandi House. Then came the great television serial slots sale. Siddharth Kak mooted the concept of *Surabhi* at a time "when nobody smiled in Doordarshan." A cultural visual magazine that ran the risk of being dismissed as experimental. In the company of actor Renuka Shahane, Kak anchored the show that took in every facet of the cultural diversity of India. The ten-year togetherness of Kak and Shahane worked like a charm, their affable presentation, making them the longest-running anchors. From 1991 to 2002, *Surabhi* recorded the largest measured audience response to television. The score of one-and-a-half million letters in a single week, prompted the postal authorities to issue a different category of "Competition Postcards" priced at two rupees each for participating in such contests. Kak would like to believe that a space could be found for info-entertainment like *Surabhi*. Television, basking in style, gloss and glamour begs to differ.

* * * * * * * * * *

Once upon a time they frowned on their poor country cousin. Though names like Mel Gibson, Tom Hanks and Denzel Washington had television careers before films found them, it took Indian stars the scent of money to lure them to 'making a compromise'. Now they are all over, straddling a domain that the original television stars painstakingly constructed for two decades. Amitabh Bachchan [*Kaun Banega Crorepati*], Salman Khan [*Big Boss, Dus Ka Dum*], Shah Rukh Khan [*Kya Aap Paanchvi Pass Se Tez Hain?, Zor Ka Jhatka* and a season of *Kaun Banega Crorepati*], Akshay Kumar and Priyanka Chopra [*Khatron Ke Khiladi*], Preity Zinta [*Guiness Book of World Records* and a *Chat Show*], Sunjay Dutt and Shilpa Shetty [*Big Boss*], Abhishek Bachchan [*National Bingo Night*] and a host of others who judge dance and music showdowns. Aamir Khan chose the socially relevant route on his Star Plus beat in *Satyameva Jayate*. Channels defend the exorbitant fees paid as a symbiotic partnership. Anil Kapoor, with his franchise of the American series *24*, has made budgets hike north. Sometimes, all it takes to change the face of Indian television is 24 hours!

* * * * * * * * * *

Following the immensely enjoyable experience of *Ghar Ki Baat Hai*, it didn't take me a minute to respond to a call from Shah Rukh Khan's office to direct the second season of *Ishaan*, a Disney channel product. Arnob Chowdhary, the channel creative head, was bent on giving the kids' show a feel of the American series *Glee*. With one-tenth of the latter's budget. His references were sourced from YouTube videos that would probably have cost a fortune to put together. After a while, it became a standing in-house joke. If YouTube ever shut down, many a creative head would be left without reference material. The bright kids, especially Tapas Mehta as *Ishaan*, made the exercise worth my efforts. But, after a while, even the kids began to see through the improbabilities that cropped up. In one particular sequence, Ishaan had to wake up feeling a strange apparition within the folds of his bedsheet. It turns out to be a glowing golden ball. I interpreted this as the sun in his bedroom, waking him up to a new dawn. But the channel creatives had fixated on, of all things, the ghastly scene of a bloodied horse's head in a similar scene in Coppola's *Godfather*. They insisted on the scene being given the shock element treatment! I couldn't get myself to comply and shot it with the warmth and wonder I had associated it with. Chowdhary instructed the Red Chillies programme driver, Samar Khan to reshoot it. It resulted in another difference-of-opinion situation that made me step down from the show.

* * * * * * * * * *

I had never met the doughty cricketer Kapil Dev before. So, we stood up for an ovation for the 1983 World Cup winning captain as he strode on to the sets of a commercial I was filming. I was persistent in breaking his taciturn nature. Here was an opportunity to feed on the great moments of his cricket. Quite expectedly, it climaxed with a debate on the IPL cricket seasons. Dev drew a comparison between paltry payments for test cricket and the fortunes heaped on players of the Premier League. He chose to equate it to the disparity in budgets of regional films and Hindi cinema. The latter was more profitable, hence huge budgets. "IPL is scripted for television. It is a television money making machine." Prophetic when one considers the Cricket Board's suggestion to hold the IPL exclusively for a television audience in the face of the Covid pandemic that ravaged the world.

* * * * * * * * * *

Aamir Khan first shared his television concept when he dropped in on the sets of my film *Life is Good*! in one of those British-raj bungalows in Panchgani. Sprawled on the ground, he indulged in the Rubik's cube and juggling coloured balls alternately. He was determined not to go the way of his contemporaries. A chat show was more up his alley. It had the scope to bring the country's ailments - bride burning, child labour, lacunae in the educational system, honour killings and the like to a wider audience. As he spoke, his eyes glistened like those of a child who had taken a detour his friends hadn't. *Satyameva Jayate,* first time on Star and Doordarshan in a simultaneous broadcast, was likened to many predecessors. From Kamleshwar's *Parikrama* in the early years of Doordarshan where he interviewed society's workhorses, to the high profile *Oprah Winfrey show,* which was more blatant and incisive. Even as aspersions were cast on the budgets and spoils of such a show, there was no doubting Khan's sincerity. He had played the star card well. It was a definitive move to increase awareness of the country's giant roadblocks. A few weeks later, I watched Tim Sebastian, the *Hard Talk* man, enter Indian television territory with *The Outsider* that debated on key issues facing India. He was articulate, well-informed and drove home bitter truths. He may be *the outsider,* but many a television host could take a leaf out of his voluminous diary of skills.

* * * * * * * * * *

New winds are blowing. From cable television to direct-to-home dish services to online viewing. The news, cricket matches and even prime time shows have found viewers on desktop computers. The online spin-off hosted the first internet show *Jay Hind*! on 15th August 2009 an amalgam of chat and spoof on the lines of CNN's *The Late Show with Jon Stewart.* Journalist Abhigyan Jha got Sumeet Raghavan to do the stand-up routine. The show ran for 4 years. So was this to be the beginning of the end of the television set as we know it? I hear the folks at YouTube sniggering "we told you so"! Considering the portability, variety and mushrooming technology of websites, television is fast yielding ground to the internet. Mobile phones incorporate a television viewing feature. The statistics are staggering. Reports of websites uploading 60 hours of video by the minute, matched by four billion videos viewed daily on an average, is not sweet music for television. This is apparently more than what three prime networks in America created over six decades! I shudder at the epitaph that is being written - "Here lies television killed by video".

* * * * * * * * * *

September 2019 marked 60 years of Doordarshan, [it began beaming on September 15th 1959] incorporating 37 years of sponsored television. I turn nostalgic about the public service broadcaster that was the vehicle for the first decade of my career. From the initial single channel, it now has a bouquet of 34 satellite arms, catering to almost every region of the country. 60 is a ripe milestone for any network and a journey that threw up a galaxy of talent including actors, directors, musicians, dancers and newscasters. From being addicts of television during the Doordarshan days to the current confession of "not having bothered to watch television for almost a decade", reflects the invaluable contribution of the channel in mothering a movement. If television was my journey, Doordarshan was my chariot.

* * * * * * * * * *

Circa 2011. The Premier Studios in Mysore. I wander around its unfamiliar new façade. An industrialist has bought over the site of the biggest tragedy on Indian television. As I venture to click pictures of its make-over, a security guard rushes out barking "no".

I explain to him my karmic connection with the place. He suspects that it could rake up a controversy and directs me to meet the manager for permission. I don't to do so. I turnaround and retrace my steps, occasionally glancing over my shoulder. The place, like my old television set, does not exist anymore. Once again, I take the long and winding road back... Then health minister Ghulam Nabi Azad [he used to affectionately address me as '*bhai*' during the Congress political rallies] has a new solution to putting the brakes on population. "Turn on the television and turn off your sex life". He reasons that if people watch television late into the night and fall asleep tired, they won't get a chance to produce children. Television as a contraceptive. Do I hear violent protests from Viagra?

* * * * * * * * * *

I move on in the hope of retrieving my missing television. It flashes from a nearby Apple electronics store, beckoning me to relate to its new form. Why would one fault Woody Allen when he says, "Today life doesn't imitate art, it imitates bad television". I steal a glance occasionally at the emperor's expensive new clothes, but like Zeami, the medieval Japanese theorist and playwright said, only "Watch with a detached gaze".

And walk slowly, silently into the fading light.